The Read-Aloud Scaffold

The Read-Aloud Scaffold

Best Books to Enhance Content Area Curriculum

Grades Pre-K–3

Judy Bradbury

LIBRARIES UNLIMITED

AN IMPRINT OF ABC-CLIO, LLC
Santa Barbara, California • Denver, Colorado • Oxford, England

Library of Congress Cataloging-in-Publication Data

Bradbury, Judy.
    The read-aloud scaffold : best books to enhance content area curriculum, grades pre-K-3 / Judy Bradbury.
        p. cm.
    Includes bibliographical references.
    ISBN 978-1-59884-684-3 (pbk. : acid-free paper) — ISBN 978-1-59884-685-0 (ebook)
    1. Reading (Elementary)—United States.   2. Language arts (Elementary)—United States.   3. Content area reading—United States.   I. Title.
    LB1573.B6918   2011
    372.47'6—dc23   2011023169

ISBN: 978-1-59884-684-3
EISBN: 978-1-59884-685-0

15   14   13   12   11   1   2   3   4   5

This book is also available on the World Wide Web as an eBook.
Visit www.abc-clio.com for details.

Libraries Unlimited
An Imprint of ABC-CLIO, LLC

ABC-CLIO, LLC
130 Cremona Drive, P.O. Box 1911
Santa Barbara, California 93116-1911

This book is printed on acid-free paper ∞

Manufactured in the United States of America

*This book is dedicated to teachers everywhere who
cherish an open book—and the world within it—
and share that love joyfully with children.*

*"Literature can carry the consciousness of human times and social life better than
anything else."—Thomas McGuane*

Contents

Introduction ix

SECTION I   **Outstanding Read-Aloud Choices to Scaffold
Instruction in the Content Areas**   **1**

SECTION II   **In the Spotlight**   **55**

SECTION III   **A Closer Look**   **121**

SECTION IV   **Poetry Pause Bookshelf**   **139**

SECTION V   **Additional Resources for Teachers and Librarians**   **145**

Author Index 157

Illustrator Index 163

Subject Index 169

Title Index 173

Introduction

The value of using children's trade books in the classroom as a vital component of the literature program has long been touted and is widely recognized as sound practice for developing lifelong readers. Reading aloud to children promotes a love of books. The more children value books and enjoy the reading experience, the more books they will read. The more they read, the better students they will be, and the better the student a child is, the more success he or she will encounter in school and in lifelong learning beyond the classroom.

Time dedicated to sowing the seeds of learning and developing an appreciation and enjoyment of rich literature is parsed when test taking overshadows the landscape of the elementary school arena. Trade books in particular are set aside in order to give full attention to standard texts, standardized tests, and rigid rubrics. Time, it is felt, is too short.

Indeed it is. All the more reason to pick up a trade book, a luscious, accessible work of art in the form of a full-color picture book, and invest fifteen minutes in suffusing a child's senses. A well-chosen book augments and enhances the institutional fare that feeds the tests. In just 15 minutes, a carefully selected, well-targeted picture book and a simply prepared read-aloud plan can scaffold learning, strengthen content area concepts, enliven the senses, and add dimension to straightforward instructional material. It makes learning memorable and thereby enhances retention.

Add another 15 to 30 seconds, yes *seconds*, at another point in your busy instructional day reading a poem that effectively connects to the concept you've taught through traditional texts and reinforced with a trade book read-aloud, and you've tripled your dosage, strengthened the scaffold, and added a layer of lovely language to the day. Simple genius, and simply gratifying—once you have the materials you need at hand.

This resource book offers teachers and librarians over 700 content area connections through carefully selected trade books representing outstanding read-aloud choices that augment content area learning. Fiction as well as nonfiction titles are referenced. Included is detailed information about outstanding children's trade books across a spectrum of genres reflecting popular themes in content area subjects, from history to holidays and special events, from biographies and memoirs to poetry and character education. Thought-provoking books, funny stories, tall tales, nursery rhymes, history, mystery, and math, as well as issues such as death, divorce, prejudice, and civil rights, are addressed. School and family matters, learning about oneself, community and friendship are prevalent themes in books written for the primary grades.

In determining which children's books to include in this resource, several criteria were used. Thousands of recently published books were evaluated in the process. Above all, the books selected can be classified as those that celebrate reading by the very excellence they bring to the picture book and early chapter book form. Each book included in this resource tells an original story in an appealing way with art that successfully merges with the text to create a memorable package for the Pre-K through third-grade child. These books are meant to nourish the spirit and encourage the pre-emergent, beginning, newly independent, and growing independent reader to embrace the wonderful world of reading while scaffolding content area instruction.

The books included in this resource are listed alphabetically by subject and alphabetically by title within subject areas in **Section I**. Books are listed in all subject areas they impact. All trade books listed include citations and annotations.

To facilitate read-aloud sessions across the content areas, complete and de-tailed read-aloud plans are offered in **Section II: In the Spotlight** and serve as templates for additional plans. Alongside these read aloud plans, highlighted with a spotlight icon, are suggested enrichment activities, writing prompts, related books, and suggested poetry for collaborative Poetry Pauses.

Each read-aloud plan follows the same format. At the top is the publication information and an estimate of the actual time it ought to take to read the book aloud (*not* including questions and follow-up activities, as these are used at the reader's discretion and the time spent on them will vary). Themes/content area connections are listed. Next you will find a brief summary of the book. The teaching plan itself consists of three parts.

The read-aloud session begins with a **Before Reading.** The plan suggests ways to introduce the book. This is an important step in the read-aloud plan because it focuses the child on the book, its format, and its subject. Discussion before reading aids in building prediction skills and nurtures experiential background by enabling children to draw on their personal experiences to bring meaning to the story. As children discuss and answer questions, they verbalize thoughts and feelings and relate their experiences. Each read-aloud plan launches the reading of the book with a **Let's read to find out** focus for listening to the story.

In the While Reading portion of the read-aloud plan, you will find questions to pose as you read the book aloud. Answers are given in parentheses to even the simplest and most obvious questions for ease in following the plan while preparing in advance for the read-aloud session. Suggestions for reading the book aloud that are specific to that title are also found in this section.

The Follow-Up discussion offers ideas for bringing the read-aloud session to a meaningful close. Questions that relate to the outcome of the story are posed. Discussion is encouraged.

Personal reflections written by the authors and illustrators on the creation of the book follow each plan. These are meant to be shared with children for added connections to text. Author and illustrator websites are also listed for each book in **Section II.**

In Section III: A Closer Look, theme-related collections of read-aloud choices receive close attention. Look for the magnifying glass icons. Within each cluster, you will find a list of recommended books, discussion points, extension activities, writing prompts, related online resources, and suggested titles for further independent study. These collections serve as examples of the wide array of choices available in children's trade books to scaffold learning in content area units of study.

In Section IV: Poetry Pause Bookshelf, a bibliography of poetry books make finding poems to connect to the curriculum simpler. Poems that are readily available and relevant aid in making the poetry pause a viable and rewarding addition to the busy day. The poetry books listed here have been chosen with content area connections in mind and offer outstanding and accessible poetry collections penned by award-winning children's poets.

Section V: Professional Resources offers recommendations of helpful websites, content-rich blogs, worthwhile reference books, and useful magazines that consistently provide professional information that aids in the quick and accurate selection and creative use of trade books for read-alouds to augment content area instruction. A selection of author and illustrator websites of particular note are also referenced here.

The indexes at the back of the book offer a variety of ways to locate information in this resource. Title, author, and subject indexes put at your fingertips what you need when you need it.

Finally, the author can be reached via her website at http://www.judybradbury.com.

"Ultimately, literature is nothing but carpentry."—García Márquez

SECTION I

Outstanding Read-Aloud Choices
to
Scaffold Instruction
in the Content Areas

Grades Pre-K–3

An Annotated List

- *Arranged alphabetically by subject*
- *Arranged alphabetically by title within subject areas*
- *Cross-referenced relevant to subject areas*

"If we want children to have access to complex ideas then the most fruitful way is the reading of whole books."—Children's Laureate, Michael Rosen

American History

> **ABRAHAM LINCOLN** written by Amy Cohn and Suzy Schmidt and illustrated by David A. Johnson; Scholastic; Grades 1–2+; a tall, slim, engaging biography with a terrific "folksy" voice. See **A Closer Look: Abraham Lincoln.**

> **ADÉLE & SIMON IN AMERICA** by Barbara McClintock; Farrar, Straus & Giroux; Grades 2–4; illustrations depict early 20th-century American cities. See **A Closer Look: Geography, Maps, and Travel**.

> **AS GOOD AS ANYBODY** written by Richard Michelson and illustrated by Raúl Colón; Knopf; Grades 2+; highlights Abraham Joshua Heschel's struggles with discrimination and civil rights in Europe, which paralleled the struggles of Martin Luther King Jr. in America, and culminates with Heschel's march toward freedom alongside the beloved American hero.

> **BACK OF THE BUS** written by Aaron Reynolds and illustrated by Floyd Cooper; Philomel; Grades 1–2; Rosa Parks's historic stand against segregation and discrimination as viewed by a fictional child witnessing the event.

> **THE BUFFALO STORM** written by Katherine Applegate and illustrated by Jan Ormerod; Clarion; Grades 1–3; Hallie and her family head west on a wagon train, leaving behind her beloved grandmother; evocative language, themes of change, family ties, nature, and the American frontier.

> **CAN YOU FIND IT? AMERICA** by Linda Falken in association with the Metropolitan Museum of Art; Abrams; Grades K–2; search to find details in works of art depicting America.

> **THE GARDENER** written by Sarah Stewart and illustrated by David Small; Farrar, Straus & Giroux; Grades 1–3; correspondence between a girl and her parents during the Depression; Caldecott Honor.

> **GOIN' SOMEPLACE SPECIAL** written by Patricia C. McKissack and illustrated by Jerry Pinkney; Atheneum; Grades 2–4; finding acceptance at the public library in America's pre–Civil Rights era.

> **HAYM SALOMON: AMERICAN PATRIOT** written by Susan Goldman Rubin and illustrated by David Slonim; Abrams; Grades 2–3; biography of an unsung hero who was "financier of the American Revolution."

> **JOHN, PAUL, GEORGE & BEN** by Lane Smith; Hyperion; Grades 1–2; zany tidbits about the famous American forefathers: John Hancock, Paul Revere, George Washington, Ben Franklin—oh, and also that "annoyingly independent" Thomas Jefferson; offers insight into why these "boys" grew up to become leaders of our nation. Full of Smith's trademark humor: fans will not be disappointed!

➤ **MARTIN'S BIG WORDS** written by Doreen Rappaport and illustrated by Bryan Collier; Hyperion; Grades K–2+; an absolutely outstanding, multiple award-winning biography of Martin Luther King Jr.

➤ **MOSES: HOW HARRIET TUBMAN LED HER PEOPLE TO FREEDOM** written by Carole Boston Weatherford and illustrated by Kadir Nelson; Hyperion; Grades 1–3; gorgeous illustrations.

➤ **NOW & BEN: THE MODERN INVENTIONS OF BENJAMIN FRANKLIN** by Gene Barretta; Henry Holt; Grades 1–3; a look at how Ben Franklin's inventions have influenced our world today.

➤ **OUR ABE LINCOLN** written by Jim Aylesworth and illustrated by Barbara McClintock; Scholastic; Grades K–2; biography of Abe Lincoln told through jaunty lyrics intended to be sung to the melody of "The Old Gray Mare." See **A Closer Look: Abraham Lincoln.**

➤ **PLAYERS IN PIGTAILS** written by Shana Corey and illustrated by Rebecca Gibbon; Scholastic; Grades 1–2+; fictional tale based on fact tells the story of a young woman who competes in the All-American Girls Professional Baseball League during World War II.

➤ **RENT PARTY JAZZ** written by William Miller and illustrated by Charlotte Riley-Webb; Lee & Low; Grades 2–4; a jazz party with free will offering enables a family to make the rent; historical perspective offered in the afterword.

➤ **SARAH MORTON'S DAY: A DAY IN THE LIFE OF A PILGRIM GIRL** written by Kate Waters with photographs by Russ Kendall; Scholastic; Grades 1–4; photographed at Plimoth Plantation, Cape Cod, Massachusetts, the story takes place in 1627. See also:

   ◦ **SAMUEL EATON'S DAY: A DAY IN THE LIFE OF A PILGRIM BOY**
   ◦ **ON THE MAYFLOWER: VOYAGE OF THE SHIP'S APPRENTICE & A PASSENGER GIRL**

➤ **STAND TALL, ABE LINCOLN** written by Judith St. George and illustrated by Matt Faulkner; Penguin; Grades 2–3; explores characteristics Abe possessed as a child. See **A Closer Look: Abraham Lincoln.**

➤ **THANK YOU, SARAH! THE WOMAN WHO SAVED THANKSGIVING** written by Laurie Halse Anderson and illustrated by Matt Faulkner; Simon & Schuster; Grades 2–4; engaging picture book biography written by an inspired award-winning author, with art by an illustrator who understands what makes a picture book stand out; biography, history, power-of-the-pen message.

➤ **WHALE PORT** written by Mark Foster and illustrated by Gerald Foster; Houghton Mifflin; Grades 2–5; history of whale towns; detailed text and illustrations.

➤ **WHATEVER HAPPENED TO THE PONY EXPRESS?** written by Verla Kay and illustrated by Kimberly Bulcken Root and Barry Root; Putnam; Grades 2–3;

the history of the short life of the Pony Express is offered in the context of a family's story told through their letters, delivered by the men on horses; spare, lyrical text.

➤ **YANKEE DOODLE AMERICA** by Wendell Minor; Puffin; Grades 2–3; an abecedary of the American Revolution; excellent introduction to the period.

The Arts

➤ **ACTION JACKSON** written by Jan Greenberg and Sandra Jordan and illustrated by Robert Andrew Parker; Roaring Brook; Grades 1–2+; adeptly conveys Jackson Pollock's spirit, talent, and influence on contemporary American art; a Robert F. Sibert Honor Book.

➤ **AN EYE FOR COLOR: THE STORY OF JOSEF ALBERS** written by Natasha Wing and illustrated by Julia Breckenreid; Holt; Grades 2–4; biography of the man who dedicated his life to studying color.

➤ **BALLYHOO BAY** written by Judy Sierra and illustrated by Derek Anderson; Simon & Schuster; Grades 2–4; contemporary fable about art, nature, and community in which a beach is saved from a high-rise; humorous, vivid illustrations; rhythmical, well-paced text.

➤ **BEAR'S PICTURE** written by Daniel Pinkwater and illustrated by D. B. Johnson; Houghton Mifflin; Grades K–2; gently and humorously considers what a picture is *supposed* to look like!

➤ **BEFORE JOHN WAS A JAZZ GIANT: A SONG OF JOHN COLTRANE** written by Carole Boston Weatherford and illustrated by Sean Qualls; Holt; Grades 1–4; the sounds John Coltrane heard growing up in the South in the 1930s helped shape the music he made; award winner.

➤ **A BOOK ABOUT COLOR: A CLEAR AND SIMPLE GUIDE FOR YOUNG ARTISTS** by Mark Gonyea; Holt; Grades 1–2+; beginning with the six primary colors and moving on to shades of color, complementary colors, hues, the emotion of color, and more, Gonyea explains in simple terms how artists see and choose colors.

➤ **BRIDGET'S BERET** by Tom Lichtenheld; Holt; Grades K–1; Bridget loves to draw and relies on her beret for inspiration—or so she thinks until the wind carries it off; amusing illustrations and a list of Bridget's "artistic observations and tips for inspiration" at the end of the book add to the appeal of this light-hearted story about artist's block.

➤ **BUTTERFLIES FOR KIRI** by Cathryn Falwell; Lee & Low; Grades 1–2; with patience and persistence, a young child creates a collage with origami.

➤ **CALLIE CAT, ICE SKATER** written by Eileen Spinelli and illustrated by Anne Kennedy; Whitman; Grades K–2; doing something you love is its own reward; sweet, whimsical art.

➤ **CAN YOU FIND IT? AMERICA** by Linda Falken in association with the Metropolitan Museum of Art; Abrams; Grades K–2; search to find details in works of art depicting America.

➤ **CELESTINE DRAMA QUEEN** by Penny Ives; Arthur A. Levine/Scholastic; Grades Pre-K–2; confidence is struck a blow after an initial experience with stage fright, but talent and reassurance save the day.

➤ **COOL CAT** by Nonny Hogrogian; Roaring Brook; Grades 1–3; a cat colors his world with the help of his friends; wordless.

➤ **DEGAS AND THE DANCE** by Susan Goldman Rubin; Abrams: Grades 1–3+; biography of the "painter of dancing girls" focuses on Degas's realization that creating and perfecting art takes dedication, hard work, and perseverance; illustrated with over 30 works of art by Degas.

➤ **DIFFERENT LIKE COCO** by Elizabeth Matthews; Candlewick; Grades 2–4; biography of Gabrielle "Coco" Chanel celebrates individuality.

➤ **THE DINOSAURS OF WATERHOUSE HAWKINS** written by Barbara Kerley and illustrated by Brian Selznick; Scholastic; Grades 2+; stunning Caldecott Honor book highlighting the life of the artist and sculptor who, in the mid-1800s, showed the world what a dinosaur looked like.

➤ **DOWN BY THE COOL OF THE POOL** written by Tony Mitton and illustrated by Guy Parker-Rees; Orchard/Scholastic; Grades Pre-K–2; rollicking, rhythmical dancing fun on the farm! See also:

- **GIRAFFES CAN'T DANCE**
- **DINOSAURUMPUS!**

➤ **FARMER JOE AND THE MUSIC SHOW** written by Tony Mitton and illustrated by Guy Parker-Rees; Orchard/Scholastic; Grades Pre-K–2; with the use of music, a resourceful farmer gets his hens to lay eggs and his crops to grow; rhythmical, jaunty text and lively illustrations.

➤ **FOGGY, FOGGY FOREST** by Nick Sharratt; Candlewick; Grades Pre-K–1; see-through "foggy" overlays suggest lurking fairy tale characters; simple text; lyrical language; predictions, fairy tales, and more. Fun!

➤ **HARRIET DANCING** by Ruth Symes and illustrated by Caroline Jayne Church; Chicken House/Scholastic; Grades K–2; sweet tale of friendship and self-acceptance; lovely, lilting illustrations.

➤ **HOW DO YOU WOKKA-WOKKA?** written by Elizabeth Bluemle and illustrated Randy Cecil; Candlewick; Grades Pre-K–2; rhythmic chant celebrates individuality, movement, dance, and multicultural friendships.

➤ **MR. GEORGE BAKER** written by Amy Hest and illustrated by Jon J. Muth; Candlewick; Grades K–2; Reading Rainbow Book; cross-generational tale about music and learning to read.

➢ **MS. MCCAW LEARNS TO DRAW** by Kaethe Zemach; Arthur A. Levine/Scholastic; Grades 2–4; inattentive, struggling student likes to doodle, and Ms. McCaw, a charming and wise teacher, finds a suitable way to celebrate that.

➢ **PETER AND THE WOLF** retold and illustrated by Chris Raschka; Atheneum; Grades 2–3; based on the work by composer Sergei Prokofiev.

➢ **THE POT THAT JUAN BUILT** written by Nancy Andrews-Goebel and illustrated by David Diaz; Lee & Low; Grades 1–2+; about Juan Quezada, "premier potter in Mexico."

➢ **RED GREEN BLUE: A FIRST BOOK OF COLORS** by Alison Jay; Dutton; Grades Pre-K–1; color and nursery rhyme recognition combine in this delightfully simple book that marries lyrical text with bright, playfully detailed illustrations; featured nursery rhymes are listed at the back of the book. See also:

    ◦ **1 2 3: A CHILD'S FIRST COUNTING BOOK**
    ◦ **A B C: A CHILD'S FIRST ALPHABET BOOK**

➢ **RED SINGS FROM TREETOPS: A YEAR IN COLORS** written by Joyce Sidman and illustrated by Pamela Zagarenski; Houghton Mifflin; Grades 1–4; poetic treatment of the colors of the seasons.

➢ **RENT PARTY JAZZ** written by William Miller and illustrated by Charlotte Riley-Webb; Lee & Low; Grades 2–4; a jazz party with free-will offering enables a family to make the rent.

➢ **SANDY'S CIRCUS: A STORY ABOUT ALEXANDER CALDER** written by Tanya Lee Stone and illustrated by Boris Kulikov; Viking; Grades 2–4; biography of the man who invented the mobile; correlates well with science unit on balance.

➢ **SCRIBBLE** by Deborah Freedman; Knopf; Grades Pre-K–1; two sisters and their scribbling rivalry!

➢ **SHAPE** by David Goodman and Zoe Miller; Tate/Abrams; Grades Pre-K–2; vivid illustrations introduce basic 2-D and 3-D shapes; simple activities and suggestions for projects encourage further exploration.

➢ **THIS JAZZ MAN** written by Karen Ehrhardt and illustrated by R. G. Roth; Harcourt; Grades Pre-K–3; playful, evocative language in a jaunty rendition of "This Old Man" pays homage to jazz greats, such as Charles Mingus, Bojangles, and Satchmo.

➢ **UNCLE ANDY'S** by James Warhola; Putnam; Grades 1–3+; amusing, child-friendly peek at Andy Warhol's world, written and illustrated by his nephew.

➢ **WHAT DO AUTHORS DO?** by Eileen Christelow; Clarion; Grades K–2; simple, straightforward explanation with charming illustrations. See also:

    ◦ **WHAT DO ILLUSTRATORS DO?**

> **WHAT'S THE BIG IDEA, MOLLY?** by Valeri Gorbachev; Philomel; Grades 1–2; in this warmly encouraging tale, collaboration spurs loads of ideas and lovely art while nurturing friendship.

> **WHEN MARIAN SANG** written by Pam Munoz Ryan and illustrated by Brian Selznick; Scholastic; Grades 2+; a Robert F. Sibert Honor Book about the African American singer's rise to fame in the 1930s despite the strictures of the times.

Bilingual Books

> **CARMEN LEARNS ENGLISH** written by Judy Cox and illustrated by Angela Dominguez; Holiday House; Grades K–1; a reassuring tale about a Latina child's first experiences in an American school.

> **EIGHT ANIMALS ON THE TOWN** written by Susan Middleton Elya and illustrated by Lee Chapman; Putnam; Grades 1–2; eight animals go to the market to find their dinner and then off to spend an evening on the town; key words are offered in Spanish with contextual clues; spunky, bright illustrations aptly reflect Latino culture.

> **GRACIAS THANKS** written by Pat Mora and illustrated by John Parra; Lee & Low; Grades K–2; text offered in both Spanish and English depicts the everyday things for which a child is thankful.

> **JUST A MINUTE: A TRICKSTER TALE AND COUNTING BOOK** by Yuyi Morales; Chronicle; Grades 1–2; tale from the Mexican culture offers an entertaining introduction to counting in both Spanish and English.

> **MIRROR** by Jeannie Baker; Candlewick; Grades K+; a creatively formatted book, largely wordless, that depicts two families across the globe from one another that nevertheless share some connections.

> **MY SHOES AND I** written by René Colato Laínez and illustrated by Fabricio Vanden Broeck; Boyds Mills Press; Grades 1–3; about a boy making his way to the United States from El Salvador in the new shoes his mother has sent to him.

> **NO MORE, POR FAVOR** written by Susan Middleton Elya and illustrated by David Walker; Putnam; Grades K–2; pitch-perfect for finicky eaters; lyrical bilingual text.

> **A PIÑATA IN A PINE TREE: A LATINO TWELVE DAYS OF CHRISTMAS** written by Pat Mora and illustrated by Magaly Morales; Clarion; Grades 1–2; traditional gifts in this version of the well-known carol are replaced with Latino-inspired offerings; find, count, and learn Spanish words and their pronunciations on each page; glossary and score are found at the back of the book.

> **SAY HELLO!** by Rachel Isadora; Putnam; Grades K–2; as Carmelita wanders through her diverse neighborhood, friends greet her in their native languages.

> **TOOTH ON THE LOOSE** written by Susan Middleton Elya and illustrated by Jenny Mattheson; Putnam; Grades K–2; bilingual; rhyming text.

> **WELCOME TO MY NEIGHBORHOOD! A BARRIO ABC** written by Quiara Alegría Hudes and illustrated by Shino Arihara; Arthur A. Levine/Scholastic; Grades K–2; key words in Spanish are highlighted throughout the simple text.

Biography/Memoir

> **ABE LINCOLN CROSSES A CREEK: A TALL, THIN TALE** written by Deborah Hopkinson and illustrated by John Hendrix; Schwartz & Wade/Random House; Grades 2–4; the mostly true tale of how Lincoln's childhood friend, Austin Gollaher, saved his life; delightful format; humorous illustrations; lively language; multiple award winner. See **A Closer Look: Abraham Lincoln**.

> **ABRAHAM LINCOLN** written by Amy Cohn and Suzy Schmidt and illustrated by David A. Johnson; Scholastic; Grades 1–2+; tall, slim, engaging biography with a terrific "folksy" voice. See **A Closer Look: Abraham Lincoln**.

> **ACTION JACKSON** written by Jan Greenberg and Sandra Jordan and illustrated by Robert Andrew Parker; Roaring Brook; Grades 1–2+; adeptly conveys Jackson Pollock's spirit, talent, and influence on contemporary American art; a Robert F. Sibert Honor Book.

> **DEGAS AND THE DANCE** by Susan Goldman Rubin; Abrams: Grades 1–3+; biography of the "painter of dancing girls" illustrated with over 30 works of art by Degas; focuses on Degas's realization that creating and perfecting art takes dedication, hard work, and perseverance.

> **THE DINOSAURS OF WATERHOUSE HAWKINS** written by Barbara Kerley and illustrated by Brian Selznick; Scholastic; Grades 1–2+; stunning Caldecott Honor book highlighting the life of the artist and sculptor who, in the mid-1800s, showed the world what a dinosaur looked like.

> **DOLLEY MADISON SAVES GEORGE WASHINGTON** by Don Brown; Houghton Mifflin; Grades 1–2; picture book about the inimitable Dolley Madison and how she saved the portrait of George Washington from being destroyed when the British burned the President's Mansion in 1814.

> **EVERY FRIDAY** by Dan Yaccarino; Grades K–1; favorite Fridays with Dad; classic picture book styling; offers model for writing memoirs.

> **GEORGE WASHINGTON CARVER** by Tonya Bolden; Abrams; Grades 2–5; richly illustrated pictorial biography.

➢ **HAYM SALOMON: AMERICAN PATRIOT** written by Susan Goldman Rubin and illustrated by David Slonim; Abrams; Grades 2–3; biography of an unsung hero who was "financier of the American Revolution."

➢ **HENRY AARON'S DREAM** by Matt Tavares; Candlewick; Grades 2–3; richly illustrated biography of one of baseball's great legends.

➢ **THE LIBRARIAN OF BASRA: A TRUE STORY FROM IRAQ** by Jeanette Winter; Harcourt; Grades 2+; story of librarian who saved 30,000 books from being destroyed during the bombing of Basra in 2003.

➢ **MAMA MITI** written by Donna Jo Napoli and illustrated by Kadir Nelson; Simon & Schuster; Grades 1–2; with the refrain, *Thayu nyumba* (Peace, my people), threaded throughout the text, able storyteller Napoli weaves the tale of the 2004 Nobel Peace Prize winner, Wangari Maathai's, far-reaching influence; beautifully depicted with collage illustrations by the Caldecott Honor artist. See **A Closer Look: Our Earth.** See also:

  ∘ **WANGARI'S TREES OF PEACE** by Jeanette Winter; Harcourt

➢ **MARTIN'S BIG WORDS** written by Doreen Rappaport and illustrated by Bryan Collier; Hyperion; Grades K–2+; outstanding, multiple award-winning book about Martin Luther King Jr.

➢ **MARY SMITH** by A. U'Ren; Farrar, Straus & Giroux; Grades 1–2+; the story within a story about "knocker-up" Mary Smith, who, in London in the 1920s before alarm clocks were widely used, shot dried peas from a rubber tube at the windows of her clients to wake them for work.

➢ **MR. LINCOLN'S BOYS** written by Staton Rabin and illustrated by Bagram Ibatoulline; Viking; Grades 2–3; as the subtitle indicates: the mostly true adventures of Lincoln's "troublemaking" sons, Tad and Willie. See **A Closer Look: Abraham Lincoln.**

➢ **OUR ABE LINCOLN** written by Jim Aylesworth and illustrated by Barbara McClintock; Scholastic; Grades K–2; biography of Abe Lincoln told through jaunty lyrics intended to be sung to melody of "The Old Gray Mare." See **A Closer Look: Abraham Lincoln.**

➢ **SO YOU WANT TO BE AN INVENTOR?** written by Judith St. George and illustrated by Caldecott artist David Small; Philomel; Grades 1–2+; short, pithy, humorous profiles; companion to Caldecott winner **SO YOU WANT TO BE PRESIDENT?**

➢ **SO YOU WANT TO BE PRESIDENT?** written by Judith St. George and illustrated by David Small; Philomel; Grades 1–2+; short, humorous anecdotes profile the American presidents through Bill Clinton; winner of the Caldecott Medal.

➢ **STEALING HOME: JACKIE ROBINSON AGAINST THE ODDS** written by Robert Burleigh and illustrated by Mike Wimmer; Simon & Schuster; Grades

1–3; picture book account of the World Series game in September 1955 in which Robinson stole home.

➢ **TEEDIE: THE STORY OF YOUNG TEDDY ROOSEVELT** by Don Brown; Houghton Mifflin; Grades 2–4.

➢ **THANK YOU, SARAH! THE WOMAN WHO SAVED THANKSGIVING** written by Laurie Halse Anderson and illustrated by Matt Faulkner; Simon & Schuster; Grades 2–4; engaging picture book biography written by an inspired award-winning author, with art by an illustrator who understands what makes a picture book stand out; biography, history, power-of-the-pen message.

➢ **UNCLE ANDY'S** by James Warhola; Putnam; Grades 1–3+; amusing child-friendly peek at Andy Warhol's world written and illustrated by his nephew.

➢ **WANGARI'S TREES OF PEACE** by Jeanette Winter; Harcourt; Grades 2–4; true story of Wangari Maathai, environmentalist and winner of the Nobel Peace Prize for her work restoring trees throughout Kenya. See **A Closer Look: Our Earth.** See also:

  ◦ **MAMA MITI** written by Donna Jo Napoli and illustrated by Kadir Nelson; Simon & Schuster

➢ **WHEN I WAS YOUNG IN THE MOUNTAINS** written by Cynthia Rylant and illustrated by Diane Goode; Dutton; Grades K–3; classic memoir of growing up in Appalachia; Caldecott Honor Award and Reading Rainbow Book.

➢ **WHEN MARIAN SANG** written by Pam Muñoz Ryan and illustrated by Brian Selznick; Scholastic; Grades 2+; a Robert F. Sibert Honor Book about the African American singer's rise to fame in the 1930s despite the strictures of the times.

➢ **YOUNG PELÉ: SOCCER'S FIRST STAR** written by Lesa Cline-Ransome and illustrated by James E. Ransome; Schwartz & Wade/Random House; Grades 1–3; story of the poor but determined Brazilian boy who always focused on his goal and never gave up his dream.

Character Education

➢ **ALL OF ME: A BOOK OF THANKS** by Molly Bang; Blue Sky/Scholastic; Grades Pre-K–K; bright, appealing collages offer a joyful look at the wonder of hands, feet, eyes, noses, and feelings.

➢ **ALL THE WORLD** written by Liz Garton Scanlon and illustrated by Marla Frazee; Beach Lane/Simon & Schuster; Grades K–2; lyrical text paired with warm, engaging art celebrates the universality of family and home.

➢ **AMAZING FACES** poems selected by Lee Bennett Hopkins and illustrated by Chris Soentpiet; Lee & Low; Grades 1–4; 16 poems featuring mulitcultural children explore universal feelings that connect us all. See **A Closer Look: All Shapes, Sizes, Shades, and Beliefs**.

➢ **BALLYHOO BAY** written by Judy Sierra and illustrated by Derek Anderson; Simon & Schuster; Grades 2–4; contemporary fable about art, nature, and community in which a beach is saved from a high-rise; humorous, vivid illustrations; rhythmical, well-paced text. See **A Closer Look: Our Earth**.

➢ **BEAR FEELS SICK** written by Karma Wilson and illustrated by Jane Chapman; McElderry Books; Grades Pre-K–1; friends take care of a sick buddy.

➢ **BEING A PIG IS NICE: A CHILD'S EYE VIEW OF MANNERS** written by Sally Lloyd-Jones and illustrated by Dan Krall; Schwartz & Wade/Random House; Grades 1–3; a humorous look at the pros and cons of poor manners.

➢ **BELLA & BEAN** written by Rebecca Kai Dotlich and illustrated by Aileen Leijten; Atheneum; Grades K–2; friends can have different interests; delightful text; warm illustrations.

➢ **BOBO AND THE NEW NEIGHBOR** by Gail Page; Bloomsbury; Grades Pre-K–2; what dog doesn't love muffins? Even so, Bobo manages to share his delectables with the new neighbor; hilarious tale about hospitality.

➢ **BRAVE CHARLOTTE** written by Anu Stohner and illustrated by Henrike Wilson; Bloomsbury; Grades K–1; shy but brave sheep saves the day. See also:

  ◦ **BRAVE CHARLOTTE AND THE WOLVES,** about bullies

➢ **BUDGIE & BOO** by David McPhail; Abrams; Grades K–1; move over, Frog and Toad, there's a new duo in town. Delightful!

➢ **BUSTER GOES TO COWBOY CAMP** by Denise Fleming; Henry Holt; Grades Pre-K–1; change can be good.

➢ **BUTTERFLIES FOR KIRI** by Cathryn Falwell; Lee & Low; Grades 1–2; with patience and persistence, a young child creates a collage with origami.

➢ **CARDBOARD PIANO** by Lynne Rae Perkins; Greenwillow; Grades 2–4; adept tale about friends respecting one another's differences.

➢ **CALLIE CAT, ICE SKATER** written by Eileen Spinelli and illustrated by Anne Kennedy; Whitman; Grades K–2; doing something you love is its own reward; sweet, whimsical art.

➢ **CELESTINE DRAMA QUEEN** by Penny Ives; Arthur A. Levine/Scholastic; Grades Pre-K–2; confidence is struck a blow after an initial experience with stage fright, but reassurance saves the day.

- ➢ **CITY DOG, COUNTRY FROG** written by Mo Willems and illustrated by Jon J. Muth; Hyperion; Grades K–2; spare reflection on friendship and the seasons of life; luminous art.

- ➢ **COMMUNICATION** by Aliki; Greenwillow; Grades K–2; interpersonal communication for the pint-sized; classic. See also:

  - ◦ **MANNERS**

- ➢ **COOL CAT** by Nonny Hogrogian; Roaring Brook; Grades 1–3; a cat colors his world with the help of his friends; wordless.

- ➢ **CROW CALL** written by Lois Lowry and illustrated by Bagram Ibatoulline; Scholastic; Grades 1–3; lyrical, beautifully rendered period piece about a girl, a dad recently home from war, and a day in which they reacquaint themselves with one another; debut picture book by the legendary children's author.

- ➢ **A DAY, A DOG** by Gabrielle Vincent; Front Street; Grades 2–4; wordless wonder about a day in the life of an abandoned dog ends with hope—and opens the door to meaningful discussion.

- ➢ **THE DAY IT RAINED HEARTS** (formerly **FOUR VALENTINES IN A RAINSTORM**) by Felicia Bond; HarperCollins; Grades Pre-K-2; perfectly rendered picture book about choosing just the right gifts for friends.

- ➢ **DIFFERENT LIKE COCO** by Elizabeth Matthews; Candlewick; Grades 2–4; biography of Gabrielle "Coco" Chanel celebrates individuality.

- ➢ **DOGKU** written by Andrew Clements and illustrated by Tim Bowers; Simon & Schuster; Grades 1–2+; story of dog adoption told in haiku; the author's note discusses haiku poetry form.

- ➢ **DO UNTO OTTERS: A BOOK ABOUT MANNERS** by Laurie Keller; Holt; Grades 1–2; the Golden Rule explained with doses of humor.

- ➢ **ERROL AND HIS EXTRAORDINARY NOSE** written by David Conway and illustrated by Roberta Angaramo; Holiday House; Grades K–1; self-esteem figures big in this book about an elephant and his talents!

- ➢ **FIVE FOR A LITTLE ONE** by Chris Raschka; Atheneum; Grades Pre-K–2; a beginner's look at the five senses features a family of rabbits.

- ➢ **FLY FREE!** written by Roseanne Thong and illustrated by Eujin Kim Neilan; Boyds Mills; Grades Pre-K–2+; a simple, kind act sets in motion a series of good deeds in a small village in Vietnam; the refrain, *Fly free, fly free in the sky so blue. When you do a good deed, it will come back to you!* sets the tone and frames the lilting, beautifully illustrated story.

- ➢ **A FRIEND LIKE YOU** by Tanja Askani; Scholastic; Grades Pre-K–1; photographs of animals and spare text effectively convey scope and depth of friendships.

➤ **GIRAFFES CAN'T DANCE** written by Giles Andreae and illustrated by Guy Parker-Rees; Orchard/Scholastic; Grades K–2; giraffe comes to realize "we can all dance when we find the music we love"; music CD included.

➤ **GRACIAS THANKS** written by Pat Mora and illustrated by John Parra; Lee & Low; Grades Pre-K–2; text offered in both Spanish and English depicts the everyday things for which a child is thankful.

➤ **THE GREAT MATH TATTLE BATTLE** written by Anne Bowen and illustrated by Jaime Zollars; Whitman; Grades 1–2; tattletale tale and math lessons.

➤ **GUTTERSNIPE** written by Jane Cutler and illustrated by Emily Arnold McCully; Farrar, Straus & Giroux; Grades 2–3; turn-of-the-century story set in Canada about a boy who learns that mistakes are part of growing up.

➤ **HARRIET DANCING** by Ruth Symes and illustrated by Caroline Jayne Church; Chicken House/Scholastic; Grades K–2; sweet tale of friendship and self-acceptance; lovely, lilting illustrations.

➤ **HAT** by Paul Hoppe; Bloomsbury; Grades Pre-K–2; a child finds a hat and considers myriad possibilities for its use.

➤ **HELLO MY NAME IS BOB** by Linas Alsenas; Scholastic Press; Grades K–1; opposites connect; simple, lighthearted language; comical illustrations.

➤ **HOPE IS AN OPEN HEART** by Lauren Thompson; Scholastic Press; Grades K–3+; spare text and inspiring photographs offer reassurance.

➤ **HOW DO YOU WOKKA-WOKKA?** written by Elizabeth Bluemle and illustrated Randy Cecil; Candlewick; Grades Pre-K–2; rhythmic chant celebrates individuality, movement, dance, and multicultural friendships.

➤ **HOW TO HEAL A BROKEN WING** by Bob Graham; Candlewick; Grades Pre-K–2; boy aids an injured bird; spare text, evocative art.

➤ **HOW TO LOSE ALL YOUR FRIENDS** by Nancy Carlson; Puffin; Grades Pre-K–3; tongue-in-cheek reminders of what makes a good friend.

➤ **HUG** by Jez Alborough; Candlewick; Grades Pre-K–K; minimal language, big message conveyed through the art; true to Alborough's distinctive, heartwarming style.

➤ **HURRY UP AND SLOW DOWN** by Layn Marlow; Holiday House; Grades Pre-K–1; two friends find common ground in a book.

➤ **I'M NOT INVITED?** by Diana Cain Bluthenthal; Atheneum; Grades K–3; told with simple, humorous understatement underscored with warm, inviting (ha ha) watercolors, this story, dedicated to "anyone, or the friend of anyone, who's ever felt left out," is a must-read before birthday invitations are permitted to be distributed in the classroom.

> **I'M NUMBER ONE** written by Michael Rosen and illustrated by Bob Graham; Grades K–2; Candlewick; a bully learns to be part of the group; stars a wind-up soldier drummer and a montage of supporting toy chest characters.

> **IT'S A SPOON, NOT A SHOVEL** written by Caralyn Buehner and illustrated by Mark Buehner; Puffin; Grades K–3; manners guide offered in a light, amusing format. See also:

   ○ **I DID IT, I'M SORRY**

> **JACK'S TALENT** by Maryann Cocca-Leffler; Farrar, Straus & Giroux; Grades K–2; everyone has a special talent. See **A Closer Look: All Shapes, Sizes, Shades, and Beliefs**.

> **JOSEPHINE WANTS TO DANCE** written by Jackie French and illustrated by Bruce Whatley; Abrams; Grades K–2; encourages children to move to their own music; charming illustrations.

> **THE JUNGLE GRAPEVINE** by John Beard; Abrams; Grades K–3; like the game of telephone, a message gets misunderstood in the jungle.

> **KISSES ON THE WIND** written by Lisa Moser and illustrated by Kathryn Brown; Candlewick; Grades 2–4; poignant tale about leaving behind those you love set in the time of the westward movement.

> **KITCHEN DANCE** by Maurie J. Manning; Clarion; Grades Pre-K–2; a celebration of family time in a Hispanic home; vibrant, joyous illustrations and foot-tapping, finger-snapping language.

> **LADYBUG GIRL AND BUMBLEBEE BOY** by David Somar and Jacky Davis; Dial; Grades Pre-K–1; working things out on the playground. Sequels available.

> **LIBRARY LION** written by Michelle Knudsen and illustrated by Kevin Hawkes; Candlewick; Grades K–2; a lion who loves the library breaks the rules and saves the day; New York Times best-seller.

> **THE LION & THE MOUSE** by Jerry Pinkney; Little, Brown; Grades Pre-K–1+; wordless rendering of Aesop fable about courage and kindness; Caldecott Medal.

> **LION'S LUNCH?** written by Fiona Tierney and illustrated by Margaret Chamberlain; Scholastic; Grades Pre-K–1; grouchy lion comes to realize how he looks to others.

> **LITTLE MOUSE'S BIG BOOK OF FEARS** by Emily Gravett; Grades Pre-K–2; everyone is afraid of something; clever book format enhances the story.

> **LOUDER, LILI** written by Gennifer Choldenko and illustrated by S. D. Schindler; Putnam; Grades 1–2; shy child gathers courage to speak up.

> **LUCY AND THE BULLY** by Claire Alexander; Albert Whitman; Grades Pre-K–2; kindness, insight, and a little help from Mom thwart the class bully.

➢ **MAMA MITI** written by Donna Jo Napoli and illustrated by Kadir Nelson; Simon & Schuster; Grades 1–2; With the refrain, *Thayu nyumba* (Peace, my people), threaded throughout the text, able storyteller Napoli weaves the tale of the 2004 Nobel Peace Prize winner, Wangari Maathai's, far-reaching influence; beautifully depicted with collage illustrations by the Caldecott Honor artist. See **A Closer Look: Our Earth**. See also:

  ◦ **WANGARI'S TREES OF PEACE** by Jeanette Winter; Harcourt

➢ **MILO ARMADILLO** by Jan Fearnley; Candlewick; Grades K–2; a tale about friendship and the things that matter; delightfully told and sweetly rendered.

➢ **MIND YOUR MANNERS, B. B. WOLF** written by Judy Sierra and illustrated by J. Otto Seibold; Knopf; Grades K–2; encourage good manners with this wacky tale starring B.B. (Big Bad) Wolf.

➢ **MOLLY WHO FLEW AWAY** by Valeri Gorbachev; Philomel; Grades Pre-K–2; going the distance for friends.

➢ **MOUSE WAS MAD** written by Linda Urban and illustrated by Henry Cole; Harcourt; Grades Pre-K–2; Mouse and his friends have different ways of expressing anger.

➢ **MS. MCCAW LEARNS TO DRAW** by Kaethe Zemach; Arthur A. Levine/Scholastic; Grades 2–4; inattentive, struggling student likes to doodle, and Ms. McCaw, a charming wise teacher, finds a way to celebrate that.

➢ **MY MOM** by Anthony Browne; Farrar, Straus & Giroux; Grades Pre-K–2; a celebration of the many talents of an everyday mom; great model for use of figurative language.

➢ **MY NAME IS YOON** written by Helen Recorvits and illustrated by Gabi Swiatkowska; Farrar, Straus & Giroux; Grades 1–3; Yoon prefers to write her name in the Korean symbols that "dance together" rather than the English letters that stand alone. Readers witness Yoon gradually making the transition to her new home in America; engaging, poignant tale; winner of the Ezra Jack Keats New Illustrator Award. See **A Closer Look: All Shapes, Sizes, Shades, and Beliefs**.

➢ **MY FATHER, THE DOG** written by Elizabeth Bluemle and illustrated by Randy Cecil; Candlewick; Grades Pre-K–2; Dad's behavior is compared to a dog's— from his snacking, lying around for hours, and roughhousing to fetching the newspaper and, yes, "tooting."

➢ **NEVER TALK TO STRANGERS** written by Irma Joyce and illustrated by George Buckett; Golden Books/Random House; Grades K–2; reissue of a classic that lightheartedly explores what a "stranger" is.

- ➤ **NEW YEAR AT THE PIER: A ROSH HASHANAH STORY** written by April Halprin Wayland and illustrated by Stephane Jorisch; Dial; Grades 2–3; family and friends take joy in the Jewish holiday; charming blend of art and text.

- ➤ **NICOLAS, WHERE HAVE YOU BEEN?** by Leo Lionni; Knopf; Grades K–2; reissue of a classic explores the theme "one bad bird doesn't make a flock."

- ➤ **OTIS** by Loren Long; Philomel; Grades Pre-K–2; a true friend is helped by those he has helped; in the style of classic picture books in tone and quality; beautifully rendered illustrations by a gifted artist.

- ➤ **PEANUT** by David Lucas; Candlewick; Grades Pre-K–1; gentle tale reminiscent of Chicken Little reminds youngsters it's silly to worry; vivid illustrations.

- ➤ **PEACE WEEK IN MISS FOX'S CLASS** written by Eileen Spinelli and illustrated by Anne Kennedy; Albert Whitman; Grades Pre-K–2; perspectives on getting along in all sorts of situations are gently offered.

- ➤ **PEARL BARLEY AND CHARLIE PARSLEY** by Aaron Blabey; Front Street; Grades Pre-K–1; opposites attract and make for solid friendships.

- ➤ **A PERFECT SNOWMAN** by Preston McDaniels; Simon & Schuster; Grades 1–3; snowman who has the best of everything receives most precious gift.

- ➤ **PLEASE IS A GOOD WORD TO SAY** written by Barbara Joosse and illustrated by Jennifer Plecas; Philomel; Grades K–2; manners basics accompanied by humorous illustrations.

- ➤ **PRINCESS PIG** written by Eileen Spinelli and illustrated by Tim Bowers; Knopf; Grades 1–2; Princess Pig realizes what makes her special.

- ➤ **PUZZLEHEAD** by James Yang; Atheneum; Grades Pre-K–2; a look at recess, playing with others, and fitting in.

- ➤ **RABBIT'S GIFT** written by George Shannon and illustrated by Laura Dronzek; Harcourt; Grades K–1; based on international folktale about friendship.

- ➤ **READY FOR ANYTHING!** by Keiko Kasza; Putnam; Grades K–2; attitude (and preparation) is everything! See also:

  - ◦ **MY LUCKY DAY**
  - ◦ **BADGER'S FANCY MEAL**
  - ◦ **THE DOG WHO CRIED WOLF**

- ➤ **READY, SET, SKIP!** written by Jane O'Connor and illustrated by Ann James; Viking; Grades Pre-K–1; rhyming text skips along as child learns to . . . skip!

- ➤ **RENT PARTY JAZZ** written by William Miller and illustrated by Charlotte Riely-Webb; Lee & Low; Grades 2–4; a jazz party with free-will offering enables a family to make the rent.

➤ **ROMAN AND LOW BLAST OFF** by Derek Anderson; Simon & Schuster; Grades Pre-K–2; the adventures of a pair of unlikely friends.

➤ **SALLY GOES TO THE VET** by Stephen Huneck; Abrams; Grades Pre-K–2; a dog's visit to the vet.

➤ **SAY HELLO** by Jack and Michael Foreman; Candlewick; Grades Pre-K–1; including others is easy and satisfying for all.

➤ **THE SCARECROW'S DANCE** written by Jane Yolen and illustrated by Bagram Ibatoulline; Simon & Schuster; Grades 2–4; recognizing one's special gifts.

➤ **SCRIBBLE** by Deborah Freedman; Knopf; Grades Pre-K–1; two sisters and their scribbling rivalry!

 ➤ **SHADES OF BLACK: A CELEBRATION OF OUR CHILDREN** written by Sandra L. Pinkney with photographs by Myles C. Pinkney; Scholastic; Grades Pre-K–2; poetic book offers affirmation. See **A Closer Look: All Shapes, Sizes, Shades, and Beliefs**.

 ➤ **SHADES OF PEOPLE** by Shelley Rotner and Sheila M. Kelly with photographs by Shelley Rotner; Holiday House; Grades Pre-K–2; people come in all shades. See **A Closer Look: All Shapes, Sizes, Shades, and Beliefs**.

 ➤ **A SICK DAY FOR AMOS MCGEE** written by Philip C. Stead and illustrated by Erin E. Stead; Roaring Brook; Grades 1–2+; a charming, gentle tale of a zookeeper whose many friends come to his aid in his time of need—as he has theirs on so many occasions; endearing, skillfully rendered illustrations make this book feel like a classic-to-be.

➤ **A SPLENDID FRIEND, INDEED** by Suzanne Bloom; Boyds Mills; Grades Pre-K–1; Theodor Seuss Geisel Honor Book celebrates reading, writing, and friendship.

➤ **SUNDAY CHUTNEY** by Aaron Blabey; Front Street; Grades Pre-K–2; gentle insight into being the new kid at school.

 ➤ **SYLVIE** by Jennifer Sattler; Random House; Grades 1–3; being yourself is the best thing to be; colorful and sprightly. See **A Closer Look: All Shapes, Sizes, Shades, and Beliefs**.

➤ **TAKING CARE OF MAMA** by Mitra Modarressi; Putnam; Grades Pre-K–1; Mama's sick and tucked in bed and her caring family intends to execute Mama's daily chores, learning along the way that taking care of the family is hard work indeed; watercolor art adds humor and delight to the simple rhyming text.

➤ **TESTING THE ICE: A TRUE STORY ABOUT JACKIE ROBINSON** written by Sharon Robinson and illustrated by Kadir Nelson; Scholastic; Grades 2–4; an incident in young Robinson's life reflects his character and courage.

> **THANK YOU, WORLD** written by Alice B. McGinty and illustrated by Wendy Anderson Halperin; Dial; Grades Pre-K–2; rich, simple rhyme expresses joys of childhood across the world. See **A Closer Look: Geography, Maps, and Travel**.

> **THAT'S WHAT FRIENDS ARE FOR** written by Florence Parry Heide and Sylvia Van Clief and illustrated by Holly Meade; Candlewick; Grades K–2; friends give advice that doesn't help; cumulative tale.

> **THOSE SHOES** written by Maribeth Boelts and illustrated by Noah Z. Jones; Candlewick; Grades 1–2; the things you have can be more valuable than the things you want.

> **TIGER AND TURTLE** by James Rumford; Roaring Brook; Grades 1–2; an unlikely duo argue over a flower until events lead them to realize how silly their behavior is.

> **TWO BOBBIES: A TRUE STORY OF HURRICANE KATRINA, FRIENDSHIP, AND SURVIVAL** written by Kirby Larson and Mary Nethery and illustrated by Jean Cassels; Walker; Grades 2–4; true story of an enduring friendship between a dog and cat.

> **VELMA GRATCH & THE WAY COOL BUTTERFLY** written by Alan Madison and illustrated by Kevin Hawkes; Schwartz & Wade/Random House Books; Grades 1–3; life cycle of the monarch and metamorphosis of a budding scientist.

> **A VERY BIG BUNNY** by Marisabina Russo; Schwartz & Wade/Random House; Grades Pre-K–2; a very big bunny who doesn't fit in befriends with a very small bunny who doesn't give up. See **A Closer Look: All Shapes, Sizes, Shades, and Beliefs**.

> **A VISITOR FOR BEAR** written by Bonnie Becker and illustrated by Kady MacDonald Denton; Candlewick; Grades Pre-K–1; bear comes to realize the value of a friend; additional titles continue tales of the unlikely but endearing friendship.

> **WANGARI'S TREES OF PEACE** by Jeanette Winter; Harcourt; Grades 2–4; true story of Wangari Maathai, environmentalist and winner of the Nobel Peace Prize for her work restoring trees throughout Kenya. See **A Closer Look: Our Earth**. See also:

> ° **MAMA MITI** written by Donna Jo Napoli and illustrated by Kadir Nelson; Simon & Schuster

> **WHAT COLOR IS CAESAR?** written by Maxine Kumin and illustrated by Alison Friend; Candlewick; Grades K–2; it's what color you are on the inside that matters. See **A Closer Look: All Shapes, Sizes, Shades, and Beliefs**.

➤ **WHAT'S THE BIG IDEA, MOLLY?** by Valeri Gorbachev; Philomel; Grades 1–2; collaboration spurs great ideas and nurtures friendship in this warmly encouraging tale.

➤ **WHEN I GROW UP** by Leonid Gore; Scholastic; Grades Pre-K–2; cutouts in pages encourage prediction in this warmhearted story of a boy who knows what he wants to be when he grows up.

➤ **WHEN RANDOLPH TURNED ROTTEN** by Charise Mericle Harper; Knopf; Grades K–2; When Randolph lets jealousy over an all-girl slumber party get the best of him, his insides turn stinky rotten despite his best friend Ivy's unflappable good humor. Mean behavior backfires, Randolph apologizes, and all's well that ends well; spunky graphic-style acrylic illustrations; Junior Literary Guild selection.

➤ **THE WORST BEST FRIEND** written by Alexis O'Neill and illustrated by Laura Huliska-Beith; Scholastic Press; Grades K–2; true-blue friend is best friend after all. See also:

　◦ **THE RECESS QUEEN**, about bullying

➤ **ZEN TIES** by Jon J. Muth; Scholastic Press; Grades K–2+; grouchy older neighbor and neighborhood children meet and grow through their interactions with one another.

Community and Families

➤ **ANGELINA'S ISLAND** by Jeanette Winter; Farrar, Straus & Giroux; Grades 1–2; Angelina misses Jamaica and the traditions there, but her involvement in a neighborhood carnival eases the transition to America.

➤ **AROUND OUR WAY ON NEIGHBORS' DAY** written by Tameka Fryer Brown and illustrated by Charlotte Riley-Webb; Abrams; Grades K–2; rhyming text celebrates neighborhood diversity as a block party gets under way.

➤ **AT THE SUPERMARKET** by Anne Rockwell; Holt; Grades Pre-K–K; a child takes a trip to the grocery store; a new edition of this classic.

➤ **BALLYHOO BAY** written by Judy Sierra and illustrated by Derek Anderson; Simon & Schuster; Grades 2–4; contemporary fable about art, nature, and community in which a beach is saved from a high-rise; humorous, vivid illustrations; rhythmical, well-paced text. See **A Closer Look: Our Earth**.

➤ **COME AND PLAY: CHILDREN OF OUR WORLD HAVING FUN** edited by Ayana Lowe with photographs by Julie Collins; Bloomsbury; Grades 2–5; children across the world are depicted playing; text is original poems of children across time and continents. See **A Closer Look: All Shapes, Sizes, Shades, and Beliefs**.

➢ **DAD AND POP: AN ODE TO FATHERS & STEPFATHERS** written by Kelly Bennett and illustrated by Paul Meisel; Candlewick; Grades Pre-K–1; dads and stepdads might be different in many ways, but in their love for this character they're very much alike; gentle message conveyed with simple text and warm watercolor, acrylic, and pastel art.

➢ **FARM** by Elisha Cooper; Orchard/Scholastic; Grades K–2; following the animals, farmers, and their children as they conduct life on a farm throughout the seasons; simply rendered panels in watercolors and pencil clearly depict the rhythm of farm life and its seasons.

 ➢ **FAMILIES** by Susan Kuklin; Hyperion; Grades K–2; children from 15 diverse families describe and celebrate their families and their place within them. See **A Closer Look: All Shapes, Sizes, Shades, and Beliefs.**

➢ **FIREKEEPER'S SON** written by Linda Sue Park and illustrated by Julie Downing; Clarion; Grades 2–3; the setting is Korea in the 1800s, but the theme is universal: choosing between the needs of others and one's own wishes; by the Newbery Award-winning author, with glowing watercolor illustrations.

 ➢ **HOW DO YOU WOKKA-WOKKA?** written by Elizabeth Bluemle and illustrated Randy Cecil; Candlewick; Grades Pre-K–2; rhythmic chant celebrates individuality, movement, dance, and multicultural friendships in an urban setting.

➢ **THE LIBRARIAN OF BASRA: A TRUE STORY FROM IRAQ** by Jeanette Winter; Harcourt; Grades 2+; story of librarian who saved 30,000 books from being destroyed during the bombing of Basra in 2003.

 ➢ **MILES TO GO** by Jamie Harper; Candlewick; Pre-K–K; a young boy takes his scooter car to school and meet his friend there. See **A Closer Look: Geography, Maps, and Travel.**

 ➢ **MIRROR** by Jeannie Baker; Candlewick; Grades K+; a creatively formatted book, largely wordless, that depicts two families across the globe from one another that nevertheless share some connections. See **A Closer Look: All Shapes, Sizes, Shades, and Beliefs.**

➢ **MY FATHER IS TALLER THAN A TREE** written by Joseph Bruchac and illustrated by Wendy Anderson Halperin; Dial; 13 everyday but special moments shared between fathers and their sons are depicted in crayon and pencil drawings and rhyming text.

 ➢ **MY PEOPLE** written by Langston Hughes and photographs by Charles R. Smith Jr.; Atheneum; Grades Pre-K–4; illustrated poem celebrates black people of all ages. See **A Closer Look: All Shapes, Sizes, Shades, and Beliefs.**

➢ **MY SHOES AND I** written by René Colato Laínez and illustrated by Fabricio Vanden Broeck; Boyds Mills Press; Grades 1–3; about a boy making his way to the United States from El Salvador in the new shoes his mother has sent to him.

- ➢ **NIGHT SHIFT** by Jessie Hartland; Bloomsbury; Grades K–2; a peek at the jobs of people who work while we sleep.

- ➢ **PEPI SINGS A NEW SONG** by Laura Ljungkvist; Beach Lane/Simon & Schuster; Grades Pre-K–1; Pepi learns new vocabulary as he searches the town for fresh things to sing about.

- ➢ **POPVILLE** by Anouck Boisrobert and Louis Rigaud; Roaring Brook; Grades 1–2; watch a city grow as you turn the pages of this clever and innovative pop-up book.

- ➢ **SALLY GETS A JOB** by Stephen Huneck; Abrams; Grades K–2; a lovable Black Lab considers jobs she would enjoy, and readers learn what the jobs entail; humorous woodcuts with color pencil illustrations; one in a series about this amiable canine.

- ➢ **SAY HELLO!** by Rachel Isadora; Putnam; Grades K–2; as Carmelita wanders through her diverse neighborhood, friends greet her in their native languages.

- ➢ **SIGN LANGUAGE: MY FIRST 100 WORDS** illustrated by Michiyo Nelson; Scholastic; Grades Pre-K–2+; great primer; includes poster.

- ➢ **SUBWAY RIDE** written by Heather Lynn Miller and illustrated by Sue Rama; Charlesbridge; Grades Pre-K–1; subways in 10 cities around the world provide the backdrop for a rhyming ride.

- ➢ **TAKING CARE OF MAMA** by Mitra Modarressi; Putnam; Grades Pre-K–1; Mama's sick and tucked in bed, and her caring family intends to take over Mama's daily chores, learning along the way that taking care of the family is hard work indeed; spare watercolor art adds humor and delight to the simple rhyming text.

- ➢ **THANK YOU, WORLD** written by Alice B. McGinty and illustrated by Wendy Anderson Halperin; Dial; Grades Pre-K–2; rich, simple rhyme expresses joys of childhood across the world. See **A Closer Look: Geography, Maps, and Travel.**

- ➢ **TWO OF A KIND** written by Jacqui Robbins and illustrated by Matt Phelan; Atheneum; Grades 1–3; explores what it means to be both a true friend and true to yourself.

- ➢ **THE VILLAGE GARAGE** by G. Brian Karas; Holt; Grades Pre-K–1; village workers use trucks in every season to keep the community clean and safe.

- ➢ **YOUR DADDY WAS JUST LIKE YOU** written by Kelly Bennett and illustrated by David Walker; Putnam; Grades Pre-K–1; Grandma recalls the ways in which her son was just like her grandson is now; warm and fuzzy and affirming; impetus for sharing family stories. See also:

  - ○ **YOUR MOMMY WAS JUST LIKE YOU**

> **ZEN TIES** by Jon J. Muth; Scholastic Press; Grades K–2+; grouchy neighbor and neighborhood children meet and grow through their gifts to one another.

English Language Arts

> **ALL OF ME: A BOOK OF THANKS** by Molly Bang; Blue Sky Press/Scholastic; Grades Pre-K–1; celebrates parts of the body; endnotes explain how a book is made.

> **BATS AT THE LIBRARY** by Brian Lies; Houghton Mifflin; Grades Pre-K—2; book-loving bats enjoy a night of bookish fun; fabulous illustrations and delightful rhyming text; begs to be read-aloud. Sequels available.

> **BELLA & BEAN** written by Rebecca Kai Dotlich and illustrated by Aileen Leijten; Atheneum; Grades K–2; friends can have different interests; delightful text; warm illustrations; one of the two characters is a terrific poet!

> **THE BEST STORY** written by Eileen Spinelli and illustrated by Anne Wilsdorf; Dial; Grades 1–3; the key to storytelling lies in the heart.

> **BILLY & MILLY SHORT & SILLY** written by Eve B. Feldman and illustrated by Tuesday Mourning; Putnam; Grades K–1; 13 funny, very short stories feature limited vocabulary; ideal for emergent readers.

> **BORN TO READ** written by Judy Sierra and illustrated by Marc Brown; Knopf; Grades K–1; Reader Sam saves the day in this fanciful rhyming tale. See also:

   ◦ **WILD ABOUT BOOKS,** winner of the E. B. White Read-Aloud Award

> **BUNNY WISHES: A WINTER'S TALE** written by Michaela Morgan and illustrated by Caroline Jayne Church; Scholastic; Grades K–2; wishes on a holiday list take on a life of their own.

> **CALENDAR** written by Myra Cohn Livingston and illustrated by Will Hillenbrand; Holiday House; Grades Pre-K–1; lyrical poem about the months of the year.

> **CRAZY LIKE A FOX: A SIMILE STORY** by Loreen Leedy; Holiday House; Grades 2–4; deftly demonstrates simile through use of popular idioms and sayings. See also:

   ◦ **MUDDY AS A DUCK PUDDLE AND OTHER AMERICAN SIMILES** written by Laurie Lawlor and illustrated by Ethan Long
   ◦ **MY BEST FRIEND IS AS SHARP AS A PENCIL AND OTHER FUNNY CLASSROOM PORTRAITS** by Hanoch Piven
   ◦ **MY DOG IS AS SMELLY AS DIRTY SOCKS AND OTHER FUNNY FAMILY PORTRAITS** by Hanoch Piven

➢ **DEAR DEER: A BOOK OF HOMOPHONES** by Gene Barretta; Henry Holt; Grades 1–2; Aunt Ant visits the zoo and describes the animal behavior she sees; entertaining as well as educational.

➢ **DEAR MRS. LARUE: LETTERS FROM OBEDIENCE SCHOOL** by Mark Teague; Scholastic; Grades 1–3+; a delightfully perfect award-winning picture book about an irascible hound sent to school to learn some manners; first in series.

➢ **DOGKU** by Andrew Clements and illustrated by Tim Bowers; Simon & Schuster; Grades 1–2+; story of dog adoption told in haiku; the author's note discusses haiku poetry form.

➢ **DOWN BY THE COOL OF THE POOL** written by Tony Mitton and illustrated by Guy Parker-Rees; Orchard/Scholastic; Grades Pre-K–2; rollicking, rhythmical dancing fun on the farm; great use of figurative language! See also:

  ◦ **GIRAFFES CAN'T DANCE**
  ◦ **DINOSAURUMPUS!**

➢ **EVERY FRIDAY** by Dan Yaccarino; Grades K–1; favorite Fridays with Dad; classic picture book styling; offers model for memoir writing.

➢ **FIREFLIES AT MIDNIGHT** written by Marilyn Singer and illustrated by Ken Robbins; Atheneum; Grades 1–2+; poems about summer's creatures; graphically enhanced photographs and collages.

➢ **FIVE FOR A LITTLE ONE** by Chris Raschka; Atheneum; Grades K–2; simple look at the five senses; useful for teaching sensory imagery.

➢ **FLIP, FLAP, FLY!** written by Phyllis Root and illustrated by David Walker; Candlewick; Grades Pre-K–K; great for teaching prediction to emergent readers.

➢ **THE GARDENER** written by Sarah Stewart and illustrated by David Small; Farrar, Straus & Giroux; Grades 1–3; correspondence between a girl and her parents during the Depression; Caldecott Honor.

➢ **GIMME CRACKED CORN & I WILL SHARE** by Kevin O'Malley; Walker; Grades 1–3+; hilarious story sprinkled with puns and word play.

➢ **GOONEY BIRD IS SO ABSURD** written by Lois Lowry and illustrated by Middy Thomas; Houghton Mifflin; Grades 1–3; early chapter book explores poetry formulas; fourth installment in popular series.

➢ **GREEDY APOSTROPHE: A CAUTIONARY TALE** written by Jan Carr and illustrated by Ethan Long; Holiday House; Grades 3–4; zany approach to the rules of apostrophe use.

➢ **HOPE IS AN OPEN HEART** by Lauren Thompson; Scholastic Press; Grades K–3+; spare text and inspiring photographs offer reassurance; metaphors.

➢ **HOW I SPENT MY SUMMER VACATION** by Mark Teague; Crown; Grades 1–3; humorous tale in verse about how one lucky boy whose imagination needed a rest spent the summer. Consider reading this before assigning the September surefire groan-getter! Nifty afterword to parents and teachers suggests extension activities.

➤ **I DON'T LIKE TO READ!** by Nancy Carlson; Viking; Grades K–1; a first grader's reluctance to read is abated when his younger brother needs his help.

➤ **THE INCREDIBLE BOOK EATING BOY** by Oliver Jeffers; Philomel; Grades K–2; clever tale and packaging celebrates books and reading. YUM!

➤ **I SPY A TO Z: A BOOK OF PICTURE RIDDLES** by Jean Marzollo and photographs by Walter Wick; Scholastic; Grades K–2; picture clues, repetition, phonics clues, and more delight emerging readers; part of a popular series.

➤ **THE JOLLY POSTMAN OR OTHER PEOPLE'S LETTERS** by Janet and Allan Ahlberg; Little, Brown; Grades 1–3; delightful interactive book celebrates snail mail; with pocket envelopes holding winsome letters. See also:

  ◦ **THE JOLLY POCKET POSTMAN**
  ◦ **THE JOLLY CHRISTMAS POSTMAN**

➤ **LIBRARY DRAGON** written by Carmen Agra Deedy and illustrated by Michael P. White; Peachtree; Grades 1–2; Dragon librarian meets nearsighted Molly, an unlikely hero who saves the day!

➤ **LOOKING FOR MOOSE** written by Phyllis Root and illustrated by Randy Cecil; Candlewick; Grades Pre-K–1; playful, evocative language. Great to pair with books by Denise Fleming.

➤ **MAX'S WORDS** written by Kate Banks and illustrated by Boris Kulikov; Farrar, Straus & Giroux; Grades 1–2; Max collects words (instead of stamps and such) and creates a story.

➤ **MEERKAT MAIL** by Emily Gravett; Simon & Schuster; Grades 1–2; Sunny is off to seek the perfect place to live, sending postcards along the way. Actual postcards affixed to pages.

➤ **MISS BROOKS LOVES BOOKS! (AND I DON'T)** written by Barbara Bottner and illustrated by Michael Emberley; Knopf; Grades 1–2; a girl who doesn't like books meets a librarian who doesn't give up; lighthearted celebration of booklovers who simply won't give up on converting the recalcitrant reader.

➤ **MISS SMITH'S INCREDIBLE STORYBOOK** by Michael Garland; Dutton; Grades 1–3; teacher makes read-aloud time magical.

➤ **THE MOON MIGHT BE MILK** written by Lisa Shulman and illustrated by Will Hillenbrand; Dutton; Grades K–2; cumulative story in which a young girl tries to discern what the moon is made of; lyrical, sensory language.

➤ **MOTHER GOOSE'S LITTLE TREASURES** collected by Iona Opie and illustrated by Rosemary Wells; Candlewick; Grades Pre-K–1; a collection of lesser-known rhymes.

➤ **MUDDY AS A DUCK PUDDLE AND OTHER AMERICAN SIMILES** written by Laurie Lawlor and illustrated by Ethan Long; Holiday House; Grades 1–2+; expressions from A to Z that tickle the funny bone gathered from across the American landscape! See also:

   ◦ **CRAZY LIKE A FOX** by Loreen Leedy
   ◦ **MY BEST FRIEND IS AS SHARP AS A PENCIL AND OTHER FUNNY CLASSROOM PORTRAITS** by Hanoch Piven
   ◦ **MY DOG IS AS SMELLY AS DIRTY SOCKS AND OTHER FUNNY FAMILY PORTRAITS** by Hanoch Piven

➤ **MY DOG IS AS SMELLY AS DIRTY SOCKS AND OTHER FUNNY FAMILY PORTRAITS** by Hanoch Piven; Schwartz & Wade/Random House; Grades K–3; lighthearted family "portraits" convey similes. See also:

   ◦ **MY BEST FRIEND IS AS SHARP AS A PENCIL AND OTHER FUNNY CLASSROOM PORTRAITS** by Hanoch Piven
   ◦ **MUDDY AS A DUCK PUDDLE AND OTHER AMERICAN SIMILES** written by Laurie Lawlor and illustrated by Ethan Long
   ◦ **CRAZY LIKE A FOX** by Loreen Leedy

➤ **MY MOM** by Anthony Browne; Farrar, Straus & Giroux; Grades Pre-K–2; a celebration of the many talents of an everyday mom; great model for use of figurative language.

➤ **ONCE UPON A BANANA** written by Jennifer Armstrong and illustrated by David Small; Simon & Schuster; Grades K–2; one small banana causes big trouble in this nearly wordless tale with rhyming street signs.

➤ **ONE DUCK STUCK** written by Phyllis Root and illustrated by Jane Chapman; Candlewick; Grades Pre-K–1; rhythmic counting story offers delightful word play!

➤ **ORANGE PEAR APPLE BEAR** by Emily Gravett; Simon & Schuster; Grades Pre-K–1; perfectly pitched emergent reader material; creative writing activity prompt.

➤ **PEPI SINGS A NEW SONG** by Laura Ljungkvist; Beach Lane/Simon & Schuster; Grades Pre-K–1; Pepi learns new vocabulary as he searches the town for fresh things to sing about.

➤ **THE PLOT CHICKENS** by Mary Jane and Herm Auch; Holiday House; Grades 3–5; slapstick humor teaches the writing process.

➤ **PUNCTUATION TAKES A VACATION** written by Robin Pulver and illustrated by Lynn Rowe Reed; Holiday House; Grades 2–4+; the punctuation marks are mad, and they're not taking it anymore. Tired of being ignored, off they go, leaving behind a befuddled class that can make no sense of their sentences now that the punctuation marks have taken a hike. Hilarious, with a definite but lighthearted mechanics lesson. See also:

- ◦ **SILENT LETTERS LOUD AND CLEAR**
- ◦ **NOUNS AND VERBS HAVE A FIELD DAY**

➤ **RED SINGS FROM TREETOPS: A YEAR IN COLORS** written by Joyce Sidman and illustrated by Pamela Zagarenski; Houghton Mifflin; Grades 1–4; poetic treatment of the colors of the seasons.

➤ **THE ROBIN MAKES A LAUGHING SOUND: A BIRDER'S JOURNAL** by Sallie Wolf; Charlesbridge; Grades 1–6; collection of poems, sketches, and paintings celebrates bird-watching and models journaling of observations as a means to learning and exploring.

➤ **THE RUNAWAY MUMMY: A PETRIFYING PARODY** by Michael Rex; Putnam; Grades Pre-K–2; pair with the classic **THE RUNAWAY BUNNY** to delight young listeners with a joke they can share with adults. See also:

- ◦ **GOODNIGHT GOON**

➤ **THE SLEEPY LITTLE ALPHABET: A BEDTIME STORY FROM ALPHABET TOWN** written by Judy Sierra and illustrated by Melissa Sweet; Knopf; Grades Pre-K–1; look, laugh, and recite!

➤ **A SPLENDID FRIEND, INDEED** by Suzanne Bloom; Boyds Mills; Grades Pre-K–1; Theodor Seuss Geisel Honor Book celebrates reading, writing, and friendship!

➤ **SUE MACDONALD HAD A BOOK** written by Jim Tobin and illustrated by Dave Coverly; Holt; Grades K–1; wonderfully rendered "vowel sing-along" intended to be read aloud to the tune of "Old MacDonald Had a Farm" and meant to forever cement the names of the vowels!

➤ **THANK YOU, WORLD** written by Alice B. McGinty and illustrated by Wendy Anderson Halperin; Dial; Grades Pre-K–2; rich, simple language in rhyme describes joys of childhood around the world. See **A Closer Look: Geography, Maps, and Travel.**

➤ **THUNDER-BOOMER!** written by Shutta Crum and illustrated by Carol Thompson; Clarion; Grades 2–4; lyrical description of a summer storm culminates with a furry surprise.

➤ **TWENTY-ODD DUCKS: WHY EVERY PUNCTUATION MARK COUNTS!** written by Lynne Truss and illustrated by Bonnie Timmons; Putnam; Grades 1–3; simple, witty examples make the point and hit the (punctuation) mark. See also:

- ◦ **EATS, SHOOTS & LEAVES: WHY, COMMAS REALLY *DO* MAKE A DIFFERENCE!**
- ◦ **THE GIRL'S LIKE SPAGHETTI: WHY YOU CAN'T MANAGE WITHOUT APOSTROPHES**

➢ **WE'RE ALL IN THE SAME BOAT** written by Zachary Shapiro and illustrated by Jack E. Davis; Putnam; Grades Pre-K–1; alphabet book set on Noah's Ark.

➢ **WE'RE GOING ON A BEAR HUNT** written by Michael Rosen and illustrated by Helen Oxenbury; McElderry; Grades Pre-K–1; enchanting family tale told with evocative language and endearing art.

➢ **WHAT DO AUTHORS DO?** by Eileen Christelow; Clarion; Grades K–2; simple, straightforward explanation with charming illustrations. See also:

  ◦ **WHAT DO ILLUSTRATORS DO?**

➢ **WHATEVER HAPPENED TO THE PONY EXPRESS?** written by Verla Kay and illustrated by Kimberly Bulcken Root and Barry Root; Putnam; Grades 2–3; history of the short life of the Pony Express and a family's story is told through the letters delivered by the men on horses.

➢ **WHAT'S THE BIG IDEA, MOLLY?** by Valeri Gorbachev; Philomel; Grades 1–2; collaboration spurs great ideas and nurtures friendship in this warmly encouraging tale.

➢ **WILL YOU READ TO ME?** by Denys Cazet; Atheneum; Grades 1–2; Pig Hamlet finds an audience for his poetry.

➢ **WORD BUILDER** written by Ann Whitford Paul and illustrated by Kurt Cyrus; Simon & Schuster; Grades 2–6; from letters to chapters, words build books; captivating art, simple text.

➢ **THE ZOO I DREW** by Todd H. Doodler; Random House; Grades Pre-K–1; rhyming abecedary celebrates zoo animals.

Fairy Tales, Folktales, Legends, Fables, Myths, and Nursery Rhymes

➢ **ABE LINCOLN CROSSES A CREEK: A TALL, THIN TALE** written by Deborah Hopkinson and illustrated by John Hendrix; Schwartz & Wade/Random House; Grades 2–4; the mostly true tale of how Lincoln's childhood friend, Austin Gollaher, saved his life; playful, humorous illustrations; lively language; multiple award winner. See **A Closer Look: Abraham Lincoln.**

➢ **BADGER'S FANCY MEAL** by Keiko Kasza; Putnam; Grades 2–4; one of many timely tales by this author/illustrator who has a knack for imparting a meaningful message in an entertaining way. See also:

  ◦ **MY LUCKY DAY**
  ◦ **READY FOR ANYTHING!**
  ◦ **THE DOG WHO CRIED WOLF**

➢ **BALLYHOO BAY** written by Judy Sierra and illustrated by Derek Anderson; Grades 2–4; contemporary fable about art, nature, and community in which a beach is saved from a high-rise; humorous, vivid illustrations; rhythmical, well-paced text. See **A Closer Look: Our Earth.**

➢ **THE CURIOUS GARDEN** by Peter Brown; Little, Brown; Grades 1–2; one person can make a difference as this gentle fable demonstrates when a boy's stitch of a garden in a most unlikely spot grows to transform a dreary cityscape; illustrations done in acrylic and gouache on board evolve from drab to magnificently bright and fresh as the story—and the garden—progresses; award winner. See **A Closer Look: Our Earth.**

➢ **DRAGON PIZZERIA** by Mary Morgan; Knopf; grades K–2; identify fairy tale celebrities in this picture book featuring fast-paced delivery!

➢ **EACH PEACH PEAR PLUM** by Janet and Allan Ahlberg; Puffin; Grades K–2; fairy tale characters take the stage in this classic cumulative tale with outstanding prediction opportunities.

➢ **FOGGY, FOGGY FOREST** by Nick Sharratt; Candlewick; Grades Pre-K–1; see-through "foggy" pages suggest lurking fairy tale characters; simple text; lyrical language; fun, predictions, fairy tales, and more!

➢ **GOLDILOCKS AND THE THREE BEARS** by Emma Chichester Clark; Candlewick; Grades Pre-K–1; a rather rude Goldilocks gets her comeuppance; great to pair with the traditional tale.

➢ **JUST A MINUTE: A TRICKSTER TALE AND COUNTING BOOK** by Yuyi Morales; Chronicle; Grades 1–2; tale from the Mexican culture offers an entertaining introduction to counting in both Spanish and English.

➢ **THE LION & THE MOUSE** by Jerry Pinkney; Little, Brown; Grades Pre-K–1+; wordless rendering of Aesop's fable; Caldecott Medal.

➢ **THE LUCK OF THE LOCH NESS MONSTER: A TALE OF PICKY EATING** written by A. W. Flaherty and illustrated by Scott Magoon; Houghton Mifflin; Grades K–3; fractured tale about how the Loch Ness Monster came to be the legendary creature will delight all manner of eaters. Don't miss the "science of it all" with the supertaster test at the back of the book.

➢ **MOTHER GOOSE'S LITTLE TREASURES** collected by Iona Opie and illustrated by Rosemary Wells; Candlewick; Grades Pre-K–1; little or lesser-known rhymes.

➢ **MIND YOUR MANNERS, B.B. WOLF** written by Judy Sierra and illustrated by J. Otto Seibold; Knopf; Grades K–2; encourage good manners with this wacky tale starring B.B. (Big Bad) Wolf.

➢ **MIRROR MIRROR** written by Marilyn Singer and illustrated by Josée Masse; Knopf; Grades 1–2+; reversible verse offers a fresh twist on old favorites.

➢ **MISS SMITH'S INCREDIBLE STORYBOOK** by Michael Garland; Dutton; Grades 1–3; teacher makes read-aloud time magical.

➢ **MOTHER GOOSE NUMBERS ON THE LOOSE** by Leo and Diane Dillon; Harcourt; Grades Pre-K–1; counting rhymes from Mother Goose illustrated by the award-winning duo.

➢ **ONCE UPON A BABY BROTHER** written by Sarah Sullivan and illustrated by Tricia Tusa; Farrar, Straus & Giroux; Grades 1–2; power of the pen overcomes tribulations of a new baby brother—almost always; a well-paced, reassuring, humorous, and satisfying story with winning illustrations.

➢ **PREVIOUSLY** written by Allan Ahlberg and illustrated by Bruce Ingman; Candlewick; Grades 1–3; What were fairy-tale characters up to *before* their well-known story took place? Clever!

➢ **THE PRINCESS AND THE PEA** by Rachel Isadora; Penguin; Grades K–2; retelling set in Africa; additional titles follow suit. See also:

   ◦ **HANSEL AND GRETEL**
   ◦ **PRETTY SALMA: A RED RIDING HOOD STORY FROM AFRICA**
   ◦ **RAPUNZEL**
   ◦ **THE TWELVE DANCING PRINCESSES**
   ◦ **THE UGLY DUCKLING**

➢ **THE RABBIT AND THE TURTLE** Aesop's Fables retold and illustrated by Eric Carle; Orchard/Scholastic; Grades K–2; one-page lessons.

➢ **RABBIT'S GIFT** written by George Shannon and illustrated by Laura Dronzek; Harcourt; Grades K–2; based on the folktale with several international versions.

➢ **THE REAL STORY OF STONE SOUP** written by Ying Chang Compestine and illustrated by Stephane Jorisch; Dutton; Grades 2–4; humorous version of the well-known folktale.

➢ **STARLIGHT GOES TO TOWN** written by Harry Allard and illustrated by George Booth; Farrar, Straus & Giroux; Grades 1–4; be careful what you wish for; hilarious!

➢ **SUCH A PRINCE** written by Dan Bar-el and illustrated by John Manders; Clarion; Grades 1–4; fractured fairy tale sure to delight contemporary students; great message about a skinny guy with no money and no confidence who has a big heart; is honest, kind, clever; and—*spoiler alert!*—wins the heart of the princess.

➢ **WYNETTA AND THE CORNSTALK: A TEXAS FAIRY TALE** written by Helen Ketterman and illustrated by Diane Greenseid; Whitman; Grades 1–2; retelling of Jack and the Beanstalk, cowgirl style!

Holidays

- **ALPHA OOPS! H IS FOR HALLOWEEN** written by Alethea Kontis and illustrated by Bob Kolar; Candlewick; Grades K–1; hilarious chaos reigns as the letters goof around.

- **A YEAR FULL OF HOLIDAYS** written by Susan Middleton Elya and illustrated by Diana Cain Bluthenthal; Putnam; Grades K–1; Nell learns to enjoy a year-long parade of fun holidays while eagerly awaiting her August birthday.

- **BEAR'S FIRST CHRISTMAS** written by Robert Kinerk and illustrated by Jim LaMarche; Simon & Schuster; Grades Pre-K–2; the joy and magic of Bear's first Christmas, shared with friends, is captured in inviting illustrations done in acrylic washes and colored pencil.

- **BUNNY WISHES: A WINTER'S TALE** written by Michaela Morgan and illustrated by Caroline Jayne Church; Scholastic; Grades K–2; wishes on a holiday list take on a life of their own.

- **THE DAY IT RAINED HEARTS** (formerly **FOUR VALENTINES IN A RAINSTORM**) by Felicia Bond; HarperCollins; Grades Pre-K–2; perfectly rendered picture book about choosing just the right gifts for friends.

- **DEAR SANTA CLAUS** written by Alan Durant and illustrated by Vanessa Cabban; Candlewick; Grades K–2; correspondence between Holly and Santa throughout the season; includes envelopes with pullout cards.

- **DRUMMER BOY** by Loren Long; Philomel; Grades K–2; builds on the classic Christmas tale; luminous illustrations.

- **THE EASTER EGG** by Jan Brett; Putnam; Grades Pre-K–1; Hoppi finds a way to make the best egg he can; trademark illustrations are as captivating as ever.

- **MY FIRST RAMADAN** by Karen Katz; Henry Holt; Grades K–1; Muslim boy observes holy month.

- **NEW YEAR AT THE PIER: A ROSH HASHANAH STORY** written by April Halprin Wayland and illustrated by Stephane Jorisch; Dial; Grades 2–3; family and friends take joy in the Jewish holiday.

- **ONE IS A FEAST FOR MOUSE: A THANKSGIVING TALE** written by Judy Cox and illustrated by Jeffrey Ebbeler; Holiday House; Grades K–2; tale about giving thanks for small things; adorable, attention-keeping illustrations paired with pleasingly descriptive language.

- **PAPA'S LATKES** written by Michelle Edwards and illustrated by Stacey Schuett; Candlewick; Grades K–2; it's the first Chanukah without Mama, and Papa's latkes are brown and lumpy. How Selma makes her way through the holiday in the midst of her feelings of loss makes for a touching story.

➢ **A PIÑATA IN A PINE TREE: A LATINO TWELVE DAYS OF CHRISTMAS** written by Pat Mora and illustrated by Magaly Morales; Clarion; Grades 1–2; traditional gifts in this version of the well-known carol are replaced with Latino-inspired offerings; find, count, and learn Spanish words and their pronunciations on each page; glossary and score are found at the back of the book.

➢ **THE SCARECROW'S DANCE** written by Jane Yolen and illustrated by Bagram Ibatoulline; Simon & Schuster; Grades 2–4; recognizing one's special gifts.

➢ **THE SEVEN DAYS OF KWANZAA** written by Melrose Cooper and illustrated by Jeremy Tugeau; Scholastic; Grades K–1; learn about the traditions of Kwanzaa with this simple story.

➢ **SHANTÉ KEYS AND THE NEW YEAR'S PEAS** written by Gail Piernas-Davenport and illustrated by Marion Eldridge; Whitman; Grades K–2; There are "chitlins, baked ham, macaroni and cheese, greens and hot corn bread, but no black-eyed peas!" Shanté moves through her multicultural neighborhood hunting for the lucky New Year's peas—and inviting everyone back to the house, where there's plenty for all the guests. Includes an afterword on ethnic New Year's traditions.

➢ **SIPPING SPIDERS THROUGH A STRAW: CAMPFIRE SONGS FOR MONSTERS** lyrics by Kelly DiPucchio and illustrated by Gris Grimly; Scholastic; Grades 2–4; boys especially delight in this book!

➢ **SHARING CHRISTMAS** written by Kate Westerlund and illustrated by Eve Tharlet; Penguin; Grades Pre-K–2; animals in the woodlands contribute to a Christmas celebration, proving that "Sharing is giving, and giving is what Christmas is all about."

➢ **THE SNOW DAY** by Komako Sakai; Arthur A. Levine/Scholastic; Grades Pre-K–1; waiting for Dad, delayed by a storm, to arrive.

➢ **THE SOUND OF KWANZAA** written by Dimitrea Tokunbo and illustrated by Lisa Cohen; Scholastic; Grades K–2; explains the meaning of the various aspects celebrated throughout Kwanzaa.

➢ **THANK YOU, SARAH! THE WOMAN WHO SAVED THANKSGIVING** written by Laurie Halse Anderson and illustrated by Matt Faulkner; Simon & Schuster; Grades 2–4; engaging picture book biography written by an inspired award-winning author, with art by an illustrator who knows what makes a picture book stand out; biography, history, power-of-the-pen message.

➢ **THE WISH** written by Elle van Lieshout and Erik van Os and illustrated by Paula Gerritsen; Front Street/Lemniscaat/Boyds Mill Press; Grades K–3; a woman makes a series of wishes ending on the night before her birthday.

Kindergarten/Preschool Readiness

➢ **ADVENTURE ANNIE GOES TO KINDERGARTEN** written by Toni Buzzeo and illustrated by Amy Wummer; Dial; Grades Pre-K–K; active, unflappable Annie makes it through the first day of kindergarten with plenty of adventures and a gentle lesson or two.

➢ **A FABULOUS FAIR ALPHABET** by Debra Frasier; Beach Lane/Simon & Schuster; Grades Pre-K–2; abecedary introduces readers to a summer fair.

➢ **MOTHER GOOSE NUMBERS ON THE LOOSE** by Leo and Diane Dillon; Harcourt; Grades Pre-K–1; counting rhymes from Mother Goose illustrated by the award-winning duo.

➢ **THE PIRATE OF KINDERGARTEN** written by George Ella Lyon and illustrated by Lynne Avril; Atheneum; Grades K–1; an irrepressible kindergartner discovers she needs corrective lenses.

➢ **PRESCHOOL DAY HOORAY!** written by Linda Leopold Strauss and illustrated by Hiroe Nakata; Scholastic; Grade Pre-K; simple rhyming text celebrates the joys of preschool.

➢ **THE SLEEPY LITTLE ALPHABET: A BEDTIME STORY FROM ALPHABET TOWN** written by Judy Sierra and illustrated by Melissa Sweet; Knopf; Grades Pre-K–1; look, laugh, and recite!

➢ **WE'RE ALL IN THE SAME BOAT** written by Zachary Shapiro and illustrated by Jack E. Davis; Putnam; Grades Pre-K–1; alphabet book set on Noah's Ark.

➢ **ZOE'S HATS: A BOOK OF COLORS AND PATTERNS** by Sharon Lane Holm; Boyds Mills; Grades Pre-K–1; simple text and bright illustrations introduce colors and patterns; a recall activity at the end of the book reinforces concepts.

➢ **THE ZOO I DREW** by Todd H. Doodler; Random House; Grades Pre-K–1; rhyming abecedary celebrates zoo animals.

Map Skills/Geography

➢ **ADÉLE & SIMON IN AMERICA** by Barbara McClintock; Farrar, Straus & Giroux; Grades 2–4; illustrations depict early 20th century American cities. See **A Closer Look: Geography, Maps, and Travel.**

➢ **AMERICA THE BEAUTIFUL** pop-up by Robert Sabuda; Candlewick; all ages; a marvel depicting the song. See **A Closer Look: Geography, Maps, and Travel.**

➢ **AROUND THE WORLD ON EIGHTY LEGS** by Amy Gibson and illustrated by Daniel Salmieri; Scholastic; Grades 1–3; lively poems and comical art describe animals found around the world. See **A Closer Look: Geography, Maps, and Travel.**

➤ **DUCK DUCK MOOSE** by Dave Horowitz; Putnam; Grades K–2; a little geography, a dash of road trip, and a large dose of slapstick make for a hilarious read-aloud! See **A Closer Look: Geography, Maps, and Travel.**

 ➤ **HOW I LEARNED GEOGRAPHY** by Uri Shulevitz; Farrar, Straus & Giroux; Grades 2–4; a boy escapes hunger and destitution through imaginary trips he takes, sparked by the colorful map his father tacks on the wall. See **A Closer Look: Geography, Maps, and Travel.**

 ➤ **HOW TO BAKE AN AMERICAN PIE** written by Karma Wilson and illustrated by Raúl Colón; McElderry; Grades K–2; warm and whimsical illustrations add to tribute to America.

 ➤ **HOW TO MAKE A CHERRY PIE AND SEE THE USA** by Marjorie Priceman; Knopf; Grades 2–3; a baker and her pup travel across the country in search of what they need to make their baking tools; map and recipe included! See **A Closer Look: Geography, Maps, and Travel.**

 ➤ **LARUE ACROSS AMERICA: POSTCARDS FROM THE VACATION** by Mark Teague; Scholastic; Grades 1–2; The irascible pup is at it again, this time on a cross-country trip. See **A Closer Look: Geography, Maps, and Travel.**

 ➤ **MAPPING PENNY'S WORLD** by Loreen Leedy; Henry Holt; Grades 2–3; a simple, direct, and pleasing introduction to maps, scale, key, and the compass rose. See **A Closer Look: Geography, Maps, and Travel.** See also:

⚬ **PROBABLY PENNY,** about probability, with the same cast of characters

 ➤ **ME ON THE MAP** written by Joan Sweeney and illustrated by Annette Cable; Crown; Grades 1–2; map skills in an accessible and appealing format. See **A Closer Look: Geography, Maps, and Travel.**

 ➤ **MY AMERICA: A POETRY ATLAS OF THE UNITED STATES** written by Lee Bennett Hopkins and illustrated by Stephen Alcorn; Simon & Schuster; Grades 1+. See **A Closer Look: Geography, Maps, and Travel.**

 ➤ **THANK YOU, WORLD** written by Alice B. McGinty and illustrated by Wendy Anderson Halperin; Dial; Grades Pre-K–2; rich, simple rhyme expresses joys of childhood across the world. See **A Closer Look: Geography, Maps, and Travel.**

 ➤ **THE TRAVEL GAME** written by John Grandits and illustrated by R. W. Alley; Clarion; Grades 1–2; a young boy from Buffalo, New York, travels the world with his aunt with the use of a globe, a book, and two creative imaginations. See **A Closer Look: Geography, Maps, and Travel.**

Math

➤ **APPLE COUNTDOWN** written by Joan Holub and illustrated by Jan Smith; Albert Whitman; Grades 1–2; countdown from 20, grouping, and simple addition.

➤ **BEAN THIRTEEN** by Matthew McElligott; Putnam; Grades 2–3; 13 beans are hard to share equally—and who wants the unlucky 13th?!

➤ **BLOCKHEAD: THE LIFE OF FIBONACCI** written by Joseph D'Agnese and illustrated by John O'Brien; Henry Holt; Grades 2–3; an appealing biography.

➤ **THE BUTTON BOX** written by Margarette S. Reid and illustrated by Sarah Chamberlain; Dutton; Grades Pre-K–1; patterns galore can be found in Grandma's button box.

➤ **BUY MY HATS!** by Dave Horowitz; Putnam; Grades K–1; advertising, money, competition, and more for the youngest of sales executives.

➤ **THE DOORBELL RANG** by Pat Hutchins; Greenwillow; Grades K–2; friends manage to share a tray of cookies even though more and more neighbors stop by; classic tale.

➤ **EACH ORANGE HAD 8 SLICES: A COUNTING BOOK** written by Paul Giganti Jr. and illustrated by Donald Crews; Greenwillow; Grades K–2; simple counting, addition, and multiplication opportunities offered through simple, straightforward text and bright illustrations. See also:

  ◦ **HOW MANY SNAILS? A COUNTING BOOK**

➤ **EIGHT ANIMALS ON THE TOWN** written by Susan Middleton Elya and illustrated by Lee Chapman; Putnam; Grades 1–2; Eight animals go to the market to find their dinner and then spend an evening on the town; key words are offered in Spanish with contextual clues; spunky, bright illustrations reflect Latino culture.

➤ **FIELD TRIP DAY** written by Lynn Plourde and illustrated by Thor Wickstrom; Dutton; Grades 1–2; sixth in the series about the students in Mrs. Shepherd's class, this story about a field trip features a wandering lad and a few silly mishaps to introduce simple math.

➤ **FOR GOOD MEASURE: THE WAYS WE SAY HOW MUCH, HOW FAR, HOW HEAVY, HOW BIG, HOW OLD** by Ken Robbins; Roaring Brook; Grades 2+; fabulous photographs help define words we use to measure.

➤ **GOBBLE GOBBLE CRASH! A BARNYARD COUNTING BASH** written by Julie Stiegemeyer and illustrated by Valeri Gorbachev; Dutton; Grades K–1; count from 1 to 10 and back again with a bevy of silly barnyard characters and a bouncy rhyming text.

➤ **GROWING PATTERNS: FIBONACCI NUMBERS IN NATURE** written by Sarah C. Campbell with photographs by Sarah C. Campbell and Richard P. Campbell; Boyds Mills; Grades 1–2; the mystery of Fibonacci numbers in nature is explored through stunning photography.

➤ **THE GREAT MATH TATTLE BATTLE** written by Anne Bowen and illustrated by Jaime Zollars; Whitman; Grades 1–2; math galore, including brainteasers at the end of the book.

➤ **HANNAH'S COLLECTIONS** by Marthe Jocelyn; Dutton; Grades 1–2; what doesn't Hannah collect?!; colorful graphics.

➤ **HOW MANY SEEDS IN A PUMPKIN?** written by Margaret McNamara and illustrated by G. Brian Karas; Schwartz & Wade/Random House; Grades 1–3; count away!

➤ **HOW MANY SNAILS? A COUNTING BOOK** written by Paul Giganti Jr. and illustrated by Donald Crews; Greenwillow; Grades K–1; simple counting, patterns; straightforward text and bright illustrations. See also:

  ◦ **EACH ORANGE HAD 8 SLICES: A COUNTING BOOK**

➤ **HOW THE SECOND GRADE GOT $8,205.50 TO VISIT THE STATUE OF LIBERTY** written by Nathan Zimelman and illustrated by Bill Slavin; Whitman; Grades 2–3; story of a drive to raise money for a field trip to the Statue of Liberty explains profits and expenses.

➤ **HOW MUCH IS A MILLION?** written by David M. Schwartz and illustrated by Steven Kellogg; HarperCollins; Grades 1–2; award-winning classic offers kid-friendly explanations of the hard-to-fathom concepts of a million, billion, and trillion. See also:

  ◦ **IF YOU MADE A MILLION**
  ◦ **MILLIONS TO MEASURE**

➤ **IT'S PROBABLY PENNY** by Loreen Leedy; Holt; Grades 2–4; probability made accessible through everyday applications.

➤ **INCH BY INCH** by Leo Lionni; Knopf; Grades 2–4; reissued classic and Caldecott Honor is a fable about one resourceful inchworm.

➤ **JUST A MINUTE: A TRICKSTER TALE AND COUNTING BOOK** by Yuyi Morales; Chronicle; Grades 1–2; tale from the Mexican culture offers an entertaining introduction to counting in both Spanish and English.

➤ **LITTLE QUACK** written by Lauren Thompson and illustrated by Derek Anderson; Simon & Schuster; Grades Pre-K–1; quack-u-lator + splendid artwork = math book winner!

➤ **MAGNUS MAXIMUS, A MARVELOUS MEASURER** written by Kathleen T. Pelley and illustrated by S. D. Schindler; Farrar, Straus & Giroux; Grades 1–2; Maximus goes from measuring to treasuring what's important in life with the help of his young friend.

- ➢ **MATH FABLES** written by Greg Tang and illustrated by Taia Morley; Scholastic; Grades K–1; grouping, simple addition, and science. See also:

  - ◦ **MATH FABLES TOO**
  - ◦ **MATH FOR ALL SEASONS**

- ➢ **MATH-TERPIECES** written by Greg Tang and illustrated by Greg Paprocki; Scholastic; Grades Pre-K–2; math functions + art masterpieces = educational fun.

- ➢ **MOTHER GOOSE NUMBERS ON THE LOOSE** by Leo and Diane Dillon; Harcourt; Grades Pre-K–1; counting collection of Mother Goose rhymes illustrated by the award-winning duo.

- ➢ **OLLY AND ME 1 2 3** by Shirley Hughes; Candlewick; Grades Pre-K–K; counting to 10; trademark illustrations engage the learner.

- ➢ **ONE BLUE FISH: A COLORFUL COUNTING BOOK** by Charles Reasoner; Little Simon/Simon & Schuster; Grades Pre-K–K; concept board book features gateleg pages that introduce numbers 1 through 10.

- ➢ **ONE BOY** by Laura Vaccaro Seeger; Roaring Brook; Grades Pre-K–K; simple counting and prediction are featured in this innovative concept book with cutout windows; Theodor Seuss Geisel Honor book.

- ➢ **ONE DUCK STUCK** written by Phyllis Root and illustrated by Jane Chapman; Candlewick; Grades Pre-K–1; rhythmic counting story offers delightful word play.

- ➢ **ONE FROG SANG** written by Shirley Parenteau and illustrated by Cynthia Jabar; Candlewick; Grades Pre-K–K; counting story offers croaking-fun word play!

- ➢ **ONE TRACTOR: A COUNTING BOOK** written by Alexandra Siy and illustrated by Jacqueline Rogers; Holiday House; Grades Pre-K–1; rhyming counting story that boys especially are sure to embrace.

- ➢ **PATTERNS IN PERU: AN ADVENTURE IN PATTERNING** written by Cindy Neuschwander and illustrated by Bryan Langdo; Holt; Grades 2–3; a math mystery centers around an ancient tunic.

- ➢ **A SECOND IS A HICCUP: A CHILD'S BOOK OF TIME** written by Hazel Hutchins and illustrated by Kady MacDonald Denton; Arthur A. Levine/Scholastic; Grades Pre-K–1; units of time effectively explained in concrete, kid-friendly terms.

- ➢ **SHAPE** by David Goodman and Zoe Miller; Tate/Abrams; Grades Pre-K–2; vivid illustrations introduce basic 2-D and 3-D shapes; simple activities and suggestions for projects encourage further exploration.

> **START SAVING, HENRY!** by Nancy Carlson; Viking; Grade 1; Henry learns to save for that big ticket item he really, *really* wants.

> **THE TWELVE DAYS OF SPRINGTIME: A SCHOOL COUNTING BOOK** written by Deborah Lee Rose and illustrated by Carey Armstrong-Ellis; Abrams; Grades Pre-K–1; a lighthearted take on "The Twelve Days of Christmas"; humorous illustrations add to the rhythmical text.

> **YOU CAN, TOUCAN, MATH** written by David A. Adler and illustrated by Edward Miller; Holiday House; Grades 1–3+; word problem fun.

> **WOMBAT WALKABOUT** written by Carol Diggory Shields and illustrated by Sophie Blackall; Dutton; Grades Pre-K–1; count along in this poem set in the Australian Outback.

> **ZOE'S HATS: A BOOK OF COLORS AND PATTERNS** by Sharon Lane Holm; Boyds Mills; Grades Pre-K–1; simple text and bright illustrations introduce colors and patterns; the recall activity at the end of the book reinforces concepts.

> **1 2 3: A CHILD'S FIRST COUNTING BOOK** by Alison Jay; Dutton; Grades Pre-K–1; number and nursery rhyme recognition combine in this delightfully simple book with lyrical text and bright, playfully detailed illustrations.

Science, Health, and Safety

> **ALL OF ME: A BOOK OF THANKS** by Molly Bang; Blue Sky Press/Scholastic; Grades Pre-K–1; celebrates parts of the body.

> **ALL PIGS ARE BEAUTIFUL** written by Dick King-Smith and illustrated by Anita Jeram; Read and Wonder series; Candlewick; Grades 1–2; science facts presented in an appealing format.

> **ANIMALS BORN ALIVE AND WELL** by Ruth Heller; Grosset & Dunlap; Grades 1–2+; classic science picture book. See also:

> - **THE REASON FOR THE FLOWER**
> - **PLANTS THAT NEVER BLOOM**

> **ANTARCTICA** by Helen Cowcher; Farrar, Straus & Giroux; Grades Pre-K–2; beautifully rendered lyrical book explores the features of the region.

> **AROUND THE WORLD ON EIGHTY LEGS** by Amy Gibson and illustrated by Daniel Salmieri; Scholastic; Grades 1–3; lively poems and comical art describe animals found around the world. See **A Closer Look: Geography, Maps, and Travel.**

> **ASTRONAUT HANDBOOK** by Meghan McCarthy; Knopf; Grades 1–3; facts about training to be an astronaut are certain to intrigue budding scientists.

➤ **BALLYHOO BAY** written by Judy Sierra and illustrated by Derek Anderson; Simon & Schuster; Grades 2–4; contemporary fable about art, nature, and community in which a beach is saved from a high-rise; humorous, vivid illustrations; rhythmical, well-paced text. See **A Closer Look: Our Earth.**

➤ **BEETLE BOP** by Denise Fleming; Harcourt; Grades Pre-K–1; simple rhymes accompanied by oversized illustrations. See also:

   ◦ **IN THE TALL, TALL GRASS**
   ◦ **IN THE SMALL, SMALL POND** (Caldecott Honor)

➤ **BIRD, BUTTERFLY, EEL** by James Prosek; Simon & Schuster; Grades 1–4; basic elements of bird, fish, and insect migration.

➤ **BORN TO BE GIANTS: HOW BABY DINOSAURS GREW TO RULE THE WORLD** by Lita Judge; Roaring Brook; Grades 1–3; from baby to giant, the dinosaurs and the details found in this book intrigue and appeal through scientific speculation and illustrations that bring their size to life.

➤ **THE BUFFALO ARE BACK** written by Jean Craighead George and illustrated by Wendell Minor; Dutton; Grades 2–4; chronicles the history of the American buffalo and its part in the balance of the American Great Plains ecosystem and its gradual and glorious comeback from the brink of extinction; inspiring. See **A Closer Look: Our Earth.**

➤ **BUYING, TRAINING & CARING FOR YOUR DINOSAUR** written by Laura Joy Rennert and illustrated by Marc Brown; Knopf; Grades K–2; a guide to choosing the right dino-pet!

➤ **CATERPILLAR CATERPILLAR** written by Vivian French and illustrated by Charlotte Voake; Read, Listen & Wonder series; Candlewick; Grades 1–2; the life cycle of the butterfly; includes read-along CD with music and additional facts.

➤ **CORAL REEFS** by Gail Gibbons; Holiday House; Grades 2+; colorful illustrations help explain this ecosystem. See **A Closer Look: Our Earth.** See also:

   ◦ **TORNADOES!,** Grades 1–2

➤ **THE CURIOUS GARDEN** by Peter Brown; Little, Brown; Grades 1–2; one person can make a difference as this gentle fable demonstrates when a boy's stitch of a garden in a most unlikely spot grows to transform a dreary cityscape; illustrations done in acrylic and gouache on board evolve from drab to magnificently bright and fresh as the story—and the garden—progresses; award winner. See **A Closer Look: Our Earth.**

➤ **THE DINOSAURS OF WATERHOUSE HAWKINS** written by Barbara Kerley and illustrated by Brian Selznick; Scholastic; Grades 1–2+; stunning Caldecott Honor book highlighting the life of the artist and sculptor who, in the mid-1800s, showed the world what a dinosaur looked like.

➤ **DINOSAURUMPUS!** written by Tony Mitton and illustrated by Guy Parker-Rees; Scholastic; Grades Pre-K–1; a dinosaur romp with facts mingled in.

➤ **DOLPHIN TALK** written by Wendy Pfeffer and illustrated by Helen K. Davie; Let's-Read-and-Find-Out Science, Stage 2; HarperCollins; Grades 1–2; appealing and informative.

➤ **EARTHLY TREASURE** written by Kate Petty and illustrated by Jennie Maizels; Dutton; Grades 2–4; pop-up book about minerals.

➤ **AN EGRET'S DAY** poems by Jane Yolen and photographs by Jason Stemple; Wordsong/Boyds Mills; Grades 2–4+; stunning photos; sensory text; side notes add interesting information and scientific fact.

 ➤ **EMI AND THE RHINO SCIENTIST** written by Mary Kay Carson with photographs by Tom Uhlman; Houghton Mifflin; Grades 1–4; a Scientists in the Field book that details the life cycle of the rhinoceros and the work being done to save rhinos across the world; includes information on how readers can help; striking photographs. See **A Closer Look: Our Earth.**

➤ **THE EMPEROR'S EGG** written by Martin Jenkins and illustrated by Jane Chapman; Read and Wonder series; Candlewick; Grades 1–2; emperor penguin's habits.

➤ **ENCYCLOPEDIA PREHISTORICA: DINOSAURS** by Robert Sabuda and Matthew Reinhart; Candlewick; Grades 1–2+; marvelous pop-up wonder.

➤ **FEEDING THE SHEEP** written by Leda Schubert and illustrated by Andrea U'Ren; Farrar, Straus & Giroux; Grades K–1; from sheep raising to sweater wearing and back to feeding the sheep, a little girl and her mom have fun with the process of making a wool sweater; lyrical language, inviting art; a fresh, and fun read-aloud.

➤ **FIREBOY TO THE RESCUE!** by Edward Miller; Holiday House; Grades Pre-K–2; graphic picture book offers young children practical lifesaving tips for staying safe in the event of a fire in their home.

➤ **FIRE DRILL** written by Paul DuBois Jacobs and Jennifer Swender and illustrated by Huy Voun Lee; Holt; Grades Pre-K–K; simple rhyming text explains a school fire drill.

➤ **FIREFLIES AT MIDNIGHT** written by Marilyn Singer and illustrated by Ken Robbins; Atheneum; Grades 1–2+; poems about summer's creatures; vivid, graphically enhanced photographs and collages.

➤ **FIVE FOR A LITTLE ONE** by Chris Raschka; Atheneum; Grades K–2; a first look at the five senses.

➤ **FLIP, FLOAT, FLY: SEEDS ON THE MOVE** by JoAnn Early Macken and illustrated by Pam Paparone; Holiday House; Grades 1–2; the journeys of seeds on the wind are explored; appealing illustrations.

➤ **GROUNDHOG WEATHER SCHOOL** written by Joan Holub and illustrated by Kristin Sorra; Putnam; Grades 1–3; weather, seasons, and related science facts are taught and learned in groundhog school; charming!

➤ **HERE COMES THE GARBAGE BARGE!** written by Jonah Winter and illustrated by Red Nose Studio; Schwartz & Wade/Random House; Grades 1–3; the mostly true story of Long Island's "garbage barge"; explores landfills, and the advent of widespread recycling; captivating art notes can be found on the inside of the book jacket. See **A Closer Look: Our Earth.** Consider pairing with:

　◦ **THE SMASH! SMASH! TRUCK: RECYCLING AS YOU'VE NEVER HEARD IT BEFORE!** by Professor Potts; David Fickling Books; Grades 1–3.

➤ **HERE'S WHAT YOU DO WHEN YOU CAN'T FIND YOUR SHOE** written by Andrea Perry and illustrated by Alan Snow; Atheneum; Grades 1–2+; poems about zany inventions kids will love.

➤ **HOW THE WORLD WORKS** written by Christiane Dorion, illustrated by Beverley Young, and paper engineering by Andy Mansfield; Templar/Candlewick; Grades 1–2+; pop-up format; features simple answers to myriad questions about how our planet works, from moving plates to weather changes to food chains. See **A Closer Look: Our Earth.**

➤ **HOW TO HEAL A BROKEN WING** by Bob Graham; Candlewick; Grades Pre-K–2; a boy aids an injured bird; spare text, evocative art.

➤ **HOW UNDERWEAR GOT UNDER THERE: A BRIEF HISTORY** written by Kathy Shaskan and illustrated by Regan Dunnick; Dutton; Grades 1–3; from Mongolian warriors to men in space, this overview covers the history of underwear with a lighthearted blend of facts, humorous stories, silliness, and lively science.

➤ **IF YOU LIVED HERE YOU'D BE HOME BY NOW** by Ed Briant; Roaring Brook; Grades 1–3; wordless tale about urban sprawl. See **A Closer Look: Our Earth.**

➤ **I'M A TURKEY!** by Jim Arnosky; Scholastic; Grades K–3; learn facts about wild turkeys through this perky picture book; includes free download of original song.

➤ **INSECT DETECTIVE** written by Steve Voake and illustrated by Charlotte Voake; Candlewick; Grades K–2; simple, straightforward primer to backyard insect life; at the end of the book, age-appropriate, fun activities for budding insect detectives are provided.

➤ **LEAF JUMPERS** written by Carole Gerber and illustrated by Leslie Evans; Charlesbridge; Grades Pre-K–2; primer for identifying leaves.

➤ **LET'S SAVE THE ANIMALS: A FLIP-THE-FLAP BOOK** by Frances Barry; Candlewick; Grades Pre-K–1; an engaging, hands-on introduction to endangered animals; end material offers suggestions of things a child can do to help protect and save endangered animals. See **A Closer Look: Our Earth.**

➤ **THE LORAX** by Dr. Seuss; Random House; Grades K–2; this Seuss classic offers a timeless environmental message; http://www.thelorax.com offers a free classroom kit. See **A Closer Look: Our Earth** for additional links to on-line materials.

➤ **LOTS OF SPOTS** by Lois Ehlert; Beach Lane/Simon & Schuster; Grades K–2; rhyming text introduces characteristics of spotted and striped animals, with a spot of humor present here and there in the verse and signature collage art.

➤ **THE MAGIC SCHOOL BUS AND THE CLIMATE CHALLENGE** written by Joanna Cole and illustrated by Bruce Degen; Scholastic; Grades 2–3; a new addition to the classic, fantastic series focuses on global warming; welcome back, Ms. Frizzle! See **A Closer Look: Our Earth.**

➤ **MAMA MITI** written by Donna Jo Napoli and illustrated by Kadir Nelson; Simon & Schuster; Grades 1–2; With the refrain, *Thayu nyumba* (Peace, my people), threaded throughout the text, able storyteller Napoli weaves the tale of the 2004 Nobel Peace Prize winner, Wangari Maathai's, far-reaching influence; beautifully depicted with collage illustrations by the Caldecott Honor artist. See **A Closer Look: Our Earth.** See also:

  ◦ **WANGARI'S TREES OF PEACE** by Jeanette Winter; Harcourt

➤ **MATH FABLES** written by Greg Tang and illustrated by Taia Morley; Scholastic; Grades K–1; grouping, simple addition, and science. See also:

  ◦ **MATH FABLES TOO**

➤ **MEET THE HOWLERS!** written by April Pulley Sayre and illustrated by Woody Miller; Charlesbridge; Grades 2–4; a rap-style text is coupled with fascinating facts about these sloppy, rude, loudmouth monkeys of the rain forest; excellent entrée to research.

➤ **MOON BEAR** written by Brenda Z. Guiberson and illustrated by Ed Young; Holt; Grades 2–4; about the slowly disappearing Asiatic black bear; lyrical text and moving illustrations. See **A Closer Look: Our Earth.**

➤ **NEVER SMILE AT A MONKEY** by Steve Jenkins; Houghton Mifflin Harcourt; Grades 1–4; creatures with not-so-obvious dangerous natures are presented along with what you should never do if you encounter one of them (such as smile at a rhesus monkey or badger a beaded lizard).

➤ **THE OLD TREE** by Ruth Brown; Candlewick; Grades K–2; charming, thoughtful tale of conservation and cooperation with a pop-up surprise at the end. See **A Closer Look: Our Earth.**

- ➤ **PLANTS THAT NEVER BLOOM** by Ruth Heller; Grosset & Dunlap; Grades 1–2+; bright, vivid art. See also:
  - ◦ **THE REASON FOR THE FLOWER**
  - ◦ **ANIMALS BORN ALIVE AND WELL**

- ➤ **POP! THE INVENTION OF BUBBLE GUM** by Meghan McCarthy; Simon & Schuster; Grades 1–2+; simple, well-crafted text is easy to follow and comprehend; extensive back material offers additional biographical information about the inventor, facts about chewing gum, and references.

- ➤ **THE REASON FOR THE FLOWER** by Ruth Heller; Grosset & Dunlap; Grades 1–2; bright, colorful illustrations accompany rhyming, factual text. See also:
  - ◦ **PLANTS THAT NEVER BLOOM**
  - ◦ **ANIMALS BORN ALIVE AND WELL**

- ➤ **RED LEAF, YELLOW LEAF** by Lois Ehlert; Harcourt; Grades Pre-K–1; a celebration of trees in autumn filled with age-appropriate facts and bold collage art.

- ➤ **THE ROBIN MAKES A LAUGHING SOUND: A BIRDER'S JOURNAL** by Sallie Wolf; Charlesbridge; Grades 1–6; collection of poems, sketches, and paintings celebrates bird-watching and models journaling of observations as a means to learning and exploring.

- ➤ **SANDY'S CIRCUS: A STORY ABOUT ALEXANDER CALDER** written by Tanya Lee Stone and illustrated by Boris Kulikov; Viking; Grades 2–4; biography of the man who invented the mobile; science/balance.

- ➤ **SCIENCE FAIR DAY** written by Lynn Plourde and illustrated by Thor Wickstrom; Dutton; Grades 1–2; chaos threatens when Ima's curiosity gets the best of her.

- ➤ **THE SHOCKING TRUTH ABOUT ENERGY** by Loreen Leedy; Holiday House; Grades 2–4; introduction to energy through zany humor, colorful illustrations, and clear diagrams that weave together physical and environmental science; tips for wise energy use; significant back matter. See **A Closer Look: Our Earth.**

- ➤ **SLOW DOWN FOR MANATEES** by Jim Arnosky; Putnam; Grades 1–3; environmental study; awareness of natural habitats. See **A Closer Look: Our Earth.**

- ➤ **THE SMASH! SMASH! TRUCK: RECYCLING AS YOU'VE NEVER HEARD IT BEFORE!** by Professor Potts; David Fickling Books; Grades 1–3; benefits of recycling simply presented; accompanied by lighthearted illustrations. See **A Closer Look: Our Earth.** Consider pairing with **HERE COMES THE GARBAGE BARGE!** (See above.)

- ➤ **SO YOU WANT TO BE AN INVENTOR?** written by Judith St. George and illustrated by Caldecott artist David Small; Philomel; Grades 1–2+; short, pithy, humorous profiles of well-known and lesser-known inventors.

- **SPINNING SPIDERS** written by Melvin Berger and illustrated by S. D. Schindler; Let's-Read-And-Find-Out Science, Level 2; HarperCollins; Grades 1–2; clear, detailed, accessible text and illustrations; excellent back matter.

- **SURPRISING SHARKS** written by Nicola Davies and illustrated by James Croft; Candlewick; Grades 1–2; informative, eco-friendly, thought provoking; well crafted. See **A Closer Look: Our Earth.**

- **TEN THINGS I CAN DO TO HELP MY WORLD: FUN AND EASY ECO-TIPS** by Melanie Walsh; Candlewick; Grades Pre-K–2; simple, straightforward commonsense tips for young children. See **A Closer Look: Our Earth.**

- **THANK YOU, WORLD** written by Alice B. McGinty and illustrated by Wendy Anderson Halperin; Dial; Grades Pre-K–2; rich, simple rhyme expresses joys of childhood across the world; environments. See **A Closer Look: Geography, Maps, and Travel.**

- **TIGRESS** written by Nick Dowson and illustrated by Jane Chapman; Read and Wonder series; Candlewick; Grades K–2; evocative language and outstanding illustrations capture the tigress's behavior. Don't miss this one!

- **TOAD BY THE ROAD: A YEAR IN THE LIFE OF THESE AMAZING AMPHIBIANS** written by Joanne Ryder and illustrated by Maggie Kneen; Holt; Grades K–3; poems chronicle the life cycle of the toad.

- **THE TURNING OF THE YEAR** written by Bill Martin Jr. and illustrated by Greg Shed; Harcourt; Grades Pre-K–1; reissue; a lyrical look at the seasons.

- **TURTLE, TURTLE, WATCH OUT!** written by April Pulley Sayre and illustrated by Annie Patterson; Charlesbridge; Grades 1–3; the challenges sea turtles face in order to survive; includes important role humans play and supplemental information on conservation efforts. See **A Closer Look: Our Earth.**

- **UP, UP, AND AWAY** written by Ginger Wadsworth and illustrated by Patricia J. Wynne; Charlesbridge; Grades 1–3; life cycle of the spider.

- **VELMA GRATCH & THE WAY COOL BUTTERFLY** written by Alan Madison and illustrated by Kevin Hawkes; Schwartz & Wade/Random House; Grades 1–3; life cycle of the monarch and metamorphosis of a budding scientist.

- **VOLCANO WAKES UP!** written by Lisa Westberg Peters and illustrated by Steve Jenkins; Holt; Grades 1–4; clever poems in alternating points of view from the lava flow crickets to ferns, the road, the sun, and the volcano itself tell the story of a day on an active volcano.

- **WANGARI'S TREES OF PEACE** by Jeanette Winter; Harcourt; Grades 2–4; true story of Wangari Maathai, environmentalist and winner of the Nobel Peace Prize for her work restoring trees throughout Kenya. See **A Closer Look: Our Earth.** See also:

  ◦ **MAMA MITI** written by Donna Jo Napoli and illustrated by Kadir Nelson; Simon & Schuster

> **WE ARE EXTREMELY VERY GOOD RECYCLERS** Charlie and Lola series by Lauren Child; Dial; Grades K–2; Charlie and Lola take up recycling; includes useful tips for youngsters and a poster. See **A Closer Look: Our Earth.**

> **WHAT IF?** by Laura Vaccaro Seeger; Roaring Brook; Grades 1–3; simple yet thought-provoking book perfect for initiating discussion of possibilities and opportunities.

> **WIRED** by Anastasia Suen and illustrated by Paul Carrick; Charlesbridge; Grades 2–3; overview of how electricity gets from the power plant to your house; accessible, straightforward facts; rhythmical text; bold illustrations.

> **YUCKY WORMS** written by Vivian French and illustrated by Jessica Ahlberg; Charlesbridge; Grades 1–3; a plethora of facts about these helpful backyard creatures; includes simple activities.

Seasons

> **ALL AROUND THE SEASONS** by Barney Saltzberg; Candlewick; Grades Pre-K–2; rhyming text and playful illustrations depict the earmarks of the seasons.

> **CALENDAR** written by Myra Cohn Livingston and illustrated Will Hillenbrand; Holiday House; Grades Pre-K–1; poem teaches the months of the year.

> **ELLEN'S APPLE TREE** by Catarina Kruusval; Farrar, Straus & Giroux; Grades 1–2; a beloved apple tree felled by a storm is eventually replaced in this story of seasons translated from Swedish.

> **MATH FOR ALL SEASONS** written by Greg Tang and illustrated by Harry Briggs; Scholastic; Grades 1–2; math riddles.

> **OLD BEAR** by Kevin Henkes; Greenwillow; Grades Pre-K–1; lyrical text pared with bright, simple renderings of the seasons.

> **RED SINGS FROM TREETOPS: A YEAR IN COLORS** written by Joyce Sidman and illustrated by Pamela Zagarenski; Houghton Mifflin; Grades 1–4; poetic treatment of the colors of the seasons.

> **THE TURNING OF THE YEAR** written by Bill Martin Jr. and illustrated by Greg Shed; Harcourt; Grades Pre-K–1; reissue; simple, lyrical look at the seasons.

> **THE VILLAGE GARAGE** by G. Brian Karas; Holt; Grades Pre-K–1; village workers use trucks in every season to keep the community clean and safe throughout the year.

> **WHAT'S THE BIG IDEA, MOLLY?** by Valeri Gorbachev; Philomel; Grades 1–2; collaboration spurs great ideas and nurtures friendship in this warmly encouraging tale.

Winter

- ➤ **BUNNY WISHES: A WINTER'S TALE** written by Michaela Morgan and illustrated by Caroline Jayne Church; Scholastic; Grades K–2; wishes on a holiday list take on a life of their own.

- ➤ **CHAUCER'S FIRST WINTER** written by Stephen Krensky and illustrated by Henry Cole; Grades Pre-K–K; it's much more fun to stay up throughout the winter than take a long winter's nap!

- ➤ **DANNY'S FIRST SNOW** by Leonid Gore; Atheneum; Grades Pre-K–1; enchanting, inspiring, glorious snow!

- ➤ **THE LONGEST NIGHT** written by Marion Dane Bauer and illustrated by Ted Lewin; Holiday House; Grades 1–2; winter night breaks at dawn with the song of the wee chickadee; lyrical, evocative, sensory.

- ➤ **A PERFECT SNOWMAN** by Preston McDaniels; Simon & Schuster; Grades 1–3; snowman who has the best of everything receives a most precious gift.

- ➤ **RABBIT'S GIFT** written by George Shannon and illustrated by Laura Dronzek; Harcourt; Grades K–2; based on an international folktale about friendship.

- ➤ **RED SLED** written by Patricia Thomas and illustrated by Chris L. Demarest; Boyds Mills Press; Grades Pre-K–1; spare, rhyming text about one happy winter eve.

- ➤ **SNOW DAY!** written by Lester L. Laminack and illustrated by Adam Gustavson; Peachtree; Grades K–2; wonderful illustrations; humorous twist at end.

- ➤ **SNOWY, BLOWY WINTER** by Bob Raczka and illustrated by Judy Stead; Albert Whitman; Grades Pre-K–2; rhythmical, poetic language celebrates the season. See also:

  - ◦ **SUMMER WONDERS**

- ➤ **SNOW! SNOW! SNOW!** by Lee Harper; Simon & Schuster; Grades Pre-K–K; the wonder and amazement of a big snowfall.

Spring

- ➤ **SPLISH, SPLASH, SPRING** written by Jan Carr and illustrated by Dorothy Donohue; Holiday House; Grades Pre-K–1; lyrical language and bold illustrations celebrate the season.

Summer

- ➤ **FIREFLIES AT MIDNIGHT** written by Marilyn Singer and illustrated by Ken Robbins; Atheneum; Grades 1–2+; poems about summer's creatures; graphically enhanced photographs and collages.

➤ **THUNDER-BOOMER!** written by Shutta Crum and illustrated by Carol Thompson; Clarion; Grades 2–4; lyrical description of summer storm ends with a furry surprise.

➤ **TO THE BEACH** by Thomas Docherty; Templar/Candlewick; Grades Pre-K–1; spare text celebrates imagination and creativity and offers a great opportunity for making predictions.

Fall

➤ **APPLESAUCE SEASON** written by Eden Ross Lipson and illustrated by Mordicai Gerstein; Roaring Brook; Grades K–2; a multigenerational urban family celebrates apple harvest.

➤ **HOW MANY SEEDS IN A PUMPKIN?** written by Margaret McNamara and illustrated by G. Brian Karas; Schwartz & Wade/Random House; Grades 1–3; count away!

➤ **IN NOVEMBER** written by Cynthia Rylant and illustrated by Jill Kastner; Harcourt; Grades Pre-K–2; lyrical and lovely.

➤ **LEAF JUMPERS** written by Carole Gerber and illustrated by Leslie Evans; Charlesbridge; Grades Pre-K–2; primer for identifying leaves.

➤ **LEAF TROUBLE** written by Jonathan Emmett and illustrated by Caroline Jayne Church; Chicken House/Scholastic; Grades Pre-K–1; Pip learns about autumn and seasonal cycles.

➤ **LEAVES** by David Ezra Stein; Putnam; Grades Pre-K–1; sweet and simple look at the seasons; a perfect picture book.

➤ **LET IT FALL** by Maryann Cocca-Leffler; Cartwheel/Scholastic; Grades Pre-K–1; light, lyrical look at a colorful season.

➤ **ONE IS A FEAST FOR MOUSE: A THANKSGIVING TALE** written by Judy Cox and illustrated by Jeffrey Ebbeler; Holiday House; Grades K–2; tale about giving thanks for small things; adorable, attention-keeping illustrations and pleasingly descriptive language.

Other

➤ **DUCK DUCK MOOSE** by Dave Horowitz; Putnam; Grades K–2; a little geography, a dash of road trip, a large dose of slapstick makes for a fantastic read-aloud! See **A Closer Look: Geography, Maps, and Travel.**

➤ **THE GREAT DOUGHNUT PARADE** by Rebecca Bond; Houghton Mifflin; Grades K–2; a boy with a doughnut on a string and a mysterious box leads a fanciful cadre of townspeople and animals to a gala affair and a simple sail in this imaginative, cumulative rhyming tale.

- ➤ **GUESS AGAIN!** written by Mac Barnett and illustrated by Adam Rex; Simon & Schuster; Grades Pre-K–1: delightful nonsensical guessing game is heightened by hilarious art.

- ➤ **HOW UNDERWEAR GOT UNDER THERE: A BRIEF HISTORY** written by Kathy Shaskan and illustrated by Regan Dunnick; Dutton; Grades 1–3; from Mongolian warriors to men in space, this overview covers the history of underwear with a lighthearted blend of facts, humorous stories, silliness, and lively science.

- ➤ **I SPY A TO Z: A BOOK OF PICTURE RIDDLES** written by Jean Marzollo and photographs by Walter Wick; Scholastic; Grades K–2.

- ➤ **IT'S PICTURE DAY TODAY!** written by Megan McDonald and illustrated by Katherine Tillotson; Atheneum; Grades K–2; crafty items get ready for class pictures, but button is late!

- ➤ **THE MYSTERY** by Maxwell Eaton III; Knopf; Grades Pre-K–1; exceptional intro to mystery genre for the youngest of listeners.

- ➤ **PSSST!** by Adam Rex; Harcourt; Grades Pre-K–2; crafty zoo animals have a deliciously sneaky plan; hilarious!

- ➤ **NOT A BOX** by Antoinette Portis; HarperCollins; Grades Pre-K–1; oh, the things a box can become when we play! New York Times Best Illustrated Book; Theodor Seuss Geisel Honor Book.

- ➤ **THE RETURN OF THE KILLER CAT** by Anne Fine; illustrated by Steve Cox; Farrar, Straus & Giroux; Grades 2–3; early chapter book about a wily cat who plays while the family is away for a week, foiling the hapless vicar and fooling mawkish Melanie (aka Little Miss Soppy).

- ➤ **THIS SCHOOL YEAR WILL BE THE BEST!** written by Kay Winters and illustrated by Renée Andriani; Scholastic; Grades Pre-K–2; wishes galore are explored in this happy look-ahead book perfect to read aloud the first week of school.

- ➤ **TILLIE LAYS AN EGG** written by Terry Golson and photographs by Ben Fink; Scholastic; Grades Pre-K–1; find the unlikely places individualist Tillie lays her eggs around the farm.

- ➤ **TOOTH ON THE LOOSE** written by Susan Middleton Elya and illustrated by Jenny Mattheson; Putnam; Grades K–2; bilingual; rhyming text.

- ➤ **WHICH SHOES WOULD YOU CHOOSE?** written by Betsy R. Rosenthal and illustrated by Nancy Cote; Putnam; Grades Pre-K–K; bright illustrations and question-and-answer format enliven this concept book.

- ➤ **WHOSE SHOES? A SHOE FOR EVERY JOB** by Stephen R. Swinburne; Boyds Mills; Grades Pre-K–K; match shoes to the job; prediction.

Wordless Books (or Almost So!)

ANNO'S JOURNEY by Mitsumasa Anno; Philomel.

ANNO'S USA by Mitsumasa Anno; Philomel.

THE ARRIVAL by Shaun Tan; Arthur A. Levine/Scholastic.

ART & MAX by David Wiesner; Clarion.

A BOY, A DOG, AND A FROG by Mercer Mayer; Dial.

    Also: FROG GOES TO DINNER
    FROG ON HIS OWN

BREAKFAST FOR JACK by Pat Schories; Boyds Mills Press.

    Also: JACK AND THE MISSING PIECE
    JACK AND THE NIGHT VISITORS
    JACK WANTS A SNACK
    WHEN JACK GOES OUT

COOL CAT by Nonny Hogrogian; Roaring Brook.

THE CROCODILE BLUES by Coleman Polhemus; Candlewick.

A DAY, A DOG by Gabrielle Vincent; Front Street.

DAWN by Uri Shulevitz; Farrar, Straus & Giroux; New York Times Outstanding Book of the Year.

DINOSAUR DAY by Liza Donnelly; Scholastic.

FLOTSAM by David Wiesner; Clarion; Caldecott Medal.

FREE FALL by David Wiesner; HarperCollins; Caldecott Honor.

GOOD DOG, CARL by Alexandra Day; Simon & Schuster.

HAVE YOU SEEN MY DUCKLING? by Nancy Tafuri; Greenwillow.

HUG by Jez Alborough; Candlewick.

IF YOU LIVED HERE YOU'D BE HOME BY NOW by Ed Briant; Roaring Brook.

LOOK! LOOK! LOOK! by Tana Hoban; Scholastic.

THE LION & THE MOUSE by Jerry Pinkney; Little, Brown; Caldecott Medal.

THE MYSTERIES OF HARRIS BURDICK by Chris Van Allsburg; Houghton Mifflin.

ONCE UPON A BANANA illustrated by David Small; Simon & Schuster.

PANCAKES FOR BREAKFAST by Tomie dePaola; Harcourt.

PEOPLE by Peter Spier; Doubleday.

RAIN by Peter Spier; Doubleday.

RAIN TALK written by Mary Serfozo and illustrated by Keiko Narahashi; Macmillan.

ROUND TRIP by Ann Jonas; Morrow.

SAIL AWAY by Donald Crews; Morrow.

THE STORM IN THE BARN by Matt Phelan; Candlewick; Scott O'Dell Award for Historical Fiction.

SUNSHINE by Jan Ormerod; Putnam.

THE THREE PIGS by David Wiesner; Clarion; Caldecott Medal.

TIME FLIES by Eric Rohmann; Crown; Caldecott Honor.

TRAINSTOP by Barbara Lehman; Houghton Mifflin.

TUESDAY by David Wiesner; Clarion; Caldecott Medal.

Wordless Books
Teaching Strategies

- Study the illustrations and discuss what is happening on each page. Note season, time of day, passage of time, foreground and background details, facial expressions, gestures, sequence of events, and colors the illustrator chose. Encourage full-sentence responses.

- Collectively create a story based on the book.

- Develop a profile/background for each of the characters and events.

- Design dialogue.

- Use expression as you read aloud the story you create!

- Predict what might happen next, after book has ended.

- Write multiple stories for the same book.

- Write stories in teams and come together to share stories with the whole group.

- Imagine: *what if?* Change key details found in the illustrations. Discuss how changes alter the story's outcome.

FIRST CHAPTER BOOKS TO JUMP-START INDEPENDENT READING

The books listed below are outstanding recently published early chapter books. They contain inviting first chapters that are sure to tickle the fancy and rouse the interest of newly independent readers. Consider occasionally reading aloud the first chapter and then leave the book on display and available for loan.

Sneaky . . . and very effective!

Grades K–1

FUNNY LUNCH (Max Spaniel books) by David Catrow; Orchard/Scholastic.

See also: **DINOSAUR HUNT**

HI! FLY GUY (Fly Guy series) written by Tedd Arnold; Scholastic; Theodor Seuss Geisel Honor Book.

I AM GOING! (Elephant & Piggie series) by Mo Willems; Hyperion.

KAT'S MYSTERY GIFT (Jon Scieszka's Trucktown Ready-to-Roll series) written by Jon Scieszka and illustrated by David Shannon, Loren Long, and David Gordon; Aladdin.

READY FOR KINDERGARTEN, STINKY FACE? Written by Lisa McCourt and illustrated by Cyd Moore; Scholastic.

See also: **IT'S THE 100TH DAY, STINKY FACE!**

Grades 1–2

AGGIE AND BEN: THREE STORIES written by Lori Ries and illustrated by Frank W. Dormer; Charlesbridge.

AMAZING MONTY (Monty Books series) written by Johanna Hurwitz and illustrated by Anik McGrory; Candlewick.

ANNIE AND BO AND THE BIG SURPRISE written by Elizabeth Partridge and illustrated by Martha Weston; Dutton.

ANT AND HONEY BEE: A PAIR OF FRIENDS AT HALLOWEEN written by Megan McDonald and illustrated by G. Brian Karas; Candlewick.

CAM JANSEN series by David A. Adler; Viking.

See also: **YOUNG CAM JANSEN**

CORK & FUZZ: GOOD SPORTS (Cork & Fuzz series) written by Dori Chaconas and illustrated by Lisa McCue; Viking.

COWGIRL KATE AND COCOA (Cowgirl Kate series) written by Erica Silverman and illustrated by Betsy Lewin; Harcourt; Theodor Seuss Geisel Honor Book.

DODSWORTH IN NEW YORK by Tim Egan; Houghton Mifflin.

HENRY AND MUDGE AND THE TALL TREE HOUSE (Henry and Mudge series; Ready-to-Read) written by Cynthia Rylant and illustrated by Carolyn Bracken in the style of Suçie Stevenson; Simon & Schuster.

HOUNDSLEY AND CATINA (Houndsley and Catina series) written by James Howe and illustrated by Marie-Louise Gay; Candlewick; E. B. White Read-Aloud Award.

PINKY AND REX (Ready-to-Read series) written by James Howe and illustrated by Melissa Sweet; Aladdin.

POPPLETON IN WINTER (Poppleton series) written by Cynthia Rylant and illustrated by Mark Teague; Scholastic.

RIP-ROARING RUSSELL (Riverside Kids series) written by Johanna Hurwitz and illustrated by Debbie Tilley; HarperCollins.

THE STORIES JULIAN TELLS written by Ann Cameron and illustrated by Ann Strugnell; Knopf; ALA Notable Children's Book; Irma Simonton Black Award.

STUART'S CAPE written by Sara Pennypacker and illustrated by Martin Matje; Orchard/Scholastic.

See also: **STUART GOES TO SCHOOL**

ZELDA AND IVY: THE BIG PICTURE (Zelda and Ivy series) by Laura McGee Kvasnosky; Candlewick.

Grades 2–3

BEING TEDDY ROOSEVELT written by Claudia Mills and illustrated by R. W. Alley; Farrar, Straus & Giroux.

BIG WHOPPER (Zigzag Kids series) written by Patricia Reilly Giff and illustrated by Alasdair Bright; Yearling/Random House.

BINK & GOLLIE written by Kate DiCamillo and Alison McGhee and illustrated by Tony Fucile; Candlewick.

THE CHILDREN WHO SMELLED A RAT written by Allan Ahlberg and illustrated by Katharine McEwen; Candlewick.

CLEMENTINE series written by Sara Pennypacker and illustrated by Marla Frazee; Hyperion; numerous awards.

DOGGONE . . . THIRD GRADE! written by Colleen O'Shaughnessy McKenna and illustrated by Stephanie Roth; Holiday House.

JAKE DRAKE: BULLY BUSTER (Jake Drake series) written by Andrew Clements; Simon & Schuster.

JUDY MOODY WAS IN A MOOD (Judy Moody series) written by Megan McDonald and illustrated by Peter H. Reynolds; Candlewick.

MARVIN REDPORT: WHY PICK ON ME? (Marvin Redpost series; Stepping Stone Books) written by Louis Sachar and illustrated by Barbara Sullivan; Random House.

MOKIE & BIK written by Wendy Orr and illustrated by Jonathan Bean; Holt.

THE PUMPKIN ELF MYSTERY (Ready, Freddy! series) written by Abby Klein and illustrated by John McKinley; Blue Sky/Scholastic.

PUPPY POWER written by Judy Cox and illustrated by Steve Björkman; Holiday House.

THE RETURN OF THE KILLER CAT written by Anne Fine and illustrated by Steve Cox; Farrar, Straus & Giroux.

ROXIE AND THE HOOLIGANS written by Phyllis Reynolds Naylor and illustrated by Alexandra Boiger; Aladdin.

THE SCHOOL MOUSE written by Dick King-Smith and illustrated by Cynthia Fisher; Hyperion.

SLY THE SLEUTH AND THE PET MYSTERIES (Sly the Sleuth series) written by Donna Jo Napoli and Robert Furrow and illustrated by Heather Maione; Dial.

SECTION II

In the Spotlight

**Detailed Plans for
Memorable Read-Aloud Experiences
Highlighting Outstanding Children's Trade Books
That Connect to the Content Areas**

*with
"The Story Behind the Story"
written by the Authors
and
"Picturing the Book"
written by the Illustrators*

IN THE SPOTLIGHT

HOW DO YOU WOKKA-WOKKA? written by Elizabeth Bluemle and illustrated Randy Cecil; Candlewick; Grades Pre-K–1.

This exuberant call-and-response is a finger-snapping, toe-tapping delight set in a city neighborhood. There's plenty of energy in the wordplay, jazzy rhythm, and upbeat oil paintings featuring multicultural characters. Repetition encourages participation and enhances multiple readings.

 This is a great book to read aloud before snack time!

Read-aloud time: 10 minutes

Themes/Content Area Connections:

Movement, dance, individuality, friendship, urban settings, multicultural diversity.

Preparation for Read-aloud:

Be sure to pre-read the wacky rhyming text so you can be-bop your way through the read-aloud without a stumble. Place the title on chart paper or the board in preparation for the Follow-Up (see below).

Note: If you have access to maracas and a picture of a flamingo (a plastic lawn ornament would be even better!) have them available.

Before Reading:

❖ Begin by asking the titular question. Following responses, show the cover of the book. Ask listeners what the characters are doing. (playing, interacting) Ask again what the title might mean. Take a closer look at the cover of the book (front and back) and the flyleaves. Where does the story take place (setting)? (urban; city) How do we know? (high-rises, cabs parked at curb, brownstones, concrete to street)

❖ **Let's read to find out** how you wokka-wokka!

While Reading:

❖ The text is best read uninterrupted so as not to spoil its rhythm and the crescendo of the text.

Follow-Up:

- ❖ Ask: So how do you wokka-wokka?

- ❖ Would you rather wokka-wokka in your shiny shoes or socka-socka?

- ❖ Put children in three groups to wokka-wokka, shimmy-shake, and shocka-shocka.

- ❖ Place the title question on chart paper or the board before the read-aloud session. Following the read-aloud, go through the book again, page by page, allowing the children to mimic the wokka-wokka-ness on each page. On the pages that ask, "How do you wokka-wokka?" point to the words on the chart paper or the board and encourage children to read along.

- ❖ End with everybody wokka-wokka-ing "in their own crazy way."

Extension Activities:

- ❖ Ask children to go home and wokka-wokka with their family. Be ready to tell about the experience (How did family members wokka-wokka?) at a special "Wokka-Wokka Show-and-Tell" the following day.

- ❖ See Writing Activity below. Once complete, line children up. Say, "How do YOU wokka-wokka?" to the first child and have him read his response. He then turns to the next child and asks: "How do YOU wokka-wokka?" and so on down the line. At the end, have all the children demonstrate their wokka-wokka together as they chant the last line of the book: "Yeah, ya gotta wokka!" Wokka away!

Writing Activity:

- ✏ Prepare sheets with "How do YOU wokka-wokka?" at the top.

- ✏ On the next line print "I wokka-wokka . . ." followed by two blank lines. Ask children to complete the stanza.

More, More, More!

For other books that celebrate neighborhood and family gatherings, see

AROUND OUR WAY ON NEIGHBORS' DAY written by Tameka Fryer Brown and illustrated by Charlotte Riley-Webb; **COME AND PLAY: CHILDREN OF OUR WORLD HAVING FUN** edited by Ayana Lowe with photographs by Julie Collins; **THE RELATIVES CAME** written by Cynthia Rylant and illustrated by Stephen Gammell; **WE HAD A PICNIC THIS SUNDAY PAST** written by Jacqueline Woodson and illustrated by Diane Greenseid; and **WHEN LIGHTNING COMES IN A JAR** by Patricia Polacco. For other books that explore community and families, see the listing in **Section I** of this resource.

THE STORY BEHIND THE STORY

From Elizabeth Bluemle, the author of HOW DO YOU WOKKA-WOKKA?:

When my nephew Will was about two years old, he started asking family members, "How do you wokka-wokka?" He had a delighted gleam in his eye, as though he knew he was asking a funny question. "Do you mean, 'how do we walk?'" we asked him. But showing him how he walked wasn't the right answer. "How do you *wokka-wokka?*" he repeated insistently. We couldn't figure out what he meant. Finally, in amused desperation, his mom made a silly flapping motion with her arms. "This is how I wokka-wokka!" she said. That was it; Will laughed and laughed and then asked each person in the room the wokka question, clearly expecting us to come up with new goofy movements—the more outrageous, the better. We obliged, and the wokka game became a regular pastime for weeks.

I was so charmed by my nephew's funny and mysterious question that I knew I wanted to write about it. But there wasn't enough material there to make a book, so I tucked the idea away in a drawer. A few years went by, and then I started thinking about that question again. Because I've always loved poetry, sometimes lines and sentences will float through my head in fragments of poems. I started hearing the rhythm of the story. Phrases came to me: "How do you wokka-wokka? How do you wokka-wokka? I wokka-wokka like a fish flop on a docka, I wokka-wokka like this." And I started seeing images of kids sharing all the different ways they like to dance. I wrote down all the words I could think of that rhymed with wokka. I also played around with using words that rhyme with "wok," like "dock" and "sock" and "tock," and adding an "a" to the end of them to make them rhyme with "wokka."

So now I had some ideas and some words, but what was the story behind them? I began thinking about the street parties in New York City that I used to love. Police would put up roadblocks so there were no cars, and people would bring out booths with tasty food and drinks, bright shirts and dresses, comic books and paintings and jewelry and toys, and even stained-glass windows to sell, and there were balloons and cotton candy and games to play. These were big summer street fairs, and everyone from the neighborhood came out to enjoy the sunshine together. It was a big rainbow of colors. What I loved most was that every person was different, an individual, but also part of a community. That's what those parties celebrated. When that memory hit me, the whole book came together: we all wokka in our own special ways, but we do it side by side, creating friendships and communities along the way.

P.S. For teachers working with kids writing poetry: I like to tell children one of my secrets for working out problematic lines in my books. I take my dogs out for a walk and pace in the rhythm of the poem I'm working on, reciting the lines out loud as I go. If there's a line I'm stuck on, I keep trying different things. There's something about walking while I think out loud that almost always solves my problem. (Note: Kids especially like this tip when you demonstrate walking and muttering to yourself.)

Visit http://www.elizabethbluemle.com to find information about Bluemle's other books as well as activities for readers and writers.

Another book written by Elizabeth Bluemle included in this resource: MY FATHER, THE DOG illustrated by Randy Cecil.

PICTURING THE BOOK

From Randy Cecil, the illustrator of HOW DO YOU WOKKA-WOKKA?:

I was thrilled to get the opportunity to illustrate **HOW DO YOU WOKKA-WOKKA?** because it was such a fun, energetic manuscript and also because so much was left open to interpretation. The openness of it left a lot of room to try different things, and the sketches went through several very different approaches.

Early on in the sketching process, the book started with a girl followed by her little brother, and adults joined in the dancing within the first few pages. As the sketches evolved the girl became a boy, the little brother became a cat, and the adults stayed out of the way until the very end!

The openness of the text also allowed me to include lots of details, as well as dances, of my own. This was great fun! If you look closely, you can find kids doing the cabbage patch, the hula, the hand jive, the lawn sprinkler, raising the roof, the robot, the wave, and probably a few other dances.

Visit http://www.randycecil.com to find more information about Cecil and his books.

Another book illustrated by Randy Cecil referenced in this resource: MY FATHER, THE DOG written by Elizabeth Bluemle.

IN THE SPOTLIGHT

THANK YOU, WORLD written by Alice B. McGinty and illustrated by Wendy Anderson Halperin; Dial; Grades Pre-K–2.

You often *can* judge a book by its cover—and its flyleaves. In the case of this book, the warm and appealing cover welcomes the reader with its bright crayon drawings of children from around the globe. Open the book, and you'll find that globe in eight plates with a country highlighted and named in each. Move into the book to meet the children who live in these lands and experience the rich, simple rhyme that expresses the joys of childhood from morning to night across the world. In a simple, affirming presentation, children are treated to ways we are different yet the same as we make our way through the day experiencing common joys. Somehow, the world doesn't feel so large and unknown when we've finished reading this book. Thank you, McGinty and Halperin.

 This is a great book to read aloud at Thanksgiving, with the multinational feast described in the **Extension Activities** below as a culminating activity.

Read-aloud time: 10 minutes

Themes/Content Area Connections:

Community, geography, cultures, natural habitats, comparison and contrast, thankfulness

Preparation for Read-aloud:

Have a globe or map of the world available for the read-aloud. On chart paper or the board, list the countries depicted.

Before Reading:

❖ Look at the cover of the book. Ask: What do you see? (children; globes) How many children are there? (eight) How many globes? (eight) What do you notice about the globes? (one country in each is highlighted)

❖ Open the book to the flyleaves (inside cover). Note the countries and their locations on the globe. Draw attention to the list on the chart paper or the board.

❖ Read the title. Predict what the book might be about. **Let's read to find out.**

While Reading:

Note: The frames correspond in placement on the page with the placement of the globes highlighting the country depicted on the flyleaves. For example, the upper left-hand frame depicts the United States, and the lower right-hand frame depicts China throughout the book.

❖ On each page take a moment to look at the illustrations and ask children to identify the differences in habitat, clothing, terrain, types of trees and flowers, homes, birds, and activities. Note things that are the same, too (all the children are playing with kites; moms tuck the children in).

❖ On the birds page, find the birds that are represented in more than one frame. See the author's note on the dedication page indicating that the barn swallow lives almost worldwide.

❖ About midway through the book, ask: What do you notice about the words being used from page to page? Did you notice words being used more than once? Ask children to pay attention to that as you read the next several pages. Ask children what they notice. (On each double-page spread, the last word becomes the "Thank you" on the subsequent page.)

Follow-Up:

❖ Ask: What are some of the things the children in the story are thankful for? (sky, breeze, trees, clouds, rain, their mothers, nighttime)

❖ What are you thankful for in your life? List these on chart paper or the board.

❖ Locate on a map or globe the countries highlighted in the book. Note the continent on which they are found, which hemisphere, and their location and direction in relation to other countries depicted in the story. Which is northernmost? Southernmost? Closest to an ocean? Closest to mountains? Landlocked? Closest to the USA? Furthest?

❖ Look closely at the homes pictured in the illustrations in **THANK YOU, WORLD.** What types of materials are used to build homes in each country? (e.g., India—thatched roofs; Mali—adobe) Why might these materials be used? (climate, natural resources, availability, location, cost) Identify the helping animals pictured for each country (donkey in Mexico; llama in Bolivia; camel in Saudi Arabia).

❖ Which country or countries in the book would you like to visit? Why?

Extension Activities:

❖ On the dedication page, the author lists the words for "thank you" from each country depicted. Prepare an 8½ by 11-inch outline for each of the countries highlighted in the story. Divide the class into groups. Assign one of the countries to each group. Ask them to find the word in that country's language for each of the following English words: sun, sky, blue, bird, grass, tree, footstep, breeze, kite, clouds, rain, flower, window, stars, Mommy, good night, and dream. Have students write the words on the country's outline.

❖ Have children ask their parents to tell them about their family's country of origin. Children will list five facts about the country similar to those depicted in the story and plan to share them with the class. As children report, locate the country on a globe or map. Display the fact sheets with maps highlighting the countries around the room.

❖ Look closely at the details of the illustrations. Research a specific detail. For example, the illustration of the people of Mali carrying baskets on their heads could prompt research on that custom. Why do people from India wear turbans or people from Mexico sombreros?

❖ Research and identify the types of trees (e.g., banyan tree in India, cactus in Mexico, pine tree in the United States, palm tree in Saudi Arabia and India) depicted for each country. Discuss: Why do you think different trees, flowers, and animals are found in different places around the world? Relate this to temperature, altitude, terrain, access to and abundance of water, and peoples' needs.

❖ Research and identify the birds pictured for each country. Research the barn swallow, found in many countries worldwide.

❖ Divide the class into eight groups. Each group will choose one country from **THANK YOU, WORLD** to research. List relevant facts about predetermined topics. Make artwork or complete a craft relating to each country. Draw the country's flags. Sing their songs. Learn a traditional dance. Dress in customary garb. Bring in toys representing that country, if possible. Culminate with a presentation by each group followed by a multinational feast in which representative dishes from each nation are served. Involve parents by requesting help with this event!

❖ Have students choose other countries they might add to this book if they were the author. Research the countries and complete pages for each country in the style of **THANK YOU, WORLD.**

Writing Activity:

✎ Distribute sheets with the skeleton or frame for a *Thank You* poem in the style of the book's text (see next page). Ask children to create a poem. Children may use words from the list generated in the Follow-Up activity (see above), but they also should be encouraged to add other words. Remind children to use the last word in each thank-you phrase as the first word in the next line. Illustrate and display.

What a Pair!

Consider pairing this book with **ALL THE WORLD** written by Liz Garton Scanlon and illustrated by Marla Frazee for a close-up focus on myriad people, places, things, and events that make up a contemporary American child's world from daybreak to day's end. Refer to the **In the Spotlight: ALL THE WORLD** for a detailed read-aloud plan and follow-up suggestions.

See additional activities for using **THANK YOU, WORLD** as part of a geography/maps unit in **SECTION III: A CLOSER LOOK.**

Thank You, _____!

Thank you, _____

for_____.

Thank you, _____

for _____.

Thank you, _____. You _____

_____.

Thank you, _____

for _____.

Thank you, _____

for _____.

Thank you _____. Your _____

_____.

Thank you, _____

for _____.

Thank you, _____

for _____.

And thank you, _____. Your _____

_____.

THE STORY BEHIND THE STORY

From Alice B. McGinty, the author of THANK YOU, WORLD:

THANK YOU, WORLD was inspired many years ago when I brought my two sons, then very young, to the public pool to swim. It was a piping-hot day, the kind where your feet burn when they touch the pavement. I remember sitting at the pool's snack bar with my boys, sweating in the humid heat, when a cool breeze blew by. It felt so wonderful and offered such relief from the heat that I said to myself, "Thank You, Breeze."

That phrase stuck with me and I began to ask myself what else I might say "Thank You" to. As I often do when I write my books, I started with a list. I included the sun, the trees, the stars, family members, and much more. I'm an outdoorsy kind of person, so most of the things I listed were part of the natural world. Next, I turned my list into a poem. I knew that in order to become a picture book, my poem would need a strong structure or story line. I gave it structure by following a child's day from morning until night. I also used structured repetition in the language, linking one verse to the next. I worked on this poem for quite some time, putting the pieces together like a puzzle, and when it was done, I submitted it to my critique group for comments. After some revisions, I began to submit it to editors and collected a good number of rejections.

Then one editor sent me, along with her rejection letter, a few suggestions to improve the manuscript. She believed that the first four or five verses should be more active. I worked on revising them but felt that I'd broken the intricate puzzle I'd put together. Unfortunately, it seemed that, like with Humpty Dumpty, I couldn't put the pieces back together again. So, I did what I sometimes do when I've "broken" a manuscript—I stuck it in a drawer and forgot about it for a while.

A couple of years later, I read the manuscript again. I still liked parts of it and decided it was worth trying to fix. I did fix it, and within a month of sending it out, this manuscript, which was at that time named "Thank You," was accepted. Hooray!

Wendy Anderson Halperin, a wonderful illustrator from Michigan, was selected to illustrate the book. I knew that her intricate, action-filled illustrations would add not only detail and life to the text but probably whole plotlines as well. I couldn't wait to see what she'd create. Still, I didn't expect what came next. Wendy decided to show other cultures and countries in her illustrations for this book—not just what she saw in her own backyard. So she created illustrations that took place in eight countries around the world. I was blown away with the illustrations she created following the stories of eight multinational children. When my editor sent me the first spread, I got tears in my eyes.

My editor suggested that we change the title to **THANK YOU, WORLD,** which I was pleased to do. It felt magical, this coming together of creative forces, and I am very pleased that teachers and librarians are using this book in their classrooms and libraries.

Alice B. McGinty is the award-winning author of over 40 books for children. Visit http://www.alicebmcginty.com to find information about McGinty's other books, advice for writers, information for teachers, and the many school programs she offers.

PICTURING THE BOOK

From Wendy Anderson Halperin, the illustrator of THANK YOU, WORLD:

THANK YOU, WORLD was for me a journey around the world. Getting ready to illustrate books always requires research. In order for an artist to draw things, it requires looking for what images will best tell the story. I wanted to illustrate the story as if the same story could be felt by children all around the world. I wanted for us all to realize how all of us, wherever we are, could relate to the words Alice McGinty chose: thank you, breeze, sunrise, kite, mom, and going to sleep.

Some of the research questions I asked myself were:

- How do the children dress?

- What is typical design in clothing patterns?

- What is a typical shoe in that country?

- What do the kites look like in that country?

- What would a bedroom look like in that country?

- Trees are different around the world. What tree should I draw for each country?

- What birds live there?

- Is there something special about each country that by drawing it I could help tell the story of that nation?

- What does the globe look like if we put the country we are featuring in the center?

Some of the answers from my research were very interesting and ended up in the book:

- The banyan tree from India is so big that it is said 10,000 people could sit under its shade. Can you see the many roots or trunks?

- Bonsai trees are an art form in China.

- In Mexico, the bottoms of trees are painted so bugs do not harm them.

- In Mexico, very often there are places in their houses to sit right by the window.

- In India, walls inside their houses are sometimes painted with beautiful designs.

- Children in India fly little tiny kites.

- African kites resemble African art.

- Some people in Africa use their heads to carry things.

- A typical scene in Mexico takes place in the town square where people gather. Even little towns have them.

- A typical swing in Saudi Arabia is in an amusement park like 6 Flags here in the United States.

- The colors of the state flower of Bolivia are also the colors of the flag for Bolivia.

- Wangari Maathai won the Nobel Peace Prize for planting trees in Africa. She was the first environmentalist to win the prize. I drew the boy in Africa planting a tree as a tribute to her cause.

- The universal shoe all around the world is the flip-flop.

- The designs of the letters for the title page of **THANK YOU, WORLD** are based on my research of typical artwork special to that region. The "U" is all of them together to represent the United States as a melting pot of so many people from so many different countries.

I had a wonderful tree house as a child, and I spent much of my childhood there. The US tree house was based on my fond memory of that special place.

Visit http://www.wendyhalperin.com to find information about Halperin's other books and the school programs she offers.

Students who would like to draw the planet with Halperin from the eight different points of view shown in THANK YOU, WORLD are invited to go to http://www.drawingchildrenintoreading.com and click on <u>Draw the Planet.</u> Students will need a box of 64 crayons, a ruler, a pencil, and 10 sheets of blank paper each.

Another book illustrated by Wendy Anderson Halperin included in this resource: MY FATHER IS TALLER THAN A TREE written by Joseph Bruchac.

IN THE SPOTLIGHT

ALL THE WORLD written by Liz Garton Scanlon and illustrated by Marla Frazee; Beach Lane/ Simon & Schuster; Grades K–2.

From the cover of the book forward, the reader is immersed in Frazee's inviting coastal California world. Her warm and playful illustrations for this book have earned Frazee a host of citations, including the Caldecott Honor Award. Paired with Scanlon's spare, lyrical text, the result is a moving celebration of the smallness and bigness of contemporary family and home.

 Pick up this book when you are introducing a unit on relationships of items within a category or group or when teaching sequence of events in addition to its obvious connection to family relationships.

Read-aloud time: 8–10 minutes

Themes/Content Area Connections:

Community, family, relationships, nature, comparative relationships

Preparation for Read-aloud:

Collect a rock, stone, pebble, and sand. Have available for read-aloud session.

Before Reading:

❖ Look at the cover of the book. Ask: What do you see? (children; sandy path; sky) How many children are there? (two) Where are they? (beach) Why do you think the boy has a pail? (to collect things on the beach) Ask: What might you find on the beach? Open the book to the title page. Note the shells.

❖ Read the title. Predict what the book's title might mean. **Let's read to find out.**

While Reading:

❖ On the first page, the children are collecting rocks, stones, pebbles, and sand. Take a moment to look at the items you've gathered and ask children to think about how these things are related. How could we arrange them? Note that the author listed them from big to small. Let's remember that as we continue to read this story.

❖ On the next page, note how the children used the rocks, pebbles, stones, and sand. Consider relationship of body, shoulder, arm, hand. Ask what a *moat* is (a trench surrounding a castle filled with water). Encourage children to use the illustrations to help determine the word's meaning. Ask children to tell about their experiences making sand castles at the beach.

❖ Pay attention to the detail in the spreads as you read the story. Find the children from the story's opening in subsequent spreads. In the double-spread panoramas, ask: What is near? What is far away?

❖ About midway through the book, note the weather change. Ask: What do you think will happen on this day? (A storm is brewing.) Ask listeners to pay attention to the weather and how it changes the day's events as you read the next few pages.

❖ The storm dampens the day's activities. Ask children to tell about their experiences when weather has altered their plans.

❖ How does the girl feel as the family goes into the restaurant? (She is hungry—and grouchy.)

❖ Read on to find out what this family does for the rest of the day.

❖ At the end of the book, ask: How did the weather change the day? (At first, the children are disappointed.) Then what happened? (The extended family gathers and enjoys indoor activities.) What do you think the girl is looking at in her hand in the last picture in the book? (a shell, perhaps)

Follow-Up:

❖ Ask: What are some of the things the children in the story did throughout their day? Which was your favorite activity? Why?

❖ The children visit a farmer's market (show illustration). What is a farmer's market? What might you find there? Has anyone been to a farmer's market? What is it like? How is it different from a grocery store? Does anyone have a garden at home? What do you grow there? Why do you think the author wrote, "All the world's a garden bed"?

❖ Look again at the double-spread illustration of the extended family gathering. What are the people doing? Who seems to be having the most fun? How many adults are there? How many children? Think of categories the people fit into. How many different categories can you name? Can a person fit in more than one category? If you were in this gathering, what would you be doing?

❖ Discuss the meaning of the words *hope, peace, love,* and *trust.* Children may define *hope* as it relates to things they want or an immediate wish (go to the playground or community pool; arrange or attend a sleepover). Encourage children to think of something they might hope for someone else. (See **HOPE IS AN OPEN HEART** by Lauren Thompson for an excellent exploration of the meaning of hope.) For *peace,* brainstorm a list of ways students can keep harmony in the classroom, the lunchroom, on the playground, and in their neighborhood. Encourage children to come up with ways to create a peaceful environment in the classroom. For *love,* have children make a list of the people they love. Ask: How do we show love for others? (offering hugs and kisses, sharing toys, helping with chores) How do we know we are loved by others? What is trust? Who do you trust? See also **Writing Activity** below.

❖ Ask: Who can remember what words followed "all the world" in the story? (wide and deep; a garden bed; old and new; sky; goes round this way; cold and hot; can hold quite still; you and me; all of us) Go back through the story to find them all. List them on chart paper or the board. Ask: How might we group these words and phrases? Place the descriptions in categories on chart paper or the board. Categories might include people, places, and descriptions. Next, look at the word lists in the story. Note how the words within the lists are arranged (large to small; small to large).

Extension Activities:

❖ Encourage children to ask their parents to tell them about a typical day in their childhood. Together with parents, children will list five things their parents liked to do. Encourage parents, if possible, to share a childhood memento, one they are willing to have their child bring in and show the class. Share during Show and Tell.

❖ For a variety of activities across the curriculum related to this book and an interview with the author, see the teacher's guide offered on the author's website at http://www.lizgartonscanlon.com/All%20The%20World%20Cur riculum%20Guide%202010.pdf.

Writing Activities:

✎ One line of the book states, "Everything you hear, smell, see . . ." Have children make a chart with Hear, Smell, See, Taste, and Touch written at the top. Ask them to categorize things they experience with their senses for a specified period of time, such as from before supper until bedtime, from wake-up until they get to school, during lunchtime, or during recess.

✎ Have children create a list poem. Encourage children to list items in order from big to small or vice versa, modeling the way lists are written in the book.

What a Pair!

Consider pairing this book with **THANK YOU, WORLD** written by Alice B. McGinty and illustrated by Wendy Anderson Halperin, which offers a peek at a child's world from daybreak to day's end in eight countries across the globe. Refer to **In the Spotlight: THANK YOU, WORLD** for a detailed read-aloud plan and follow-up suggestions.

Other books to pair with **ALL THE WORLD: HOPE IS AN OPEN HEART** by Lauren Thompson and **PEACE WEEK IN MISS FOX'S CLASS** written by Eileen Spinelli and illustrated by Anne Kennedy. For additional books in the realm of world communities, see **Section I** of this resource.

THE STORY BEHIND THE STORY

From Liz Garton Scanlon, the author of ALL THE WORLD:

When I started writing this book, I had this phrase in my head—*All the World*—and a vague sense that if I explored the connections between the things in the world that I loved, that would lead to other connections. Larger ones.

So I began making lists of words that felt important to me, even if they referred to things that are quite ordinary—things like sand and corn on the cob, crickets and curtains.

And all of those lists started coming out in rhyme, which is both a joyful and terrible puzzle—especially if someone asks you to change any of them (which my editor, Allyn Johnston, did)! Because, of course, if you change half a rhyme, you have to change the other half, too. They need to fit together like seashells in the end.

I have dozens of versions of some of the stanzas in this book, all pounded out as I worked to find the right imagery and the right rhyme with the right words at the same time. There were hats and boots and burrows and dens and chicks and cheeps that *didn't* make it into the final manuscript, while tree trunks and bird feathers and big black pots did.

My editor asked me things like, "Is this rhyme perfect enough?" which meant, of course, she thought it wasn't, and "Is this too similar to the previous stanza?" which meant, of course, she thought it was. And I tried to respond to those questions while staying true to my original impulse.

Meanwhile, Marla Frazee had begun to illustrate the text. We passed countless messages back and forth, trying to mesh the words with the pictures—my rhymes with her art. She, too, kept some sketches and tossed others away, in an effort to draw this daunting subject—ALL the world. (You can read about Marla Frazee's process on the following page.)

But really, in the end, it was not so overwhelming. Because at its heart, **ALL THE WORLD** is simply a book about those things we have in common—those things we *love* in common—with people everywhere. Which is what I think I hoped it would be about when I started.

Visit http://www.lizgartonscanlon.com to find information about Scanlon's other books for children, teacher resources, a link to her blog, and information about the school programs she offers.

PICTURING THE BOOK

From Marla Frazee, the illustrator of ALL THE WORLD:

The idea of illustrating a book titled **ALL THE WORLD** was scary. I mean, it's supposed to be about all the world. I was totally overwhelmed. But when I thought about the times I've felt most connected to the big wide world, I realized that none of us ever inhabit all the world but rather our own small place in it. So I focused on one of the places I love the most—the central coast of California—and set the book there.

ALL THE WORLD was written by Liz Scanlon, and I love her words because they celebrate the small things, the big things, children, and grown-ups in equal measure. And I love how it is all mixed up and jumbled together and interconnected and personal *and* universal.

The illustrations in **ALL THE WORLD** are inspired by things that mean a lot to me. The grandfather under the oak tree reminds me of my own immigrant grandfather, who had enough patience and faith in the future to grow oaks from acorns—trees he knew he would never live to see taller than himself. The little tree in front of the café is a mulberry tree he planted 70 years ago to remind him of his childhood in Lebanon. After he died, we carefully transplanted the tree to my parent's house, and its berries have sweetened many summers and stained eight great-grandchildren's clothes. The café was inspired by my hike to the Phantom Ranch Cantina, which sits at the bottom of the Grand Canyon. I drew my zippy orange 2007 Honda Fit and my faithful dog, Rocket, in its front seat, pulling out of the farmer's market. The tulips, the Mediterranean architecture, the pink house, the purple-and-yellow sunset, the beach ball—all of it means something to me. I hope that readers will find many things in *All the World* that mean something to them, too. (For photos of the things that inspired the art for this book, go to http://blaine.org/sevenimpossiblethings/?p=1783.)

Creating the illustrations for a book requires that I do a lot of thinking, doodling, gathering up research, making up characters, figuring out the page turns, emptying the dishwasher very slowly, eating tortilla chips out of the bag, reading all the fine print on the junk mail, talking up the neighbors, driving long distances by myself with the music blaring, returning home with odd purchases that no one needs, and then circling back to the thinking and doodling. It is very scientific!

My studio is in our backyard under an avocado tree, and I adore it. It's got a plywood floor and no running water. I run into the house often, where we are indeed lucky enough to have indoor plumbing. I love spending the day drawing or painting in my studio, but when I write, I go to various coffeehouses in Pasadena or sit at my dining room table.

I knew I wanted to be a children's book illustrator from the time I was in first or second grade. I loved books, loved to read, and, most of all, loved to draw. Every day I get to do the things I love most in the world. I wish that for all my readers!

Visit http://www.marlafrazee.com to find information about Marla Frazee's other books and the school programs she offers.

For a video of Frazee talking about picture books, go to http://books.simo nandschuster.com/All-the-World/Liz-Garton-Scanlon/9781416985808.

Other books illustrated by Marla Frazee included in this resource: the Clementine series written by Sara Pennypacker.

IN THE SPOTLIGHT

RED SINGS FROM TREETOPS: A YEAR IN COLORS written by Joyce Sidman and illustrated by Pamela Zagarenski; Houghton Mifflin; Grades 1–4.

Walk with the author and the illustrator through the seasons of the year with this richly sensory collection of poems on the seasons and the colors they showcase. Even winter sparks the senses in this inspiring collection.

 Rather than reading this book of poems in its entirety from beginning to end, refer to the corresponding poems in the book throughout the year as each season commences. Use the poems as a springboard for examining the richness of color in nature throughout the seasons and as a stimulus for composing seasonal poems throughout the school year.

Read-aloud time: 30 seconds per poem

Themes/Content Area Connections:

Colors, nature, seasons of the year

Preparation for Read-aloud:

For each season, collect items from nature referenced in the poems. For example, in spring find a bit of moss, an abandoned nest, or white spring flowers. In fall, find dried green leaves and brightly colored ones, apples, berries, and pumpkins. Have items available for read-aloud sessions.

Before Reading:

❖ Ask: What season is it? What are some things that remind you of this season? What will we see, smell, hear, feel, taste, and touch that are special this season? What colors do you think of when you think of this season? Look out the window. Is there anything else this season brings?

❖ Look at the cover of the book. Notice that there are four trees on the cover. Which tree do you think is the tree for this season?

❖ Plan to read a poem or two at a time. Consider reading the poems throughout the day on the first day of the season or sprinkle the reading of them throughout the season. Predict what colors will be mentioned in the poem(s) and what the colors will represent. **Let's read to find out.**

While Reading:

❖ Show the illustration. Pick out the predominant color. On the first page, for example, the color is red. There are cardinals, a red door, musical notes, a phone, and worms. Ask children what color they think the poem will be about. Why do you think the poet chose this color? Look at other aspects of the illustration. Here, for example, we should note that the tree is bare, there are no flowers in bloom, the grass is green, and there are no flowers in the pots beside the house's doors.

❖ Read the poem. Identify the items that are represented in the color the poem is about.

❖ What is the girl in the illustration doing? (singing)

❖ As you move through the seasons, ask listeners to pay attention to how the character's outfits change. Ask: What else do you notice?

Follow-Up:

❖ The colors stand for certain things in all the poems. Ask children to identify what they personify. Find it in the illustration. Ask: Which was your favorite thing mentioned? Why? Which line did you like best? Explain. What are some other things we will see in this color this season?

❖ As you progress through the seasons, look again at the illustrations from poems already read and compare the seasonal changes. What is the character doing differently? Consider her clothing and props. What is different; what is the same?

❖ List the senses the poem appeals to. What senses are used most? Least? What would you add to the poem to include another sense?

Extension Activities:

❖ Find the dog on each page. What is he up to? Find the red bird on most pages. What other animals can you find in the illustrations?

❖ To hear the author read one of her poems, go to http://www.joycesidman. com/Listen.html.

Writing Activities:

✐ Write a poem about the season and one of its best colors. Try to use as many senses as you can in your poem. Use color pens or markers to depict or highlight color words.

✐ For more ideas from the author and publisher on writing poems associated with this book and Sidman's other books of poetry, go to http://www.

joycesidman.com/redsingsTG.html and http://www.scribd.com/full/309 34526?access_key=key-257blpkjxm5e1uq8ntym.

🖉 Sidman's encourages young poets on the "Young Voices" page on her website. Go to http://www.joycesidman.com/youngvoicespage.html.

More, More, More!

Other poetry books that celebrate the seasons include **ANNA'S GARDEN SONGS** and **ANNA'S SUMMER SONGS**, poems by Mary Q. Steele and illustrated by Lena Anderson; **AUTUMNBLINGS, SUMMERSAULTS,** and **WINTER EYES** by Douglas Florian; **CALENDAR** written by Myra Cohn Livingston and illustrated by Will Hillenbrand; **A CHILD'S CALENDAR** written by John Updike and illustrated by Trina Schart Hyman; **A CIRCLE OF SEASONS** written by Myra Cohn Livingston and illustrated by Leonard Everett Fisher; **FESTIVALS**, poems by Myra Cohn Livingston and illustrated by Leonard Everett Fisher; **HOLIDAY STEW: A KID'S PORTION OF HOLIDAY AND SEASONAL POEMS** by Jenny Whitehead; **PIECES: A YEAR IN POEMS & QUILTS** by Anna Grossnickle Hines; and **WINTER POEMS** selected by Barbara Rogasky and illustrated by Trina Schart Hyman.

For a poetry book about colors, see **HAILSTONES AND HALIBUT BONES** written by Mary O'Neill and illustrated by John Wallner. For a listing of poetry books about other aspects of nature, see **Section IV: Poetry Pause Bookshelf.**

See also the read-aloud choices listed under **Seasons** in **Section I** of this resource and **RAIN** by Peter Spier and **RAIN TALK** written by Mary Serfozo and illustrated by Keiko Narahashi listed in **Wordless Books** in **Section I.**

THE STORY BEHIND THE STORY

From Joyce Sidman, the author of RED SINGS FROM TREETOPS:

Often it takes the collision of two ideas to get a book rolling, and that was the case with **Red Sings.**

I had wanted to write about color for a long time, but I wasn't sure how to go about it. There have been so many books about color. Color is so important to me that I couldn't bear to write a second-rate book about it. I wanted mine to be new and different, to really express the deep emotional connection I felt when I saw a flaming red maple or a brilliant blue sky. Walking in the woods with my dog every day, I tried out lots of different ways of expressing my feelings about color—in fact, I talked to myself a lot! (Fortunately, no one caught me at it—except my dog, who is used to it.) But an emotion or image is not enough—I had to figure out a "voice" for the book: a way to write it so that it captures that original emotion. I played around with all sorts of color poems, touching on this idea or that, and then retreating when it didn't feel right. With poetry, sometimes you have to go slowly. If you force it, it's just bad poetry. And you have to give it time to rest, so you can look at it with fresh eyes and see if it still works.

Finally one spring day, I looked down at some tracks in the mud, and a line came into my head: "Look down—brown. Deer were here, and a dainty raccoon." That line isn't even in the book anymore, but I knew that I'd found a way to talk about color. I could connect it to the seasons!

After that, my woodland walks were full of what I called the "color hunt." I made lists of everything I found: red maple buds, green moss, gray bark, blue snow shadows. It was like finding treasure! Every day I'd rush back and write down all my ideas. As I wrote, the colors took on their own voices. I began to personify each color—write about it as though it were alive, changing personality in each season.

The collision of two ideas, Color and Seasons, gave me the framework of the book. Personifying each color gave me the voice I needed. After that, it was pure joy to write these poems.

 *Visit http://www.joycesidman.com to find tips for young writers and creative suggestions for writing poetry. Listen to the author read her poetry, learn about Sidman's other books, and peruse the reading guides, teacher guides, and array of activities designed to be used in conjunction with Sidman's award-winning books.*

PICTURING THE BOOK

From Pamela Zagarenski, the illustrator of RED SINGS FROM TREETOPS:

While illustrating any children's book (or creating any painting for that matter), I allow myself become that painting.

I become the words, and then the words flow in and through me, and I transform them into feelings and then back out into this world as image and color.

I live in that very world created by the author, much like an actor or actress takes on a role in a play. (Lucky me, I play all the parts—grasses and trees and leaves and skies and suns and moons and people and animals—and no, I would *never* get up on a stage to perform!)

In my imagination, I fill the white spaces that are snuggled in between and all around the text with the minute details of the characters' lives and their feelings.

I become a conductor, orchestrating with my paintbrush their worlds. Strangely enough, I even fall in love with the characters, often becoming quite attached to them.

Illustrating **RED SINGS FROM TREETOPS** was not any different; it was the little white dog that I particularly became quite fond of. To me, he was sort of serious and silly, old and young, and quite content to just walk along with. As dogs are, he was wise beyond his years and all the time knowing secrets about the mysteries of this world.

In the original text, the dog was written in the text as a different color, and I boldly asked my editor and Joyce Sidman if I could change him to be a white dog with tan spots.

A white dog just seemed to fit better with all the colors in the book, and I saw him as an integral part of every page. (White is all color.) Joyce was so kind to agree with my bold request!

At the time I painted **RED SINGS FROM TREETOPS,** I was without a dog in my life. I had a golden retriever for almost 17 years and he had died about a year and a half before. The pain of losing him was very, very hard, and in that pain, I swore I would never again have a dog in my life.

It was early spring when I finished the paintings for **RED SINGS FROM TREETOPS.** In July of that very same year, a friend of mine decided to adopt a rescue dog as a companion for the dog she already had.

She called me at work and said, "Pam, do you want a dog?"

I said, "No, absolutely not!"

She said, "But you want this dog. I can't keep him, and I just can't return him, but my other dog hates him."

I said, "No more dogs! No!"

Before I could get in another "No" she said, "I'm bringing him in to show you!" (Remember, I was at work!)

About an hour later, after giving him a good scrubbing and a blow dry, she showed up at the gallery that I work in with a fluffy white and tan spotted little knowing dog and placed him in my arms.

She had no knowledge of **RED SINGS FROM TREETOPS.** She had never seen one illustration.

When she handed him to me, I knew that dog. I was already in love with that dog. Instantly he was mine. He was already part of all of our lives, our world.

His name is Basho. We named him after the famous Haiku poet. His favorite thing is just to walk along with. He is knowing and completely and utterly loved.

Yes, you see I do believe in the magic of this world!

Zagarenski works in mixed media, acrylic, colored pencil, collage, and sometimes computer graphics. She describes her illustrations as "a little of everything, usually painted on wood."

Of working on poetry written by Joyce Sidman, Zagarenski says, "It is an illustrator's dream to have such inspiring words to play with!"

View more of Pamela Zagarenski's artwork as part of an interview on the children's book blog, Seven Impossible Things Before Breakfast: Why Stop at Six?, at http://blaine.org/sevenimpossiblethings/?p=1707.

IN THE SPOTLIGHT

A SICK DAY FOR AMOS MCGEE written by Philip C. Stead and illustrated by Erin E. Stead; Roaring Brook; Grades K–2.

Come meet the instantly lovable zookeeper and his menagerie of animal friends for whom he cares day in and day out—until one day they return the favor.

 Use this book as an introduction to character study.

Read-aloud time: 7–10 minutes

Themes/Content Area Connections:

Friendship, caring for friends, sick days

Preparation for Read-aloud:

What is a sick day? How you feel when you are sick and have to stay home from school? How do you feel when one of your friends is sick and doesn't come to school? When someone in your family is sick? How can we help a sick friend or family member feel better? What makes you feel better when you are sick?

Before Reading:

❖ Read the title. Ask: What do you think this story is about?

❖ Look at the cover of the book. Ask: What do you notice? (wild animals—elephant, penguin, mouse—and a man in his pajamas playing cards) Look at the back cover. (other animals—turtle, owl, rhinoceros) Discuss what might be happening here. (Animals are leaving zoo; going to visit Amos.)

❖ Ask: What is a zookeeper? What does a zookeeper do? (takes care of animals in a zoo)

❖ **Let's read to find out** about Amos McGee and the animals.

While Reading:

❖ Read the first page. Ask: What is an early riser? (one who gets up early) What words do you especially like: words that make the story interesting? (Note vivid verbs: *clanged, swapped.*) What is colored in this picture? (walls, blanket, collar and cuffs of pajamas, uniform)

❖ Read the next page. Ask: Do you have a morning routine as Amos does? Discuss.

❖ Read the next several pages in which Amos's friends are introduced. Note details in illustrations.

❖ After reading the page on which Amos wakes up sick, discuss student's experiences waking up not feeling well. Note placement of splashes of color.

❖ Read the next page. Discuss why each animal is doing what he is doing.

❖ Read the next page (Later that day . . .) Look at the back cover. Look at the double-page spread. Ask: Where are the animals? (bus stop) Where do you think the animals are going? (to see Amos) Turn to the next spread.

❖ Read the next page. Ask: How does Amos feel when his friends arrive? Note the full color in this spread.

❖ Read to the end of the book. Note how Amos' friends help him to feel better. Enjoy the last illustration!

Follow-Up:

❖ Ask children to think about the qualities of each of Amos's friends. Review. Ask: Which of Amos's friends would you most like to have? Which was your favorite? Why?

❖ What qualities does Amos possess? Discuss. Would you like to have Amos as a friend? Why?

❖ Do you know anyone like Amos? Each of the animals? Discuss.

❖ What other animals would you add if you were to extend this story. What qualities would the animal possess?

Extension Activities:

❖ Make a list of things to do for a friend or family member the next time he or she gets sick.

❖ As a class, prepare a Get Well Soon packet to send home to classmates when they are sick during the school year.

Writing Activities:

🖉 Write a get-well wish to a sick friend or classmate or to children in an acute care facility.

✏ Break into groups. Research the animals in the story. Write about why each of the animals might have the quality it possesses.

✏ Write about the qualities a pet or favorite animal possesses. How can you be a special friend to this animal? How is this animal a special friend to you?

More, More, More!

For poetry about animals, see **ANIMALS ANIMALS**, poems selected and illustrated by Eric Carle; **ANIMAL FRIENDS: A COLLECTION OF POEMS FOR CHILDREN** illustrated by Michael Hague; **CREATURES OF EARTH, SEA, AND SKY**, poems by Georgia Heard and illustrations by Jennifer Owings Dewey; **DOGKU** by Andrew Clements and illustrated by Tim Bowers; **DOG POEMS** written by Dave Crawley and illustrated by Tamara Petrosino; **HOOFBEATS, CLAWS & RIPPLED FINS: CREATURE POEMS** edited by Lee Bennett Hopkins and illustrated by Stephen Alcorn; **IF NOT FOR THE CAT**, haiku by Jack Prelutsky and illustrated by Ted Rand; **LITTLE DOG POEMS** written by Kristine O'Connell George and illustrated by June Otani; **LOOSE LEASHES** written by Amy Schmidt and photographs by Ron Schmidt; and **SCRANIMALS,** poems by Jack Prelutsky and illustrated by Peter Sis.

For a listing of poetry books about other aspects of nature, see **Section IV: Poetry Pause Bookshelf.**

See also the following read-aloud choices listed under **Character Education** in **Section I** of this resource: **BEAR FEELS SICK** written by Karma Wilson and illustrated by Jane Chapman, **CITY DOG, COUNTRY FROG** written by Mo Willems and illustrated by Jon J. Muth, **THE DAY IT RAINED HEARTS** (formerly **FOUR VALENTINES IN A RAINSTORM**) by Felicia Bond, **HUG** by Jez Alborough, **MILO ARMADILLO** by Jan Fearnley, **MOLLY WHO FLEW AWAY** by Valeri Gorbachev, **RABBIT'S GIFT** written by George Shannon and illustrated by Laura Dronzek, **A SPLENDID FRIEND, INDEED** by Suzanne Bloom, **TAKING CARE OF MAMA** by Mitra Modarressi, **THAT'S WHAT FRIENDS ARE FOR** written by Florence Parry Heide and Sylvia Van Clief and illustrated by Holly Meade, and **TWO BOBBIES: A TRUE STORY OF HURRICANE KATRINA, FRIENDSHIP, AND SURVIVAL** written by Kirby Larson and Mary Nethery and illustrated by Jean Cassels.

THE STORY BEHIND THE STORY

From Philip C. Stead, the author of A SICK DAY FOR AMOS MCGEE:

A question I get a lot is, So what are you working on next? The truth is, a lot of times I don't know. I have very little control over when and how a story will come to me. Often they come at inopportune times. For example, an entire story outline once came to me in a flash while driving on Interstate 94 from Ann Arbor to Detroit, Michigan. Driving 70 miles per hour without a pen or pencil in reach, I was desperate to get home before the ideas disappeared to that special place where forgotten things go to live—a place not reachable via I-94.

A SICK DAY FOR AMOS MCGEE was different. It was the first time I ever sat down with the thought: I am going to write a story today. I wanted to write a story specifically for my wife, Erin. Nobody draws animals (especially elephants!) quite like Erin. She has a knack, too, for illustrating the unusual relationships that people can have with animals. I thought about the things Erin draws best, and the story characters came to me with no effort at all—an elephant, a penguin, a rhinoceros, a tortoise, an owl, and their good friend Amos McGee, an elderly zookeeper. **A SICK DAY FOR AMOS MCGEE** is a simple, quiet story about Amos and his daily routine—chess with the elephant, races with the tortoise, story time with the owl. On a day when Amos is feeling under the weather, his good friends board a bus and come over for a visit. The animals do for Amos all of the things that Amos normally does for them. It's a story about friendship, it's a story about the unusual but strong relationships that a person can have with animals, and it's a story I really couldn't have illustrated myself, at least not as well as Erin, who I think has done a beautiful job.

Philip C. Stead is also an artist. Visit his website at http://www.philip stead.com. View Stead's artwork and enjoy an interview on the children's book blog, Seven Impossible Things Before Breakfast: Why Stop at Six?, found at http://blaine.org/sevenimpossiblethings/?p=1708.

Stead rhymes with bed or red.

PICTURING THE BOOK

From Erin E. Stead, the illustrator of A SICK FOR AMOS MCGEE:

I came home from work one day and Phil handed me a story. Just out of the blue. Since we hadn't discussed him writing me a story for a very, very long time, I was a little surprised and maybe a little nervous. Once I read the story, I was obviously hooked. He had written me a beautiful story with characters I was eagerly looking forward to getting to know and draw. I felt lucky.

Eventually, I was signed up to make the book, and I spent the next 16 months or so doing just that. There were days when it was hard and days when I was maybe being too picky. But those days were minor compared to how much I enjoyed creating the cast of characters. To me, every one of them has a different personality and movement. I was able to spend my days drawing with Phil creating books next to me. We had a great time.

Follow Erin E. Stead on her blog at http://erinstead.com. Read an enlightening interview of Stead on the children's book blog, Seven Impossible Things Before Breakfast: Why Stop at Six?, found at http://blaine.org/sevenimpossiblethings/?p=1723.

Stead rhymes with bed or red.

IN THE SPOTLIGHT

GRACIAS THANKS written by Pat Mora and illustrated by John Parra; Lee & Low; Grades K–2.
Through bilingual text, we meet and come to know a sweet and gentle child who expresses his thanks for the simple things he experiences throughout his busy day.

 Consider using this book at the beginning of each season. Compare what children note they are thankful for from season to season throughout the year.

Read-aloud time: 5–7 minutes

Themes/Content Area Connections:

Thankfulness, ELL, commonality of childhood experiences and activities, multicultural awareness

Preparation for Read-aloud:

Write the work *thanks* on the board or on chart paper or the board.

Before Reading:

❖ Ask: What does it mean to be thankful?

❖ Ask children to name things for which they are thankful. Encourage them to think of small things as well as big things. List and discuss.

❖ Look at the cover of the book. Notice the details in the illustration, front and back. Note that the title is in Spanish and English.

❖ Read the word *gracias*. Ask children if they know what this means. (thanks)

❖ **Let's read to find out** why this book has is titled as it is.

While Reading:

❖ Read the boy's comments. Note the many details in the illustrations. Consider reading the book's text in both languages.

❖ Take note of the boy's descriptions and sensory language.

❖ As you move through the boy's day, ask listeners to think about similar things they are thankful for.

Follow-Up:

❖ Categorize the things the boy is thankful for. Similarly, categorize the class list.

Extension Activities:

🖉 Children can interview their parents, or principal, custodian, librarian, or other school staff about what they were most thankful for when they were young.

Writing Activity:

🖉 Find the word that means *thanks* in other languages. Have children use the word for *thanks* from their family's country of origin as the label for an illustration depicting something they are thankful for.

More, More, More!

Other books listed in this resource that focus on thankfulness include **ONE IS A FEAST FOR MOUSE: A THANKSGIVING TALE** written by Judy Cox and illustrated by Jeffrey Ebbeler, **ALL OF ME: A BOOK OF THANKS** by Molly Bang, **THE DAY IT RAINED HEARTS** (formerly **FOUR VALENTINES IN A RAINSTORM**) by Felicia Bond, and **THANK YOU, WORLD** written by Alice B. McGinty and illustrated by Wendy Anderson Halperin.

See also: **KITCHEN DANCE** by Maurie J. Manning for a celebration of shared family time in a Hispanic home with vibrant, joyous illustrations, and foot-tapping, finger-snapping language, and **CARMEN LEARNS ENGLISH** written by Judy Cox and illustrated by Angela Dominguez, a reassuring tale about a Latina child's first experiences in an American school.

For a list of other books with text in both English and Spanish, go to **Section I: Bilingual Books.**

THE STORY BEHIND THE STORY

From Pat Mora, the author of GRACIAS THANKS:

School visits are often occasions for me to hear interesting questions from teachers, librarians and students. Occasionally before 2008, some boys asked, 'Why don't you write more books about boys?" I was surprised by the question and mentioned **THE GIFT OF THE POINSETTIA: EL REGALO DE LA FLOR DE NOCHEBUENA; PABLO'S TREE;** and **TOMÁS AND THE LIBRARY LADY** as examples that I had written such books. I have a son and two daughters, so I have always been interested in writing about protagonists of both genders, but it's true I've always had a particular interest in writing about spunky girls and women—like my mom.

I don't remember what prompted the idea for a picture book on gratitude, but I do remember that I knew the speaker was a boy, a sweet boy like my son who's now grown. I loved the challenge of finding and conveying this boy's voice, imagining his days and life, his family, his setbacks, and his triumphs. I was delighted when my editor at Lee & Low Books, Louise May, who's always a pleasure to work with, quickly took an interest in the manuscript—not that common an experience. She invited me to join her for breakfast and I remember sitting across from Louise, full of excitement to hear her comments.

In her ever-positive way, Louise said, "We all immediately liked the voice of this girl."

"Girl, girl?" I asked. "The protagonist is a boy!"

"It is? We somehow all assumed it is a girl, and we wanted a book about a girl."

"But look at the opening page that says, 'For the sun that wakes me up so I don't sleep for years and years and grow a long, white beard, thanks.'"

"Hmm. Yes," said Louise.

"It's a boy," I said. "I know it is."

Luckily, Louise and my friends at Lee & Low went along with me. Then there was the issue of the illustrator. Louise sent me some wonderful web sites to visit. The illustrators were talented, but oh, they didn't draw sweet-looking boys, and I so wanted readers to love this boy as I do.

Louise kindly asked me to suggest an illustrator. I was at the Seattle Public Library for a Día event, and they had a grand Día display of books about the diverse children of our country. I said to the helpful librarians, "Let's go out there and find the perfect illustrator for this manuscript."

Again, we saw the work of many talented illustrators, but we all agreed that John Parra would be perfect. I didn't know John (which is usually the case with my illustrators), but Louise and the book designer both liked the suggestion. Lucky for me and **GRACIAS,** John said yes. *Gracias,* Louise.

Visit http://www.patmora.com to link to Mora introducing GRACIAS THANKS on http://www.TeachingBooks.net and to find information on her other books for children, young adults, and adults.

PICTURING THE BOOK

From John Parra, the illustrator of GRACIAS THANKS:

It is a wonderful feeling to be a children's book artist and illustrator. I happily get to spend hours and days drawing and painting my way through many books and stories. My imagination runs wild with ideas for characters, colors, scenes, and designs. I fall into the work so completely at times that I forget I am still at home in my studio and not in some faraway land. Once the work is all finished and the art and stories are made into a book and published, I am able to share it and enjoy it with others.

Working on **GRACIAS THANKS** was a thrill for me. A big part of why I connected to this project begins with writer Pat Mora's beautifully written story. It tells of a young boy growing up in a multicultural Hispanic home and being thankful for all the special people and things in his life. The story closely reflects my own life growing up. Many of the scenes are events and memories that I had as a child, and many of the characters are modeled after my own family. The main character is really a portrait of me and how I saw life.

My two favorite pages from the book are the scene at the beach where the waves are crashing and chasing the kids as they play, and the other is where the family is dancing and enjoying their guitar-playing uncle. For me, **GRACIAS THANKS** is a family photo album of life, love, and heartfelt gratitude.

Many people have asked me when and how I learned to become an artist. I would have to say it all began many years ago. I always loved to draw. I was drawing even before I was in school. I would spend hours looking around, examining people and landscapes, birds and bugs, robots and fantastic creatures. I also set up still life compositions in my room of toys, blocks, books and various objects. I would draw with my brothers and friends as we shared sketches. Once a teacher showed me how to draw perspective, and I drew pages and pages of railroad tracks and buildings that would disappear off into the distance. Art always brought out a creative and positive energy in me.

For those who would like to be an artist, the first step is draw and draw and draw so you practice and get your ideas out on paper. Next, make sure to have a special place or area in your home where you can do art, with your supplies ready to go. Lastly, remember to feed your imagination for art by reading books, visiting museums, and observing the world. You will then see a path to where your creativity and energies lie in becoming an artist.

John Parra won the 2010 SCBWI Award for Picture Book Illustration for GRACIAS THANKS. This book was also awarded the 2010 ALA Pura Belpré Honor Award and the 2010 ALA Notable Book Award. Visit http://www. johnparraart.com to view more of Parra's art and to learn more about the artist.

IN THE SPOTLIGHT

THOSE SHOES written by Maribeth Boelts and illustrated by Noah Z. Jones; Candlewick; Grades 1–3. In this touching and telling realistic fiction story about needs versus wants, young Jeremy comes to understand that a loving grandparent, sturdy boots, and a true friend have value that far outlasts trends and fads.

 A useful prop for the read-aloud of this book would be an old (and hopefully funny-looking!) fad item, now outdated.

Read-aloud time: 7–10 minutes

Themes/Content Area Connections:

Needs, wants, fads, friendship; caregivers other than parents

Preparation for Read-aloud:

Show listeners a fad item or a photograph of one from bygone days. Note the photograph on Boelts's website of the pair of sneakers she wanted as a youngster that spurred the creation of this story. (http://www.maribethboelts.com/news.html; see also "The Story Behind the Story" following this plan). Prepare to tell listeners about the fad item you brought in after they participate in the "Before Reading" segment of this plan.

Before Reading:

❖ Discuss *needs* and *wants*. Ask children to name things they need. List these in one column on easel chart paper or the board. In a parallel column, list wants. Discuss the difference between needs and wants.

❖ Look at the cover of the book. Read the title. Note that there are four boys on the cover and a close-up of "those shoes." Call attention to the facial expressions of the boys on the cover. Discuss. Look at back cover. Ask: Who do you think is the main character of this story? Why? Which one is different? (frowning boy) What do you think this book is about?

❖ Talk about fads. What is a fad? (a fashion, notion, or behavior followed enthusiastically by a large number of people; a craze) Discuss current fads, past fads. Ask: What makes something popular? Why do you want (name items mentioned by children)? How do you feel when you don't have/aren't able to get something that is popular with your classmates? Discuss.

❖ Look at the front endpapers. What season is it? (fall)

❖ Look at the back endpapers. What season is it? (winter) Let's keep that in mind as we read the story.

❖ Look at the title page spread. Where does this story take place? (in a city) How do we know? (tall, large buildings; expanse of concrete)

❖ **Let's read to find out** about the boy on the cover and why he is frowning.

While Reading:

❖ Show the first full-page spread. What is our character looking at? (billboard ad)

❖ Read aloud the first several pages. Discuss how Jeremy is feeling. (frustrated, sad, embarrassed, left out)

❖ Read about Jeremy's visit to Mr. Alfrey and the next page, when he returns to the classroom. How do you think Jeremy is feeling? What clues in the illustrations help us to know how Jeremy is feeling? (facial expressions, his affect-hunched shoulders at door to classroom)

❖ How would you feel if you were Jeremy? Discuss.

❖ What clues in the words help us to know how Jeremy is feeling? (". . . my grip is so tight on my pencil I think it might bust.")

❖ Read aloud the next several spreads in which Jeremy and his grandmother are shopping and he purchases a pair of "those shoes" that are too small for him. Ask: How would you feel if you were Jeremy and you realized that your grandmother thinks those shoes are too expensive? Do you think Jeremy made a wise decision buying those shoes at the thrift store? Discuss. Have you ever done anything like this? Explain.

❖ Read aloud the next part of the story when we see Antonio and his worn-out shoes. Jeremy makes a tough decision about his too-small shoes. Discuss Jeremy's decision.

❖ Read aloud the next page. Discuss: The next day at school Jeremy feels both happy for Antonio and mad about the Mr. Alfrey shoes. Can we feel both happy and sad at the same time? Explain, using personal experiences.

❖ Read to the end of the story. Discuss.

❖ Compare the endpapers at the front and back of the book again and discuss why the endpapers are different. (elapsed time of story)

Follow-Up:

❖ Return to the class-generated list of needs and wants. In a different color, list Jeremy's needs and wants as we know them from the story.

❖ Discuss in detail the friendship between Antonio and Jeremy.

❖ Discuss qualities of a true friend.

Extension Activities:

❖ Read about children from other parts of the world who are less fortunate and discuss their needs.

🖊 Discuss ways in which we can help those in need.

🖊 Make a list of the qualities a true friend possesses.

Writing Activities:

🖊 On prepared paper cutouts of "those shoes" with the title *I Am Lucky Because . . .*, have students list their most important needs that are met and for which they are thankful. Post around the room.

🖊 Have students interview each other about their wants and write feature stories. Who, what, why questions could be explored and the answers included in the feature story.

🖊 Have students interview their parents about a fad they loved when they were the age of the student. Students will report back to class. Encourage them to bring in the item, if possible! Share Boelts's "Story Behind the Story" with children to start off or cap class reports.

What a Pair!

Consider reading **MY SHOES AND I** written by René Colato Laínez and illustrated by Fabricio Vanden Broeck about a boy making his way from El Salvador to the United States in the new shoes his mother has sent to him. For activities about children emigrating to America, go to http://activities.macmillanmh.com/read ing/treasures/stories/olteachres/2101085.html.

Also consider pairing with **WHICH SHOES WOULD YOU CHOOSE?** written by Betsy R. Rosenthal and illustrated by Nancy Cote and **WHOSE SHOES? A SHOE FOR EVERY JOB** by Stephen R. Swinburne.

More, More, More!

See **Section I: Character Education** for other books about friendship and peer relationships.

For a poetry book about school friendships, see **RUFUS AND FRIENDS: SCHOOL DAYS** by Iza Trapani.

See also **BAREFOOT: POEMS FOR NAKED FEET** written by Stefi Weisbud and illustrated by Lori McElrath-Eslick for a compilation of poems about "feet at their freest."

THE STORY BEHIND THE STORY

From Maribeth Boelts, the author of THOSE SHOES:

THOSE SHOES was written from a series of memory snapshots. The first memory that played into its creation happened when I was in sixth grade. All the kids in my class were getting blue-and-white-striped sneakers, made popular by the *Starsky and Hutch* TV show. My parents couldn't afford them, so I got a pair of look-alike "knockoffs" that were much cheaper. I remember hoping that the kids wouldn't notice that my shoes weren't *those shoes,* but when I walked into the classroom, they sure did!

The second event happened while I was going to college to get an education degree. I was to observe an elementary classroom for a week. One boy in the class had a pair of shoes in rough shape, and at recess, one of the soles came apart. The teacher sent him to the guidance counselor, Mr. Alfrey, to get a different pair, and the boy came back in wearing a pair of black dress shoes. Some of the other kids made fun of him for wearing "Mr. Alfrey Shoes," and I remember clearly identifying with how that child must have felt.

The third event occurred a few years ago. I was volunteering in an elementary school. One of my tasks was tidying a clothes closet set aside for the students. I was organizing the shelves one morning when a young boy came to me saying he needed a new pair of shoes. I looked at his feet and saw they were stuffed into a ripped-out pair of cheap water shoes that were at least two sizes too small. I found a brand new pair of cool sneakers that fit perfectly, and that boy left to go back to his classroom with a big smile on his face, and cool new shoes on his feet.

It was when I took into account all three of these snapshots that I knew I needed to write a story about a kid who wants the latest pair of shoes. He doesn't just *want* those shoes—he dreams about them, begs his grandma, and gets more and more desperate to have them as the kids in his class come to school sporting the "black shoes with two white stripes."

But I also knew I wanted this story to go beyond a child's desire for the latest fad. I wanted to get into what it's like to sacrifice something precious for a friend. Jeremy may have given up what he thought he had to have, but he got what he truly needed—a growing friendship with a great kid named Antonio.

Visit http://www.maribethboelts.com to find information on Maribeth Boelts' other books for children. Email the author for lesson plans related to her books. Go to http://www.maribethboelts.com/classroom.html for more information.

PICTURING THE BOOK

From Noah Z. Jones, the illustrator of THOSE SHOES:

When I was working out the illustrations for **THOSE SHOES,** I really wanted to capture that *longing* that all kids feel when all their friends have something that they want more than anything in the world. Each time Jeremy catches a glimpse of those black and white sneakers, he feels pangs of want deep in his belly.

My other goal for the artwork in **THOSE SHOES** was to evoke the spirit of an urban environment. I made sure to keep the art raw and imperfect. I'm particularly happy with the color of the sky when Jeremy is lying in bed. When, as a child, I would visit my grandmother in Chicago, I remember the night sky always having a strange orange/grey cast.

 It was a delight to work with Maribeth and to bring this book to life. **THOSE SHOES** is a book I have always been proud of.

Visit Noah Z. Jones at http://www.noahzjones.com, where he spotlights his newest projects and offers a glimpse of his character designs. Jones's silly side can be enjoyed at http://www.almostnakedanimals.com and http://www.idlemonsters.com. Jones's cartoon series is featured on the Disney Channel.

IN THE SPOTLIGHT

BUNNY WISHES: A WINTER'S TALE written by Michaela Morgan and illustrated by Caroline Jayne Church; Scholastic; Grades 1–3.

In this delightfully warm and witty wintry tale of wishes and friends, bunnies Teeny and Tino (for short) make wish lists that end up torn and worn, but all the better for it.

 A timely read-aloud for the beginning of the winter holiday season or the first days of wintry weather.

Read-aloud time: 7–10 minutes

Themes/Content Area Connections:

Wishes, friendship; word choice, vivid verbs; winter weather

Preparation for Read-aloud:

Have a pad of small sheets of notepaper available for the prereading and follow-up activities. Have a large cutout of a tree ready for the follow-up activity. (Keep this hidden until the end of the story!)

Before Reading:

❖ Discuss what **wishes** are. Ask children to each think of one special wish. Ask them to write their wish on a piece of notepaper. Share wishes orally. Collect the wish pieces for use with the follow-up activity.

❖ Look at the cover of the book. Ask: What season is it? (winter) Read the title. Ask: What do you think bunnies might wish for in the winter? Discuss.

❖ What do you like about winter? What makes it special?

❖ What words would you use to describe winter?

❖ Look at the back cover. Note mice and scraps of paper with words written on them. Ask: What do you notice? Read the words on the scraps of paper. Ask: What have the mice done with the scraps of paper? (made fun objects out of them)

❖ **Let's read to find out** about the bunny wishes and the mice with the pieces of paper.

While Reading:

❖ Be sure to enjoy the playful placement of words on the page throughout the story.

❖ Read aloud the first several pages. When you get to the page when Tino and Teeny decide to pin their list of wants to the hollow log, ask the children what they think the bunnies will wish for. Make a list.

❖ Read the lists Tino and Teeny made. Compare to the predictions the children made,

❖ Continue reading. When you finish the page on which the mice make toys of the lists, ask children to predict what will happen next.

❖ Continue reading. Ask: Why do the little mice cry? (They feel bad for having wrecked the bunnies' wish lists.)

❖ Read aloud to the end of the story. Ask: How would you feel if you were Tino and Teeny?

❖ Read the words on the tree and then return to the beginning of the story and find them on the original lists Tino and Teeny made.

Follow-Up:

❖ Return wishes notes to the class. Have students work together or in groups to make a "wishes message" of their own.

❖ Place the wishes message on the tree. Display!

Extension Activities:

🖉 Discuss ways in which we can help those in need who have wishes for food and warm clothing. Coordinate a collection of food and used clothing.

🖉 Have students interview each other to find out about the wishes they wrote down initially and why that was their one special wish.

Writing Activities:

🖉 Create a wish list that the mice might make.

🖉 Create a wish list that Tino and Teeny might make for each of the other seasons.

🖉 Have students write about the wish they wrote down during the prereading portion of the read-aloud and why that was their one special wish.

More, More, More!

See **Section I: Character Education** for other books about friendship.

See **Section I: Seasons** for other books about winter.

For poetry about winter, see **WINTER EYES** by Douglas Florian, **WINTER POEMS** selected by Barbara Rogasky and illustrated by Trina Schart Hyman, **LITTLE TREE** written by e.e. cummings and illustrated by Deborah Kogan Ray, and **UNDER THE KISSLETOE: CHRISTMASTIME POEMS** written by J. Patrick Lewis and illustrated by Rob Shepperson.

Find poems about other seasons and calendar events in **Section IV: Poetry Pause Bookshelf.**

THE STORY BEHIND THE STORY

From Michaela Morgan, the author of BUNNY WISHES:

It's sometimes hard to know where an idea comes from, but I have always used *bunny* as a term of endearment, and one day I started singing "My Funny Valentine" and turned it into "My Bunny Valentine." This was the teeny tiny seed of an idea that led me to write **DEAR BUNNY**—originally called Bunny Valentine. (The publishers liked the story, but they changed the title.)

The plot ideas came tiptoeing up to me when I was in a semi-doze on a beach. I seem to spend some part of every day in a daydream. As the ideas came, I scribbled them down. I am very good at getting ideas, but I am VERY bad at remembering them, so I always make a note.

The first bunny book really did start out as very messy scribblings (complete with ideas for pictures) on the back of an envelope. It was a BIG envelope and there were many hours spent rewriting and improving, but that's where it all started. I still have the envelope.

After **DEAR BUNNY,** which is a springtime story, I wrote **BUNNY WISHES.** This is a winter's tale, which features the same two rabbits and the same family of mice that were introduced in the first book. For me, it contains the essence of this very special time of year.

If you look you will find cold days, warm shelter, snowflakes, a snowman (or mouse), tasting snowflakes, making snow angels, playing snowballs, and . . . thinking about presents.

You'll find making a list. You'll find waiting and hoping, you'll find sledging and sliding and skating, and you'll find a sort of Santa's workshop with candles. (There should have been some mistletoe, but the illustrator forgot that bit.) You'll find three gift-bearing mice travelling in the night, and you'll find presents delivered on a sledge, pulled (of course) by mice. The leading mouse has a Rudolph-like red nose.

On the last page of the book, you'll find waking up on a crisp and sparkly winter's day to discover a Christmas tree with everything anyone could ever want—not just toys and THINGS, but love, warmth, friendship, and the very best of best wishes. I know not everybody celebrates Christmas, but I do, and I have strong memories. I tried to capture here all the things that meant Christmas to me.

It's also fun to think that even though an accident happened and the lists were destroyed, something good came out of the disaster. And, although the bunnies did not get exactly what they wished for, they got something that made them really happy—the great ideas and kind wishes of some very good friends who worked hard, cared deeply, and spent time to make sure the bunnies had a surprise and got the things that really counted. Who wouldn't be happy with snuggles and hugs and love and warmth?

It was really hard for me to make up lists that I could put together to make the Christmas tree poem of wishes. My desk was littered with scraps of paper as I tried to work it all out. I write poetry as well as stories and I love words, and I love moving them around to make new meanings. I am always surrounded by bits of paper with words or notes or scribbled down ideas. There is a page in **DEAR BUNNY** where the mice sleep surrounded by words. My life is a bit like that. I practically live in a nest of paper! Words, sentences, scribbled ideas surround me.

So now you know where the Bunny Books came from. I hope you enjoy them, and I send my best **bunny wishes** to you. May all your best wishes come true, too!

Visit http://www.michaelamorgan.com to find information on Morgan's other books for children.

PICTURING THE BOOK

From Caroline Jayne Church, the illustrator of BUNNY WISHES:

The story, **BUNNY WISHES,** was wonderful to illustrate. I find that my best books include some drama, a sad bit, a happy bit, and a warm ending! **BUNNY WISHES** was a follow on to **DEAR BUNNY.** I think this companion book is unusually detailed for me, but I felt the outdoor/seasonal aspect lent itself to more intricate artwork.

The artwork in **BUNNY WISHES** is done in collage. It's quite hard work creating the first sketches because the book has to flow and have clarity for young children. When these drawings are resolved, I really enjoy turning them into full-color artwork! In **BUNNY WISHES** I tried to capture the sweet friendship between the bunnies and the playfulness of the little mice. Whilst making some of the spreads look cold and blustery, I made others cosy and warm. I liked that contrast.

How do I work? My studio is full of hundreds of pieces of paper that I use—all in beautiful colours, textures, and patterns. I create textures, too, and also use line and ink in my artwork.

I scribble down ideas and new characters, just in case I forget them at a later date!

I'm always trying to make my pictures look special in some way. I want them to be filled with life and for children to be able to "get lost" in them. Characters need to jump off the pages!

My little rescue dog, Maddie, is with me when I work. She keeps a watchful eye on what I'm doing. I listen to the radio, too, and sometimes stop to daydream!

Caroline Jayne Church lives in Farnham, Surrey, UK.

Visit her on her website at http://www.carolinejaynechurch.com.

Other books illustrated by Caroline Jayne Church referenced in this resource: HARRIET DANCING written by Ruth Symes and LEAF TROUBLE written by Jonathan Emmett.

IN THE SPOTLIGHT

GROUNDHOG WEATHER SCHOOL written by Joan Holub and illustrated by Kristin Sorra; Grades 1–3. In this hilarious tale chock-full of interesting facts about weather, the seasons, hibernation, and animal characteristics, we meet a cast of characters doing their best to predict the weather.

A fun read-aloud for Groundhog Day that is also perfect for launching a weather unit.

Read-aloud time: 10–12 minutes

Themes/Content Area Connections:

Weather; seasons; hibernation; Groundhog Day; animal characteristics; character traits

Preparation for Read-aloud:

Have a set of the *"Have You Got What It Takes To Be A Weather Forecaster?"* quizzes ready so children can fill them out! Have a few flashlights for making shadows and a copy of the BIG test for each student.

Before Reading:

❖ Ask: What do you know about Groundhog Day? What is a groundhog?

❖ Look at the cover of the book. Ask: What mood does the cover of this book put you in? (humorous cover) Read the title. Ask: What do you think you would learn at Groundhog Weather School? **Let's read to find out!**

❖ What do you like about winter? What makes it special?

While Reading:

❖ Read aloud to the quiz. Have students take the quiz and then continue reading.

❖ Have students stand up and hold their right hand up. Have them repeat the Pledge of Hog-Allegiance.

❖ Read the next page in which the characters are introduced. Discuss their characteristics.

❖ Read the next page. List the groundhog facts on chart paper or the board.

❖ Continue reading. When you finish the page on which "Nature's Weather Predictors" are listed, add these to the list of facts.

❖ Continue reading, adding pertinent facts to the list.

❖ After reading "Shadow Studies" make shadows!

❖ Take the BIG test.

❖ Read to the end of the story. Ask: Why do you think it is hard to predict the weather?

Follow-Up:

❖ Read the author's afterword. Discuss.

Extension Activities:

🖉 Have students take the parts of the characters in Groundhog School. Develop a Readers' Theater script for the characters. Consider props or simple costume pieces.

🖉 Have students listen to weather forecasts for the next week. Note predictions and chart how often the predictions are correct. Compare those with Holub's facts at the end of the book.

🖉 Keep a weather log from February 2 six weeks hence. Was the groundhog correct this year?

Writing Activities:

🖉 Have students write a weather forecast for circle time.

🖉 Create character trait charts for each of the students in Groundhog School and the professor. Be sure to read the artist's reflection following this read-aloud plan to the children.

🖉 Have students write a letter to the Weather Groundhog (see Rabbit's letter). Post.

More, More, More!

See **Section I: Science** for other books about the weather.

See **Section I: Seasons** for books about winter and the other seasons of the year.

For poetry about winter, see **WINTER EYES** by Douglas Florian and **WINTER POEMS** selected by Barbara Rogasky and illustrated by Trina Schart Hyman.

Find poems about the other seasons of the year and calendar events in **Section IV: Poetry Pause Bookshelf.**

THE STORY BEHIND THE STORY

From Joan Holub, the author of GROUNDHOG WEATHER SCHOOL:

When I asked my seven-year-old niece if she thought she could predict the weather for all of North America by popping out of a burrow and looking around for her shadow on February 2, her answer was, "I think not!" It turns out that even groundhog weather predictions are only right about one-third of the time. TV forecasters often fare no better despite their sophisticated equipment.

It's just plain hard to predict the weather! This undeniable fact is the theme of **GROUNDHOG WEATHER SCHOOL.**

Groundhog Day provides a great opportunity to begin discussions with children about weather predictors in nature as well as about other animal, nature, and weather facts. I wanted to write a funny story about this day that was strong enough to live and be enjoyed on its own but that also seamlessly included such facts.

I kept looking for the right hook, and it eventually grew out of my theme. I decided to let Professor Groundhog be fallible. To have him get his prediction wrong on February 2. When that happens, there is an outcry. He gets letters. Lots of letters. Rabbit is not happy that her sunny play day turns out to be snowy.

Recognizing that he needs help with his predictions, Professor Groundhog creates a school where he will train other weather forecasters that he'll disburse throughout North America to help him watch for shadows on the following Groundhog Day.

What a great opportunity! Just think—you, too, could attend Groundhog Weather School and have an illustrious future as a weather forecaster. To determine if you're a suitable candidate for the school, simply take the quiz titled **Have You Got What It Takes To Be A Weather Forecaster?** found on page 4 of the book. If you make it in, you'll learn how to build a better burrow; the reasons for seasons and for hibernation; and you'll meet some famous forecasters.

Wow! Of course you want to go. But beware—the quiz includes tough questions. And if you are a rat or a monkey, forget it.

Luckily, there are also hints accompanying the questions to help you out, for instance, Are You An Herbivore? (If you only eat plants, you are.) That one was easy, but I was stumped by question number 2: Are You Furry? (You be the judge.)

Since I am not particularly furry, it looks like I will have to continue on as an author instead of a weather forecaster!

Joan Holub is the author and/or illustrator of over 120 books for children. Visit Holub online at the following sites: http://www.joanholub.com, http://reader totz.blogspot.com, and http://joanholub.blogspot.com.

Other books by Joan Holub included in this resource:

RIDDLE-ICULOUS MATH illustrated by Regan Dunnick; Albert Whitman, **GEOGRA-FLEAS!: RIDDLES ALL OVER THE MAP** illustrated by Regan Dunnick; Albert Whitman, and **HAUNTED STATES OF AMERICA: HAUNTED HOUSES AND SPOOKY PLACES IN ALL 50 STATES AND CANADA, TOO!;** Aladdin.

PICTURING THE BOOK

From Kristin Sorra, the illustrator of GROUNDHOG WEATHER SCHOOL:

When our editor, Tim Travaglini, sent me the manuscript for **GROUNDHOG WEATHER SCHOOL,** it was unlike any other I had ever read.

The story was not formatted like a traditional picture book. Joan Holub, an illustrator herself, wrote the story accompanied by simple layouts. The text was full of dialogue, placed in word balloons, of a variety of colorful characters that contrasted with the sprinkling of more factual passages about the weather.

The aim was to make learning about Groundhog Day and the weather entertaining and informative. It was an ambitious project, and my most challenging yet. Parts of the manuscript offered suggestions of characters and facts to include, and it was during the sketch stages that we hammered out just how many groundhogs, how much information, and how many jokes we could fit on each spread.

Initially, I was asked to illustrate the story in pen and ink, similar to another title I had done for Penguin called **TURKEY RIDDLES.** However, my style has changed a lot since I illustrated that book. I discussed this with Tim, who was open to the idea of a different approach, and from that point I spoke with the art director, Cecilia Yung, who encouraged me to work in whatever style would bring out my best work. Many illustrators aren't given such creative freedom, so it was wonderful, and I felt privileged, but I did feel pressure to prove myself.

The book is illustrated digitally, with a variety of mixed media, including photographic and hand-painted textures, as well as a wide variety of layout techniques Joan suggested, including comiclike panel art, maps, and report papers. I also incorporated fun patterns and line work for visual interest.

Because there is so much information on each page, I think the variety makes the experience of reading **GROUNDHOG WEATHER SCHOOL** fun and interesting instead of overwhelming.

Also, I thought using a different art style for the straight factual elements, such as the school reports, in "Famous Furry Hognosticators," helped to break up the potential monotony of busy spreads.

I loved developing the personalities for each of the groundhogs. The more I sketched, the more ideas for little jokes and distinct story events arose. For example, we have one groundhog that is always a bit confused. I thought, as a funny touch, that we show him sleeping through Groundhog Day and snoring through the actual reports. It was a last minute addition, and I was pleased that it was approved.

My favorite character is the skunk. I thought it would be funny if his regular profession would be that of an actor since he has to disguise himself throughout the story. So, naturally, it is he who is assigned to predict the weather in California. When he reveals himself, it is behind velvet ropes in front of many "fans" wearing sunglasses and reporting through a distinct set of white earbuds. Very "Hollywood."

Working on **GROUNDHOG WEATHER SCHOOL** was such a rewarding experience! Parts of the story evolved organically, and the creative process was never stifled. It helped to bring out some of my best work to date.

To learn more about Kristin Sorra and her art, visit http://www.kristin sorra.com.

IN THE SPOTLIGHT

THE FOGGY, FOGGY FOREST written and illustrated by Nick Sharratt; Candlewick; Grades Pre-K–2.
In this creatively formatted book, fairy-tale characters romp, tromp, and laze the night away in a fanciful forest. Fog is effectively conveyed through sheer, tracing paper–like overlays that cleverly reveal the characters as the very simple rhyming story develops. Perfect for prediction practice with emerging readers and identifying fairy-tale characters, the story also provides effective repetition in its economical text.

Have variants of fairy tales featuring the characters in this book on display and available for children to look through following the read-aloud (Goldilocks and the Three Bears, Cinderella, Snow White). As a follow-up activity, encourage children to compare and contrast how the characters are depicted in this book with how they are drawn in other books.

Read-aloud time: 5–7 minutes

Themes/Content Area Connections:

Fairy-tale characters, friendship, night, fog, forests, prediction, emergent reader skills

Preparation for Read-aloud:

Collect and display fairy-tale books (see above).

Before Reading:

❖ Show the cover of the book. Ask: Where do you think this story takes place? (forest) How do you know? (trees) What time of day is it? (night)

❖ Read the title. Ask: What word is repeated in the title? (foggy) What does *foggy* mean? (hard to see) What is fog? (a cloud near the ground; water vapor in the air close to the ground) Have you ever been in fog? What was it like? (Encourage sensory description.) What color is fog? How does it feel? (damp) Do you know what causes fog? (moisture and cooling of the air near the ground) When do we usually have fog? (early morning or night)

❖ Show front and back cover of book. Ask: Besides the title, what colors do you see on the cover of this book? (black and gray) Why do you think the cover of this book is mainly black and gray? (foggy night)

❖ What else do you see on the cover? (characters) **Let's read to find out** who they are and what they are doing in the foggy, foggy forest. (Point to the words in the title.)

While Reading:

❖ Read the title page. Show the first full-page spread. Read the text. Allow students to predict what this might be. (elf)

❖ Read the next spread. Ask for predictions on whose shadows these might be. (the Three Bears) What do you think they are doing? (sitting and eating)

❖ Turn the page. Note what the bears are doing and eating. Ask: Who do they remind you of? (fairy-tale characters) Let's keep that in mind!

❖ Look at the next page. Note the trampoline. Ask: What do you think is jumping in the air above the trampoline? (fairy queen)

❖ Point out what we can see through the tracing paper beyond the next page. (unicorn with horn; trees)

❖ Turn the page. Read the text. Turn back to the previous page so children can compare the fairy queen on both pages. Ask: What do we know about fairies? Discuss.

❖ Look at the page with the unicorn with the horn. Point to the text. Encourage children to read the repetitive text along with you. Ask: What do you think we will find on the next page?

❖ Turn the page. Revel in the correct predictions. Read the text.

❖ On the next page, note the girl in the tree. Ask: Who can that be? (Goldilocks) Ask: What is she doing? (eating)

❖ Recall three bears earlier in the story. Briefly summarize fairy tale.

❖ What else can you see beyond Goldilocks in the tree? (witch on broom)

❖ Turn the page. Read the text. Cheer for correct predictions. Encourage reading along of repetitive line.

❖ Note detail in illustration behind the broom. Ask: What could that be? (motor on broom) Let's turn the page and find out.

❖ Turn the page; read the text. Enjoy the ogre! Make predictions.

❖ Turn the page; read the text. Review fairy tale stories about Cinderella and Snow White. Make predictions.

❖ Turn the page; read the text. Note the details of the scene. Review the tale of Red Riding Hood. Make predictions. Note color beyond!

❖ Turn the page. Read the text.

❖ Turn to last page. Note rising sun.

Follow-Up:

❖ Review who we met in the story. Flip through the pages to aid in recall.

❖ See the Follow-Up activity suggested above.

Extension Activities:

🖉 Read fairy tales about the characters featured in the book. (Goldilocks and the Three Bears, Snow White, Cinderella)

🖉 Make books collaboratively or design individual overlay illustrations using tracing paper like that used in the book. Display.

Writing Activities:

🖉 Write extended text for each illustration in the book.

🖉 Create dialogue for the characters on each page.

🖉 Have students write about their favorite fairy-tale character. Who is it? Why is the character your favorite? What characteristics does the character have that you like best?

🖉 Similarly, have students write about their favorite fairy tale. Why is the tale your favorite? Which character do you like best in the tale? Why? Which character do you like least? Why? What is your favorite part? Which is your least favorite part? How would you change it?

More, More, More!

For other books about fairy tales, folk tales, legends, fables, myths, and nursery rhymes, refer to the listing in Section I.

For a creative book of poetry about fairy tales, see **MIRROR MIRROR: A BOOK OF REVERSIBLE VERSE** written by Marilyn Singer and illustrated by Josée Masse, in which fairy tales are turned upside down, literally, for a whole new perspective.

THE STORY BEHIND THE STORY AND THE ART

From Nick Sharratt, the author and illustrator of THE FOGGY, FOGGY FOREST:

I am the kind of author/illustrator who doesn't actually like having complete freedom when it comes to thinking up ideas for new books. If a publisher tells me I can do anything I like, I panic at all that choice and find it really difficult to settle on anything at all. I respond much better when I'm given a problem to solve. It might be a specific theme to tackle, or an unusual format, or a novelty device that has to be exploited, but once I have the challenge of a restriction or two, I'm happy, and I'm able to think creatively.

THE FOGGY, FOGGY FOREST is a case in point. My British publishers gave me a printer's dummy of a book made with tracing paper and said, "Come up with a use for this!" I thought of fog the minute I started turning the translucent pages and saw the effect of one layer on top of another. It took rather longer to work out a story based around the subject, but once I'd settled on a forest setting (because silhouettes of trees seen through fog were such a pleasing thing to draw), the idea quickly followed to create a guessing game involving fairy-tale characters emerging from and sinking back into the mists. A rhyming text completed the fun.

When it came to the illustrations, the artwork was a lot more complicated than I anticipated because of the need to make sure that four layers of pictures at a time, left page and right, interacted properly with one another. I spent an enormous amount of time jiggling trees and character shapes around so that they would overlap to the best advantage. It was also quite a departure for me to produce a book predominantly in black and shades of grey, as my usual palette is one of dazzlingly bright colours. In addition, technically **THE FOGGY, FOGGY FOREST** made big demands on the printers. This was true not only because the images on either side of each tracing paper page had to match up with absolute precision (otherwise, the crisp silhouette effect would have been ruined) but also because we discovered that the ink took considerably longer to dry than it would have on normal paper. In fact, in addition to other awards, the book won a trade prize for the quality of its printing.

I always enjoy sharing this book with children. My favourite bit is when the ogre doing yoga is revealed. Just about every time, without any prompting, the kids will take up the same yoga position, close their eyes, and start humming, and a little meditative interlude is enjoyed by all!

Nick Sharratt lives in Brighton, on the southern coast of the United Kingdom. Visit http://www.nicksharratt.com to learn more about Sharratt and other books he has written and/or illustrated and to tour his studio and meet his studio mate!

Sharratt rhymes with carrot or parrot.

IN THE SPOTLIGHT

ZOE'S HATS: A BOOK OF COLORS AND PATTERNS written and illustrated by Sharon Lane Holm; Boyds Mills Press; Grades Pre-K–K.
   A simple, rhythmic, and fun introduction to colors and patterns.

 Have children bring in their favorite hat for the follow-up activity.

Read-aloud time: 5 minutes

Themes/Content Area Connections:

Colors, patterns, dress-up

Preparation for Read-aloud:

Collect and display hats (see above). Also have a colander on hand.

Before Reading:

❖ Show the cover of the book. Ask: Here is Zoe. What do you think is a favorite thing of hers? What is a favorite thing you like to collect?

❖ You all brought in hats today. Tell me about your hat.

❖ Read the title. **Let's read to find out** about Zoe's hats.

While Reading:

❖ Count the hats on Zoe's head in the first picture.

❖ Read the first page. Discuss what kind of hat she has on. Find something else in the room that is red.

❖ Read the second page. Find someone who is also wearing blue.

❖ Read the next page. Discuss what this might be a "zoo" hat.

❖ Continue reading. Ask: What kind of hat is the brown hat? (cowboy)

❖ What is silly about Zoe in the green hat? (She has it on sideways.)

❖ Does anyone know what the plaid hat is called? (a beret)

❖ What does the white hat remind you of? (a bunny rabbit) Why do you think Zoe looks like this in the picture? (She is frowning.)

❖ When might Zoe wear the black hat? (Halloween) Why? (It's a witch's hat.)

❖ What is the gray hat? (a colander) Show one.

❖ Do you think the purple hat is Zoe's? (no) Why do you think that? (too big on her) Whose hat might the purple hat be? (Mom's)

❖ What does the orange hat make Zoe look like? (tiger)

❖ The turquoise hat is a lot like the plaid hat (go back to plaid hat page). Do you remember what this type of hat is called? (beret)

❖ Continue reading in this fashion to the end of the book.

❖ Have children name the colors.

❖ Have children name the patterns.

Follow-Up:

❖ Have children try on the hats and have fun with them.

❖ Have children put the hats into categories according to colors or patterns.

❖ Have children explain why they brought in the hat they did and when they like to wear it.

Extension Activities:

🖉 Review the silly and bright hats Zoe wears near the end of the book. Have children make silly, bright hats!

Writing Activities:

🖉 Write extended text for each illustration in the book.

🖉 Have children write labels for the hats that were collected.

What a Pair!

Consider pairing with **BRIDGET'S BERET** by Tom Lichtenheld in which Bridget, who loves to draw and relies on her beret for inspiration—or so she thinks—loses her beret to the wind.

More, More, More!

Other books about hats include the classic **THE CAT IN THE HAT** by Dr. Seuss, **HAT** by Paul Hoppe, **BUY MY HATS!** by Dave Horowitz, and **BLUE HAT, GREEN HAT** by Sandra Boynton.

Other books about patterns include **GROWING PATTERNS: FIBONACCI NUMBERS IN NATURE** written by Sarah C. Campbell with photographs by Sarah C. Campbell and Richard P. Campbell, **BLOCKHEAD: THE LIFE OF FIBONACCI** written by Joseph D'Agnese and illustrated by John O'Brien, **PATTERNS IN PERU: AN ADVENTURE IN PATTERNING** written by Cindy Neuschwander and illustrated by Bryan Langdo, **HANNAH'S COLLECTIONS** by Marthe Jocelyn, and **THE BUTTON BOX** written by Margarette S. Reid and illustrated by Sarah Chamberlain.

THE STORY BEHIND THE STORY AND THE ART

From Sharon Lane Holm, the author and illustrator of ZOE'S HATS:

I am one of those lucky people who has always known what I wanted to be when I "grew up." I wanted to be an artist, to draw pictures and write stories. As a published illustrator in the children's market, I had told many stories with my illustrations—other people's stories. I was ready to write my own stories, and draw the pictures too!

I saw a little girl wearing her mother's hat. It was so big, it kept slipping down over her nose, down to her chin, covering her little face. She kept pushing it back up, giggling! I sketched that little face and hat. (*Could it be a great idea for a children's book?*) I pinned the sketch on my studio "idea" wall alongside my many other ideas on many other scraps of paper.

Shortly thereafter, I took an adult education class, the instructor of which was the president of Boyds Mills Press, a small trade publisher. Having to stand to explain why we were there, I boldly blurted, "I came to meet you and show you my illustrations, and I'd love an opportunity to illustrate children's books for your publishing company." (*How brave of me to spout like that!*) I wasn't thinking of writing the books, but I wanted to.

The president was impressed with my boldness! He requested I submit my illustration work along with a manuscript (*An opportunity to write and illustrate my own book?*)

I pulled the hat sketch off the wall. What about a book about hats—too big, too silly, too flowery, defiantly too bright . . . brown, black, and white . . . red, yellow, green and blue. But what else do these hats do? I wrote, rewrote, edited, and eventually created a fresh, funny, novel way to introduce the concept of colors!

My illustrative style is geared toward a very young audience. All my illustrations of children look like me at four years old, all chubby faced with pudding cheeks!

I happened to know a little girl, Zoe; she liked to wear hats, too. She modeled my hat collection for "our" book and **ZOE'S HATS** was created! (The book is dedicated to her. Look and see!)

With blessings and luck, that publisher did purchase **ZOE'S HATS.** (Zoe and I both wore our favorite hats to our book signing.)

I, that chubby-faced, pudding-cheeked little girl who refuses to grow up, always hope to enlighten and inspire by sharing my experiences. If success is measured by doing work that one loves to do, then I am truly blessed and a success. I love what I do.

I share my process of creating **ZOE'S HATS** at school visits, library visits, presentations, and conferences. I share my struggles, my mistakes, and my passion for writing and drawing, with the hope that all in attendance learn that with passion, patience, and persistence we can all follow our dreams.

I am still very passionate and persistent, hoping to make more of my dreams come true.

There are many more good ideas pinned to my idea wall . . .

Visit Sharon Lane Holm at http://www.sharonholm.com to learn more about her books and to view her art.

SECTION III

A Closer Look

Subject-Related Collections
of
Read-Aloud Choices
with
Multiple Content Area
Connections

Including
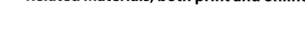

- **Discussion Points**
- **Cross-Curricular Activities**
- **Writing Suggestions**
- **Related Materials, both print and online**

"I never teach my pupils: I only attempt to provide the conditions in which they can learn."—Albert Einstein

A CLOSER LOOK

ABRAHAM LINCOLN

Outstanding Read-Aloud Choices

➢ **ABE LINCOLN CROSSES A CREEK: A TALL, THIN TALE*** written by Deborah Hopkinson and illustrated by John Hendrix

➢ **ABRAHAM LINCOLN** written by Amy Cohn and Suzy Schmidt and illustrated by David A. Johnson

➢ **MR. LINCOLN'S BOYS** written by Staton Rabin and illustrated by Bagram Ibatoulline

➢ **OUR ABE LINCOLN**** written by Jim Aylesworth and illustrated by Barbara McClintock

➢ **STAND TALL, ABE LINCOLN** written by Judith St. George and illustrated by Matt Faulkner

Themes/Content Area Connections:

History, Social Studies, Biography, Civil War, Historic Figures, Leadership, Presidency, Presidents' Day, Slavery, Books & Reading, *Tales, **Music

Discussion Following Read-Aloud Session:

Ask students to pick their favorite event from Lincoln's life. List key words on chart paper or the board.

Ask: Have you experienced anything similar to something Lincoln experienced? Explain. How did you feel? What would you have done in Lincoln's place?

After reading **STAND TALL, ABE LINCOLN,** discuss how books were important to Lincoln as he was growing up. Ask children to name a favorite book. List titles on chart paper or the board. Display books with one-sentence endorsements by students. Encourage children to read books of interest and add their comments to the original endorsements. After several weeks, hold a "Pick of the Picks" contest using a student-designed ballot listing the books. Design book award ribbons or stickers. Have an awards celebration!

After reading in **MR. LINCOLN'S BOYS** about Tad and Willie's life in the White House, ask: How were Tad and Willie's lives the same as other children's lives? What things did the boys do that other children would not have been able to do? Of the things Tad and Willie did, what seemed the most fun to you? What would you do if you lived in the White House? How would you describe the kind of dad Abraham Lincoln was? In what ways is your dad, uncle, granddad, or big brother alike or different from Lincoln?

Sally Bush Johnson, Lincoln's stepmom, brought books to Abe Lincoln, and in that way she changed his life. After reading **STAND TALL, ABE LINCOLN,** ask children to name an important person in their life and tell how that person helps them.

Activities:

Create a timeline of key events in Lincoln's life using words generated in discussion (see above).

Following the read-aloud, discuss the qualities or distinctive traits Lincoln possessed. Accept physical traits, but prompt personal characteristics as well. When students suggest a word, ask them to point out something in the book that supports assigning that quality or trait to Lincoln.

➢ Compare and contrast Lincoln's personality traits as highlighted in each book.

➢ Create posters or collaborative collages depicting Lincoln's distinctive traits.

Trace Abraham Lincoln's steps from the simple log cabin with a dirt floor to the most impressive house and most important job in our country. Place the key points in Lincoln's life on paper "footprints" and place them in order clockwise circling the room.

For directions on how to make a Lincoln-style stovepipe hat, go to http://www.ehow.com/how_2224624_stove-pipe-hat.html.

After reading **OUR ABE LINCOLN,** sing the song! Make a recording and send the book and recording home with children. Encourage parents to read the book to their child and then sing the song before bed!

Write Away!

✎ Write about the event in Lincoln's life that means the most to you. Describe the event in detail in the first paragraph and tell why it's important to you in the following paragraph.

✎ After reading **MR. LINCOLN'S BOYS,** write about something fun you and your brother(s) or sister(s) do with your dad, uncle, granddad, or big brother.

✎ Books were important to Lincoln as he was growing up. After reading **STAND TALL, ABE LINCOLN**, ask children to write on silhouettes of Lincoln's face, the title, author, illustrator, and a few sentences about a favorite book of theirs. Follow-up or alternative book: **ABE LINCOLN: THE BOY WHO LOVED BOOKS** written by Kay Winters and illustrated by Nancy Carpenter; Aladdin.

✎ Ask children to write about a book they have enjoyed reading that they think Lincoln would have liked. Tell why.

On the Web:

McElmeel, Sharron L. "In the Spotlight: Abraham Lincoln: Bicentennial 1809–2009." Offers curriculum connections for a selection of books about Abraham Lincoln. *Library Sparks* (February 2009); Online: http://www.highsmith.com/pdf/librarysparks/2009/lsp_feb09_spotlight.pdf

Shelftalker: A Children's Bookseller's Blog. *"A Whole Lotta Lincoln Going On"* (July 9, 2008) by Alison Morris: http://www.publishersweekly.com/blog/ShelfTalker_A_Children_s_Bookseller_s_Blog/29077-A_Whole_Lotta_Lincoln_Going_On.php

Directions on how to make a Lincoln-style stovepipe hat: http://www.ehow.com/how_2224624_stove-pipe-hat.html

Related Titles:

➤ **SO YOU WANT TO BE PRESIDENT**? written by Judith St. George and illustrated by David Small

➤ **THANK YOU, SARAH! THE WOMAN WHO SAVED THANKSGIVING** written by Laurie Halse Anderson and illustrated by Matt Faulkner

More, More, More!

Listed below are suggested titles for children to explore on their own, with peers, or with their families.

ABE LINCOLN LOVED ANIMALS written by Ellen Jackson and illustrated by Doris Ettlinger; Whitman.

ABE LINCOLN: THE BOY WHO LOVED BOOKS written by Kay Winters and illustrated by Nancy Carpenter; Aladdin.

ABE LINCOLN'S HAT (Step into Reading 3) written by Martha Brenner and illustrated by Donald Cook; Random House.

GRACE'S LETTER TO LINCOLN (Hyperion Chapters) written by Peter and Connie Roop and illustrated by Stacey Schuett; Hyperion.

LINCOLN TELLS A JOKE: HOW LAUGHTER SAVED THE PRESIDENT (AND THE COUNTRY) written by Kathleen Krull and Paul Brewer and illustrated by Stacy Innerst; Harcourt.

MR. LINCOLN'S WHISKERS by Karen B. Winnick; Boyds Mills Press.

A CLOSER LOOK

ALL SHAPES, SIZES, SHADES, AND BELIEFS

Outstanding Read-Aloud Choices

➢ **AMAZING FACES** poems selected by Lee Bennett Hopkins and illustrated by Chris Soentpiet

➢ **COME AND PLAY: CHILDREN OF OUR WORLD HAVING FUN** poems by children and edited by Ayana Lowe

➢ **FAMILIES** by Susan Kuklin

➢ **I LIKE BEING ME: POEMS FOR CHILDREN ABOUT FEELING SPECIAL, APPRECIATING OTHERS, AND GETTING ALONG** by Judy Lalli with photography by Douglas L. Mason-Fry

➢ **JACK'S TALENT** by Maryann Cocca-Leffler

➢ **MIRROR** by Jeannie Baker

➢ **MY NAME IS YOON** written by Helen Recorvits and illustrated by Gabi Swiatkowska

➢ **MY PEOPLE** written by Langston Hughes with photographs by Charles R. Smith Jr.

➢ **SHADES OF BLACK: A CELEBRATION OF OUR CHILDREN** written by Sandra L. Pinkney with photographs by Myles C. Pinkney

➢ **SHADES OF PEOPLE** by Shelley Rotner and Sheila M. Kelly with photographs by Shelley Rotner

➢ **SYLVIE** by Jennifer Sattler

➢ **A VERY BIG BUNNY** by Marisabina Russo

➢ **WHAT COLOR IS CAESAR?** written by Maxine Kumin and illustrated by Alison Friend

Themes/Content Area Connections:

Self-esteem; ethnic pride, identity; acceptance; inclusion

Discussion Following Read-Aloud Session:

Ask students to describe themselves. Explore: How are we all alike, and how are we different?

Ask children to describe their families. Explore: How are you like other members of your family? How are you different from other members of your family?

How are you like your friends? How are you different?

After reading **MY NAME IS YOON,** ask: Have you experienced anything similar to what Yoon experiences in the story? Explain. How did you feel? If not, how do you think you would feel if you were the new child in a classroom? What could you do to welcome a new child, whether in the classroom, the school, or in your neighborhood?

Activities:

After reading **MY PEOPLE** explore other poems written by Langston Hughes. See **THE NEGRO SPEAKS OF RIVERS** illustrated by E. B. Lewis; Hyperion; and **THE DREAM KEEPER AND OTHER POEMS** illustrated by Brian Pinkney; Knopf.

Following the read-aloud of **FAMILIES** ask children to take a photo with their family. (Loan a classroom digital camera or purchase inexpensive disposable cameras for this activity.) Ask children to interview family members in the style of the book and create a page about their family for a classroom book. Invite families to a FAMILIES celebration in which children will introduce their families to their classmates.

Create family collages and display on Family Night.

After reading **MIRROR** have children make a diorama depicting their family.

After reading **COME AND PLAY,** play the games popular with the children from across the world depicted in this book.

Write Away!

✎ After sampling the poems in **I LIKE BEING ME: POEMS FOR CHILDREN ABOUT FEELING SPECIAL, APPRECIATING OTHERS, AND GETTING ALONG**, have students write a poem titled "I Like Being Me!" in which they describe themselves. (Teacher and librarians, do this, too!) Collect the poems and read them aloud. Have children guess who the author of the poem is. Take photos of the children and make a class book or display the photos around the room.

✎ After reading **MIRROR** and making the diorama depicting their family, ask children to write a short paragraph describing what is happening in the scene.

✎ After reading **COME AND PLAY,** have children research the different places depicted in the scenes to complete a profile of each country or area listing specifics, such as weather, what a school looks like, typical clothing, and types of food and pets.

On the Web:

Go to http://www.maryanncoccaleffler.com/activity/JacksAward.pdf for an "I Have Talent" award ribbon activity sheet to use with **JACK'S TALENT** and http://www.maryanncoccaleffler.com/activity/JacksTalent.pdf for an activity sheet of a spiffy frame in which to place an illustration of each child's talent.

Read an interview with Lee Bennett Hopkins and Chris Soentpiet (pronounced soon peet) on the making of **AMAZING FACES** at http://www.leeandlow.com/p/amazing.mhtml.

For additional activities for use with the book **MY NAME IS YOON** go to https://www.roundrockisd.org/docs/17-yoon.pdf, http://www.kansasread.org/pdf/BMJ_2004/yoon2.pdf, and http://blazers.k12.ar.us/~kshipp/Lesson%20Plans%20Week%203.htm.

For additional activities about children emigrating to America, go to http://activities.macmillanmh.com/reading/treasures/stories/olteachres/2101085.html.

Related Titles:

➢ **THE DREAM KEEPER AND OTHER POEMS** written by Langston Hughes and illustrated by Brian Pinkney

➢ **POETRY FOR YOUNG PEOPLE: LANGSTON HUGHES** edited by David Roessel and Arnold Rampersad and illustrated by Benny Andrews

More, More, More!

Listed below are suggested titles for children to explore on their own, with peers, or with their families.

THE NAME JAR by Yangsook Choi; Dragonfly Books.

I HATE ENGLISH! written by Ellen Levine and illustrated by Steven Björkman; Scholastic.

ONE GREEN APPLE written by Eve Bunting and illustrated by Ted Lewin; Clarion.

THE OTHER SIDE written by Jacqueline Woodson and illustrated by E. B. White; Putnam.

A CLOSER LOOK

GEOGRAPHY, MAPS, AND TRAVEL

Outstanding Read-Aloud Choices

➤ **ADÉLE & SIMON IN AMERICA** by Barbara McClintock

➤ **AMERICA THE BEAUTIFUL** by Robert Sabuda

➤ **ANNO'S JOURNEY** by Mitsumasa Anno; Philomel

➤ **ANNO'S USA** by Mitsumasa Anno; Philomel

➤ **AROUND THE WORLD ON EIGHTY LEGS** written by Amy Gibson and illustrated by Daniel Salmieri

➤ **DUCK DUCK MOOSE** by Dave Horowitz

➤ **HOW I LEARNED GEOGRAPHY** by Uri Shulevitz

➤ **HOW TO BAKE AN AMERICAN PIE** written by Karma Wilson and illustrated by Raúl Colón; McElderry.

➤ **HOW TO MAKE A CHERRY PIE AND SEE THE USA** by Marjorie Priceman

➤ **LARUE ACROSS AMERICA: POSTCARDS FROM THE VACATION** by Mark Teague

➤ **MAPPING PENNY'S WORLD** by Loreen Leedy

➤ **ME ON THE MAP** written by Joan Sweeney and illustrated by Annette Cable

➤ **MILES TO GO** by Jamie Harper

➤ **MY AMERICA: A POETRY ATLAS OF THE UNITED STATES** selected by Lee Bennett Hopkins and illustrated by Stephen Alcorn

➤ **THE SCRAMBLED STATES OF AMERICA** by Laurie Keller

➤ **THE SCRAMBLED STATES OF AMERICA TALENT SHOW** by Laurie Keller

➤ **THANK YOU, WORLD** written by Alice B. McGinty and illustrated by Wendy Anderson Halperin

➤ **THE TRAVEL GAME** written by John Grandits and illustrated by R. W. Alley

➤ **UNITED TWEETS OF AMERICA: 50 STATE BIRDS THEIR STORIES, THEIR GLORIES** by Hudson Talbott

Themes/Content Area Connections:

Maps, map features, map reading, geography of the United States, world geography, natural resources, travel; state symbols; state characteristics; features of countries across the world

Discussion Following Read-Aloud Session:

Ask students why maps are useful and why knowing how to read a map is important. Discuss the features of a map.

Use a large and colorful map of the United States to highlight and discuss parts of the country, climates, directions, and physical features. Discuss where children have traveled to visit relatives or on vacation. How was that part of the country different from where we live? How was it the same?

Post a large and detailed map of the world following the reading of **HOW I LEARNED GEOGRAPHY, THE TRAVEL GAME,** and **THANK YOU, WORLD.** Have children choose a country and describe it location. See also **ATLAS OF THE WORLD: THE ULTIMATE INTERACTIVE,** listed below.

Discuss ways we travel. Compare those to travel in the past. Why is travel fun?

Activities:

After reading **MILES TO GO,** have children design a large map in the classroom with roads, landmarks, homes, and a school. (See endpapers for a useful model.) Make large arrows and have children place them along the path from home to school. Similarly, have them find the way to the store, the library, the fire station, the supermarket, and the police station. Read books related to community workers, such as **THE VILLAGE GARAGE** by G. Brian Karas, **AT THE SUPERMARKET** by Anne Rockwell, **FARM** by Elisha Cooper, **NIGHT SHIFT** by Jessie Hartland, **PEPI SINGS A NEW SONG** by Laura Ljungkvist, and **POPVILLE** by Anouck Boisrobert and Louis Rigaud.

After reading **MAPPING PENNY'S WORLD,** have students make a 3-D map as shown in the book of their favorite place.

After reading **MAPPING PENNY'S WORLD,** have students use pedometers to measure distances between common places in the school, such as the library, the cafeteria, the gymnasium, the lavatories, and the main office. Make a map to scale. Make a key.

Following the read-aloud of **MAPPING PENNY'S WORLD** and **ME ON THE MAP,** have children make a map of their bedroom to scale and label it. Make a key and place a scale and compass rose in upper and lower corners.

> ➢ Compare and contrast maps.

After reading **HOW TO MAKE A CHERRY PIE AND SEE THE U.S.A.**, follow the recipe from the back of the book and make a cherry pie!

After reading **HOW TO MAKE A CHERRY PIE AND SEE THE U.S.A.**, refer to the map on the endpapers and discuss the natural resources found in various parts of the country.

After reading **HOW I LEARNED GEOGRAPHY** and **THE TRAVEL GAME**, use a globe and book of pictures from around the world and play the travel game!

Post a large and colorful map of the world following the reading of **HOW I LEARNED GEOGRAPHY, THE TRAVEL GAME**, and **THANK YOU, WORLD**. Have children choose a country and describe it location. See also **ATLAS OF THE WORLD: THE ULTIMATE INTERACTIVE**, listed below. Research specific features of the country. List relevant facts about the predetermined topics. Make artwork or complete a craft relating to each country. Draw the country's flags. Sing their songs. Learn a traditional dance. Dress in customary garb. Bring in toys representing that country, if possible. Culminate with a presentation by each group followed by a multinational feast in which representative dishes from each nation are served. Involve parents by requesting help with this event!

Using a map of the United States, have children trace the path Duck Duck and Moose traveled in the book **DUCK DUCK MOOSE**. Figure out compass directions from place to place.

Have children make a vacation collage from photos, postcards, or pictures taken from old magazines.

Use the map on the endpapers of **LARUE ACROSS AMERICA: POSTCARDS FROM THE VACATION** to write specific directional details of the comical trip across the country.

After reading **THE SCRAMBLED STATES OF AMERICA, THE SCRAMBLED STATES OF AMERICA TALENT SHOW,** and **UNITED TWEETS OF AMERICA: 50 STATE BIRDS THEIR STORIES, THEIR GLORIES** and completing the writing activity listed below, have students label a map of the United States with state birds, flags, key crops, natural resources, and so on (See also **GO, GO AMERICA, OUR FIFTY STATES: A FAMILY ADVENTURE ACROSS AMERICA,** and **GREETINGS FROM THE 50 STATES: HOW THEY GOT THEIR NAMES**). Read poems from the various states in **MY AMERICA: A POETRY ATLAS OF THE UNITED STATES**.

Write Away!

✎ After reading **HOW I LEARNED GEOGRAPHY** and **THE TRAVEL GAME**, play the travel game (see above) and write about the place you visited. Describe the event in detail, modeling the authors' descriptions.

✎ After reading **THE TRAVEL GAME,** make a list of what you would take if you were going on a trip around the world.

✎ After reading **DUCK DUCK MOOSE,** devise classroom "road" signs and post. Explain what they indicate and place in a classroom "driving" manual.

✎ After reading **LARUE ACROSS AMERICA: POSTCARDS FROM THE VA-CATION**, have children add to Ike's correspondence as he grumpily tours the country with Mrs. LaRue, accompanied by Mrs. Hibbins's annoying felines.

✎ After reading **HOW TO MAKE A CHERRY PIE AND SEE THE U.S.A.** and discussing the natural resources found in various parts of the country (see above), have children research natural resources and report to the class.

✎ After reading **THE SCRAMBLED STATES OF AMERICA, THE SCRAMBLED STATES OF AMERICA TALENT SHOW,** and **UNITED TWEETS OF AMERICA: 50 STATE BIRDS THEIR STORIES, THEIR GLORIES,** have students choose a state and describe its size, shape, location, state symbols, and a few unusual facts. See also **GO, GO AMERICA, OUR FIFTY STATES: A FAMILY ADVEN-TURE ACROSS AMERICA,** and **GREETINGS FROM THE 50 STATES: HOW THEY GOT THEIR NAMES,** listed below.

On the Web:

Visit the site dedicated to **ADÉLE AND SIMON IN AMERICA**, filled with activities for use in the classroom and at home: http://www.adeleandsimon.com.

For a solid collection of activities for teachers using **THE SCRAMBLED STATES OF AMERICA TALENT SHOW**, visit Laurie Keller's "School Stuff" page: http://www.lau riekeller.com/schoolstuff_talent.html. There are also a puzzle and book set, a card game, and a board game to go along with **THE SCRAMBLED STATES OF AMER-ICA**. Go to http://www.lauriekeller.com/links.html for more information.

For a set of activities to accompany **HOW TO MAKE A CHERRY PIE AND SEE THE U.S.A.**, go to http://www.randomhouse.com/catalog/teachers_guides/9780375812 552.pdf.

For a lesson plan using **MAPPING PENNY'S WORLD**, go to http://www.lesson planspage.com/printables/PSSLAMappingPennysWorldK2.htm.

Go to http://school.discoveryeducation.com/lessonplans/programs/exploringgeo graphy for a library of suggestions and resources related to geography that can be adapted for use with younger children. See also http://www.nationalgeographic. com/xpeditions/lessons/02/gk2 for lessons and suggestions complete with stan-dards compliance and http://blog.richmond.edu/openwidelookinside/archives/ category/geography.

For interactive map activities, go to http://activities.macmillanmh.com/OralLan guageActivities/main1.php?activityID=126 and http://activities.macmillanmh.com/ OralLanguageActivities/main1.php?activityID=176.

Related Titles:

- ➢ **ATLAS OF THE WORLD: THE ULTIMATE INTERACTIVE** written by Elaine Jackson and paper engineering by Alan Brown; Scholastic.

- ➢ **GEOGRA-FLEAS!: RIDDLES ALL OVER THE MAP** written by Joan Holub and illustrated by Regan Dunnick; Albert Whitman.

- ➢ **GO, GO AMERICA** by Dan Yaccarino; Scholastic.

- ➢ **GREETINGS FROM THE 50 STATES: HOW THEY GOT THEIR NAMES** written by Sheila Keenan and illustrated by Selina Alko; Scholastic.

More, More, More!

Listed below are suggested titles for children to explore on their own, with peers, or with their families.

THE AMAZING POP-UP GEOGRAPHY BOOK written by Kate Petty and illustrated by Jennie Maizels; Dutton.

BACKSEAT BOOKS: KIDS' U.S. ROAD ATLAS; Rand McNally.

HAUNTED STATES OF AMERICA: HAUNTED HOUSES AND SPOOKY PLACES IN ALL 50 STATES AND CANADA, TOO! by Joan Holub; Aladdin.

OUR FIFTY STATES: A FAMILY ADVENTURE ACROSS AMERICA written by Lynne Cheney and illustrated by Robin Preiss Glasser; Simon & Schuster

A CLOSER LOOK

OUR EARTH

Outstanding Read-Aloud Choices

- ➢ **BALLYHOO BAY** written by Judy Sierra and illustrated by Derek Anderson

- ➢ **THE BUFFALO ARE BACK** written by Jean Craighead George and illustrated by Wendell Minor

- ➢ **CORAL REEFS** by Gail Gibbons

- ➢ **THE CURIOUS GARDEN** by Peter Brown

- ➢ **EMI AND THE RHINO SCIENTIST** written by Mary Kay Carson with photographs by Tom Uhlman

- ➢ **HERE COMES THE GARBAGE BARGE!** written by Jonah Winter and illustrated by Red Nose Studio

- ➢ **THE SMASH! SMASH! TRUCK: RECYCLING AS YOU'VE NEVER HEARD IT BEFORE!** by Professor Potts

- ➢ **HOW THE WORLD WORKS** written by Christiane Dorion, illustrated by Beverley Young, and paper engineering by Andy Mansfield

- ➢ **IF YOU LIVED HERE YOU'D BE HOME BY NOW** by Ed Briant

- ➢ **LET'S SAVE THE ANIMALS: A FLIP-THE-FLAP BOOK** by Frances Barry

- ➢ **THE LORAX** by Dr. Seuss

- ➢ **THE MAGIC SCHOOL BUS AND THE CLIMATE CHALLENGE** written by Joanna Cole and illustrated by Bruce Degen

- ➢ **MAMA MITI** written by Donna Jo Napoli and illustrated by Kadir Nelson

- ➢ **MOON BEAR** written by Brenda Z. Guiberson and illustrated by Ed Young

- ➢ **THE OLD TREE** by Ruth Brown

- ➢ **THE SHOCKING TRUTH ABOUT ENERGY** by Loreen Leedy

- ➢ **SLOW DOWN FOR MANATEES** by Jim Arnosky

- ➢ **SURPRISING SHARKS** written by Nicola Davies and illustrated by James Croft

- ➤ **TEN THINGS I CAN DO TO HELP MY WORLD: FUN AND EASY ECO-TIPS** by Melanie Walsh

- ➤ **TURTLE, TURTLE, WATCH OUT!** written by April Pulley Sayre and illustrated by Annie Patterson

- ➤ **WE ARE EXTREMELY VERY GOOD RECYCLERS** Charlie and Lola series by Lauren Child

- ➤ **WANGARI'S TREES OF PEACE** by Jeanette Winter

Themes/Content Area Connections:

Environmental awareness, conservation, endangered species, extinction, energy conservation, recycling, ecology, Earth Day

Discussion Following Read-Aloud Session:

Ask children to describe ways they recycle at home and in school. Explore: How can we improve the way we recycle at home and in the classroom?

Discuss why trees are important and what we can do to protect them.

Discuss the difference between endangered and extinct animals and the repercussions of endangered species on the environment.

After reading aloud **THE SHOCKING TRUTH ABOUT ENERGY**, generate discussion points. Develop a take home sheet from the class brainstorm. Children will discuss the book with their parents and report back to the class about the conversation the following day.

Activities:

Plant and manage a classroom or school garden.

Begin a classroom recycling program.

Following the read-aloud of **MAMA MITI, WANGARI'S TREES OF PEACE** and **THE OLD TREE**, plan the planting of trees in the school yard. For an informative book on planting trees, read aloud **RED LEAF, YELLOW LEAF** by Lois Ehlert.

Write Away!

- 🖉 After reading **LET'S SAVE THE ANIMALS, BALLYHOO BAY, EMI AND THE RHINO SCIENTIST, SLOW DOWN FOR MANATEES, SURPRISING SHARKS, TURTLE, TURTLE, WATCH OUT!,** and **THE BUFFALO ARE BACK,** choose an endangered species and write a report on the animal and what is being done to save it. Pair reports with photos; present to class and display around the room.

✏ After reading **TEN THINGS I CAN DO TO HELP MY WORLD: FUN AND EASY ECO-TIPS**, have children make their own lists things they can do to help their world.

On the Web:

There are several resources online to correlate with **THE LORAX.** On the publisher's site at http://www.randomhouse.com/teachers/themes, you will find a teacher's guide.

Go to http://www.homeschoolshare.com/lorax.php for cross-curricular activities. See also http://teacherlink.ed.usu.edu/tlresources/units/byrnes-literature/alleman.html,

http://www2.scholastic.com/browse/lessonplan.jsp?id=1244&print=1,

http://www.seussdude.com/pdfs/activity-the-lorax.pdf,

http://www.lessonplanet.com/directory_articles/teacher_education_lesson_plans/20_April_2010/325/earth_day_and_the_lorax_lesson_plans,

http://www.lessonplanet.com/search?keywords=dr.+seuss%27s+the+lorax&media=lesson,

http://www.atozteacherstuff.com/pages/250.shtml#lorax,

http://teachers.net/lessons/posts/2786.html,

and http://www.associatedcontent.com/article/1529967/free_green_lesson_plans_dr_seuss_the.html.

Play "The Lorax's Save the Trees" game at http://www.randomhouse.com/teachers/themes.

For Earth Day activities, go to http://holidays.kaboose.com/earthday-activities.html. For Earth Day games, go to http://funschool.kaboose.com/globe-rider/earth-day. For Earth Day crafts, activity sheets, games, songs, and more, go to http://www.dltk-kids.com/crafts/earth.html.

Following the read-aloud of **THE MAGIC SCHOOL BUS AND THE CLIMATE CHALLENGE**, take a virtual field trip to the Liberty Science Center in Jersey City, New Jersey, and find related resources to accompany the webcast at http://www.scholastic.com/magicschoolbuswebcast/resources.htm.

Visit Loreen Leedy's website at http://www.loreenleedy.com/books/energy.html for downloadable materials and a project idea to accompany **THE SHOCKING TRUTH ABOUT ENERGY**.

Related Poetry:

- ➤ **ANIMALS ANIMALS** poems selected and illustrated by Eric Carle
- ➤ **ANIMAL FRIENDS: A COLLECTION OF POEMS FOR CHILDREN** illustrated by Michael Hague
- ➤ **ANNA'S GARDEN SONGS** poems by Mary Q. Steele and illustrated by Lena Anderson
- ➤ **CREATURES OF EARTH, SEA, AND SKY** poems by Georgia Heard and illustrations by Jennifer Owings Dewey
- ➤ **HOOFBEATS, CLAWS & RIPPLED FINS: CREATURE POEMS** edited by Lee Bennett Hopkins and illustrated by Stephen Alcorn
- ➤ **LITTLE TREE** written by e.e. cummings and illustrated by Deborah Kogan Ray
- ➤ **NEST, NOOK & CRANNY** poems by Susan Blackaby and illustrated by Jamie Hogan
- ➤ **OCEAN SOUP: TIDE-POOL POEMS** written by Stephen R. Swinburne and illustrated by Mary Peterson
- ➤ **OLD ELMS SPEAKS: TREE POEMS** written by Kristine O'Connell George and illustrated by Kate Kiesler
- ➤ **SCRANIMALS** poems by Jack Prelutsky and illustrated by Peter Sis
- ➤ **SILVER SEEDS: A BOOK OF NATURE POEMS** by Paul Paolilli and Dan Brewer and illustrated by Steve Johnson and Lou Francher
- ➤ **A WHIFF OF PINE, A HINT OF SKUNK: A FOREST OF POEMS** by Deborah Ruddell and illustrated by Joan Rankin

More, More, More!

Listed below are suggested titles for children to explore on their own, with peers, or with their families.

Magic Tree House #6: AFTERNOON ON THE AMAZON written by Mary Pope Osborne and illustrated by Sal Murdocca; Random House.

Magic Tree House Research Guide #9: DOLPHINS AND SHARKS written by Mary Pope Osborne and Natalie Pope Boyce and illustrated by Sal Murdocca; Random House.

ONE HEN: HOW ONE SMALL LOAN MADE A BIG DIFFERENCE written by Katie Smith Milway and illustrated by Eugene Fernandes; Kids Can Press.

BEATRICE'S GOAT written by Page McBrier and illustrated by Lori Lohstoeter; Aladdin.

THE FANTASTIC UNDERSEA LIFE OF JACQUES COUSTEAU by Dan Yaccarino; Random House.

BABY BELUGA written by Raffi and illustrated by Ashley Wolff; Random House.

THE GOOD GARDEN: HOW ONE FAMILY WENT FROM HUNGER TO HAVING ENOUGH written by Katie Smith Milway and illustrated by Sylvie Daigneault; Kids Can Press.

BREAD COMES TO LIFE written by George Levenson and photographs by Shmuel Thayer; Random House.

COMPOST STEW written by Mary McKenna Siddals and illustrated by Ashley Wolff; Random House.

SECTION IV

Poetry Pause Bookshelf

A Selection of Poetry Books
to Connect with Content Areas

"There is no Frigate like a Book To take us Lands away Not any coursers like a Page Of prancing Poetry"—Emily Dickinson

AMAZING FACES poems selected by Lee Bennett Hopkins and illustrated by Chris Soentpiet; Lee & Low.

ANIMALS ANIMALS poems selected and illustrated by Eric Carle; Philomel.

ANIMAL FRIENDS: A COLLECTION OF POEMS FOR CHILDREN illustrated by Michael Hague; Holt.

ANNA'S GARDEN SONGS poems by Mary Q. Steele and illustrated by Lena Anderson; HarperCollins.

ANOTHER JAR OF TINY STARS: POEMS BY MORE NCTE AWARD-WINNING POETS edited by Bernice E. Cullinan and Deborah Wooten and portraits by Marc Nadel; Wordsong/Boyds Mills.

ANNA'S SUMMER SONGS poems by Mary Q. Steele and illustrated by Lena Anderson; Harper-Collins.

AUTUMNBLINGS by Douglas Florian; Greenwillow; see also:
> **SUMMERSAULTS**
> **WINTER EYES**

BAREFOOT: POEMS FOR NAKED FEET written by Stefi Weisbud and illustrated by Lori McElrath-Eslick; Wordsong/Boyds Mills Press.

BEAT THE DRUM INDEPENDENCE DAY HAS COME: POEMS FOR THE FOURTH OF JULY selected by Lee Bennett Hopkins and illustrated by Tomie dePaola; Wordsong/Boyds Mills Press.

BECAUSE I COULD NOT STOP MY BIKE AND OTHER POEMS by Karen Jo Shapiro and illustrated by Matt Faulkner; Charlesbridge.

BEHIND THE MUSEUM DOOR: POEMS TO CELEBRATE THE WONDERS OF MUSEUMS selected by Lee Bennett Hopkins and illustrated by Stacey Dressen McQueen; Abrams.

BIG TALK: POEMS FOR FOUR VOICES written by Paul Fleischman and illustrated by Beppe Giacobbe; Candlewick.

THE BILL MARTIN JR. BIG BOOK OF POETRY edited by Bill Martin Jr. with Michael Sampson; Simon & Schuster.

BIRDS ON A WIRE renga poems by J. Patrick Lewis and Paul B. Janeczko and illustrated by Gary Lippincott; Wordsong/Boyds Mills Press.

BLACKBERRY INK poems by Eve Merriam and illustrated by Hans Wilhelm; Morrow.

BLAST OFF! POEMS ABOUT SPACE selected by Lee Bennett Hopkins and illustrated by Melissa Sweet; Harper I Can Read Level 3; HarperCollins.

CALENDAR written by Myra Cohn Livingston and illustrated Will Hillenbrand; Holiday House.

A CHILD'S CALENDAR written by John Updike and illustrated by Trina Schart Hyman; Holiday House.

A CIRCLE OF SEASONS written by Myra Cohn Livingston and illustrated by Leonard Everett Fisher; Holiday House; see also:
> **SKY SONGS**
> **EARTH SONGS**
> **SEA SONGS**
> **SPACE SONGS**

COME AND PLAY: CHILDREN OF OUR WORLD HAVING FUN edited by Ayana Lowe with photographs by Julie Collins; Bloomsbury.

CREATURES OF EARTH, SEA, AND SKY poems by Georgia Heard and illustrations by Jennifer Owings Dewey; Boyds Mills Press.

DEAR MOTHER, DEAR DAUGHTER: POEMS FOR YOUNG PEOPLE by Jane Yolen and Heidi Y. Stemple and illustrated by Gil Ashby; Wordsong/Boyds Mills Press.

DEAR WORLD by Takayo Noda; Dial.

DIRTY LAUNDRY PILE: POEMS IN DIFFERENT VOICES poems selected by Paul B. Janeczko and illustrated by Melissa Sweet; Greenwillow.

DOGKU by Andrew Clements and illustrated by Tim Bowers; Simon & Schuster; haiku meets dogs.

DOG POEMS written by Dave Crawley and illustrated by Tamara Petrosino; Wordsong/Boyds Mills Press.

THE DREAM KEEPER AND OTHER POEMS written by Langston Hughes and illustrated by Brian Pinkney; Knopf.

THE EVERYTHING BOOK by Denise Fleming; Holt.

FARMER'S DOG GOES TO THE FOREST: RHYMES FOR TWO VOICES by David L. Harrison and illustrated by Arden Johnson-Petrov; Wordsong/Boyds Mills Press.

FATHERS, MOTHERS, SISTERS, BROTHERS: A COLLECTION OF FAMILY POEMS written by Mary Ann Hoberman and illustrated by Marylin Hafner; Penguin.

FESTIVALS poems by Myra Cohn Livingston and illustrated by Leonard Everett Fisher; Holiday House.

FIREFLIES AT MIDNIGHT written by Marilyn Singer and illustrated by Ken Robbins; Atheneum.

FLY WITH POETRY: AN ABC OF POETRY by Avis Harley; Wordsong/Boyds Mills Press.

GOOD BOOKS, GOOD TIMES! poems selected by Lee Bennett Hopkins and illustrated by Harvey Stevenson; HarperCollins.

GOOD LUCK GOLD AND OTHER POEMS by Janet S. Wong; McElderry.

THE GOOF WHO INVENTED HOMEWORK AND OTHER SCHOOL POEMS by Kalli Dakos and illustrated by Denise Brunkus; Dial.

HAILSTONES AND HALIBUT BONES written by Mary O'Neill and illustrated by John Wallner; Doubleday; reissue of classic book of poems about colors.

HERE'S A LITTLE POEM: A VERY FIRST BOOK OF POETRY collected by Jane Yolen and Andrew Fusek Peters and illustrated by Polly Dunbar; Candlewick.

HERE'S WHAT YOU DO WHEN YOU CAN'T FIND YOUR SHOE: INGENIOUS INVENTIONS FOR PESKY PROBLEMS written by Andrea Perry and illustrated by Alan Snow; Atheneum.

HEROES AND SHE-ROES: POEMS OF AMAZING AND EVERYDAY HEROES written by J. Patrick Lewis and illustrated by Jim Cooke; Dial.

HIST WHIST written by e.e. cummings and illustrated by Deborah Kogan Ray; Crown.

HOLIDAY STEW: A KID'S PORTION OF HOLIDAY AND SEASONAL POEMS by Jenny Whitehead; Holt.

HOOFBEATS, CLAWS & RIPPLED FINS: CREATURE POEMS edited by Lee Bennett Hopkins and illustrated by Stephen Alcorn; HarperCollins.

THE ICE CREAM STORE poems by Dennis Lee and illustrated by David McPhail; Scholastic.

IF I WERE IN CHARGE OF THE WORLD AND OTHER WORRIES written by Judith Viorst and illustrated by Lynne Cherry; Aladdin.

IF NOT FOR THE CAT haiku by Jack Prelutsky and illustrated by Ted Rand; Greenwillow.

I LIKE BEING ME: POEMS FOR CHILDREN ABOUT FEELING SPECIAL, APPRECIATING OTHERS, AND GETTING ALONG by Judy Lalli, photography by Douglas L. Mason-Fry; Free Spirit Publishing.

IN THE LAND OF WORDS: NEW AND SELECTED POEMS written by Eloise Greenfield and illustrated by Jan Spivey Gilchrist; HarperCollins.

IT'S VALENTINE'S DAY poems by Jack Prelutsky and illustrated by Yossi Abolafia; HarperCollins.

JOYFUL NOISE: POEMS FOR TWO VOICES written by Paul Fleischman and illustrated by Eric Beddows; HarperCollins.

A KICK IN THE HEAD: AN EVERYDAY GUIDE TO POETIC FORMS selected by Paul B. Janeczko and illustrated by Chris Raschka; Candlewick.

KIDS PICK THE FUNNIEST POEMS: POEMS THAT MAKE KIDS LAUGH selected by Bruce Lansky and illustrated by Stephen Carpenter; Meadowbrook.

LAUGH-ETERIA by Douglas Florian; Penguin.

LET THERE BE LIGHT: POEMS AND PRAYERS FOR REPAIRING THE WORLD compiled and illustrated by Jane Breskin Zalben; Dutton.

LITTLE DOG POEMS written by Kristine O'Connell George and illustrated by June Otani; Clarion.

LITTLE TREE written by e.e. cummings and illustrated by Deborah Kogan Ray; Crown.

LOCUST POCUS! A BOOK TO BUG YOU written by Douglas Kaine McKelvey and illustrated by Richard Egielski; Philomel.

LOOSE LEASHES written by Amy Schmidt, photographs by Ron Schmidt; Random House; endearing dog poems and photos.

LUNCH BOX MAIL AND OTHER POEMS by Jenny Whitehead; Holt.

LUNCH MONEY AND OTHER POEMS ABOUT SCHOOL written by Carol Diggory Shields and illustrated by Paul Meisel; Dutton.

MAMA SAYS: A BOOK OF LOVE FOR MOTHERS AND SONS by Rob D. Walker and illustrated by Leo & Diane Dillon; Scholastic.

MARVELOUS MATH: A BOOK OF POEMS selected by Lee Bennett Hopkins and illustrated by Karen Barbour; Aladdin.

MATHEMATICKLES! poems by Betsy Franco and illustrated by Steven Salerno; McElderry.

MATH FOR ALL SEASONS written by Greg Tang and illustrated by Harry Briggs; Scholastic.

MESSING AROUND ON THE MONKEY BARS AND OTHER SCHOOL POEMS FOR TWO VOICES written by Betsy Franco and illustrated by Jessie Hartland; Candlewick; offers "adventurous ways to read the poems" at the back of the book.

MIRROR MIRROR: A BOOK OF REVERSIBLE VERSE written by Marilyn Singer and illustrated by Josée Masse; Dutton.

MY AMERICA: A POETRY ATLAS OF THE UNITED STATES poems selected by Lee Bennett Hopkins and illustrated by Stephen Alcorn; Simon & Schuster.

MY FUNNY BOOK OF VALENTINES written by Margo Lundell and illustrated by Nate Evans; Scholastic.

MY PEOPLE poem by Langston Hughes and photographs by Charles R. Smith Jr.; Atheneum.

MOTHER GOOSE'S LITTLE TREASURES collected by Iona Opie and illustrated by Rosemary Wells; Candlewick; a collection of lesser-known rhymes.

THE NEGRO SPEAKS OF RIVERS poem by Langston Hughes and illustrated by E. B. Lewis; Disney.

THE NEW KID ON THE BLOCK poems by Jack Prelutsky and illustrated by James Stevenson; Greenwillow.

NEST, NOOK & CRANNY poems by Susan Blackaby and illustrated by Jamie Hogan; Charlesbridge; habitat poems, excellent back matter offers details on habitats and explains poem construction.

NO MORE HOMEWORK! NO MORE TESTS! KIDS FAVORITE FUNNY SCHOOL POEMS selected by Bruce Lansky and illustrated by Stephen Carpenter; Meadowbrook.

NONSENSE poems by Edward Lear and illustrated by Valorie Fisher; Atheneum.

NOT A COPPER PENNY IN ME HOUSE: POEMS FROM THE CARIBBEAN written by Monica Gunning and illustrated by Frané Lessac; Boyds Mills Press.

OCEAN SOUP: TIDE-POOL POEMS written by Stephen R. Swinburne and illustrated by Mary Peterson; Charlesbridge.

OLD ELMS SPEAKS: TREE POEMS written by Kristine O'Connell George and illustrated by Kate Kiesler; Clarion.

OOPS! poems by Alan Katz and illustrated by Edward Koren; McElderry.

PAINT ME A POEM: POEMS INSPIRED BY MASTERPIECES OF ART by Justine Rowden; Wordsong/ Boyds Mills.

PAUL REVERE'S RIDE written by Henry Wadsworth Longfellow and illustrated by Ted Rand; Dutton.

PENCIL TALK AND OTHER SCHOOL POEMS written by Anastasia Suen and illustrated by Susie Lee Jin; Lee & Low.

PIECES: A YEAR IN POEMS & QUILTS by Anna Grossnickle Hines; HarperCollins.

POCKET POEMS selected by Bobbi Katz and illustrated by Marylin Hafner; Dutton; see also:
> **MORE POCKET POEMS**

POETRY FOR YOUNG PEOPLE: LANGSTON HUGHES edited by David Roessel and Arnold Rampersad and illustrated by Benny Andrews; Sterling.

A POKE IN THE I: A COLLECTION OF CONCRETE POEMS selected by Paul B. Janeczko and illustrated by Chris Raschka; Candlewick.

READ A RHYME WRITE A RHYME edited by Jack Prelutsky and illustrated by Meilo So; Knopf; includes "poemstarts" as prompts.

THE REASON FOR THE PELICAN by John Ciardi and illustrated by Dominic Catalano; Wordsong/ Boyds Mills Press.

 RED SINGS FROM TREETOPS: A YEAR IN COLORS written by Joyce Sidman and illustrated by Pamela Zagarenski; Houghton Mifflin.

THE ROBIN MAKES A LAUGHING SOUND: A BIRDER'S JOURNAL by Sallie Wolf; Charlesbridge; Grades 1–6; collection of poems, sketches, and paintings.

ROSES ARE PINK, YOUR FEET REALLY STINK by Diane de Groat; HarperCollins.

RHYME TIME (Rufus and Friends) traditional poems extended and illustrated by Iza Trapani; Charlesbridge.

SCHOOL DAYS (Rufus and Friends) traditional poems extended and illustrated by Iza Trapani; Charlesbridge.

SCRANIMALS poems by Jack Prelutsky and illustrated by Peter Sis; Greenwillow.

SHAPE ME A RHYME: NATURE FORMS IN POETRY poems by Jane Yolen and photographs by Jason Stemple; Wordsong/Boyds Mills Press.

SILVER SEEDS: A BOOK OF NATURE POEMS by Paul Paolilli and Dan Brewer and illustrated by Steve Johnson and Lou Fancher; Puffin.

SING A SONG OF POPCORN: EVERY CHILD'S BOOK OF POEMS selected by Beatrice Schenk de Regniers, Eva Moore, Mary Michaels White, and Jan Carr and illustrated by nine Caldecott Medal artists; Scholastic.

THE SNACK SMASHER AND OTHER REASONS WHY IT'S NOT MY FAULT written by Andrea Perry and illustrated by Alan Snow; Atheneum.

SOMETHING BIG HAS BEEN HERE poems by Jack Prelutsky and illustrated by James Stevenson; Greenwillow.

SQUEEZE: POEMS FROM A JUICY UNIVERSE by Heidi Mordhorst and photographs by Jesse Torrey; Wordsong/Boyds Mills Press.

STEADY HANDS: POEMS ABOUT WORK written by Tracie Vaughn Zimmer and illustrated by Megan Halsey and Sean Addy; Clarion.

SUMMERSAULTS by Douglas Florian; Greenwillow.

TAKE SKY by David McCord and illustrated by Henry B. Kane; Little, Brown; a classic.

TAP DANCING ON THE ROOF: SIJO (POEMS) written by Linda Sue Park and illustrated by Istvan Banyai; Clarion.

THIS PLACE I KNOW: POEMS OF COMFORT selected by Georgia Heard and illustrated by eighteen picture book artists; Candlewick.

TOASTING MARSHMALLOWS: CAMPING POEMS written by Kristine O'Connell George and illustrated by Kate Kiesler; Clarion.

TODAY AT THE BLUEBIRD CAFÉ: A BRANCHFUL OF BIRDS written by Deborah Ruddell and illustrated by Joan Rankin; McElderry.

TRUCKERY RHYMES written by Jon Scieszka and illustrated by David Shannon, Loren Long, and David Gordon; Simon & Schuster; truck rhymes based on classic nursery rhymes.

UNDER THE KISSLETOE: CHRISTMASTIME POEMS written by J. Patrick Lewis and illustrated by Rob Shepperson; Wordsong/Boyds Mills Press.

THE UNDERWEAR SALESMAN AND OTHER JOBS FOR BETTER OR VERSE poems by J. Patrick Lewis and illustrated by Serge Bloch; Atheneum.

VOICE FROM AFAR: POEMS OF PEACE by Tony Johnston and illustrated by Susan Guevara; Holiday House.

VOLCANO WAKES UP! written by Lisa Westberg Peters and illustrated by Steve Jenkins; Holt; Grades 1–4; poems in alternating points of view from the lava flow crickets to ferns, the road, the sun, and the volcano itself tell the story of a day on an active volcano.

WHAT'S THE WEATHER INSIDE? poems by Karma Wilson and illustrated by Barry Blitt; McElderry.

A WHIFF OF PINE, A HINT OF SKUNK: A FOREST OF POEMS by Deborah Ruddell and illustrated by Joan Rankin; McElderry.

WINTER POEMS selected by Barbara Rogasky and illustrated by Trina Schart Hyman; Scholastic.

WONDERFUL WORDS: POEMS ABOUT READING, WRITING, SPEAKING, AND LISTENING selected by Lee Bennett Hopkins and illustrated by Karen Barbour; Simon & Schuster.

A WRITING KIND OF DAY: POEMS FOR YOUNG POETS written by Ralph Fletcher and illustrated by April Ward; Wordsong/Boyds Mills Press.

YOU KNOW WHO by John Ciardi and illustrated by Edward Gorey; Wordsong/Boyds Mills Press.

YOU READ TO ME, I'LL READ TO YOU by John Ciardi and illustrated by Edward Gorey; HarperCollins.

Useful references for teachers and librarians:

A WRITING KIND OF DAY: POEMS FOR YOUNG POETS by Ralph Fletcher; Boyds Mills Press.

FLY WITH POETRY: AN ABC OF POETRY by Avis Harley; Wordsong/Boyds Mills Press.

PASS THE POETRY, PLEASE! 3rd edition by Lee Bennett Hopkins; HarperCollins.

POEM-MAKING: WAYS TO BEGIN WRITING POETRY by Myra Cohn Livingston; HarperCollins.

POETRY FROM A TO Z: A GUIDE FOR YOUNG WRITERS compiled by Paul B. Janeczko; Simon & Schuster.

POETRY MATTERS: WRITING A POEM FROM THE INSIDE OUT by Ralph Fletcher; HarperCollins.

TEACHING 10 FABULOUS FORMS OF POETRY by Paul B. Janeczko; Scholastic.

SECTION V

Additional Resources
for
Teachers and Librarians

- *Suggested Read-Aloud Plan Format*
- *Professional Reference Books and Magazines*
- *Children's Book-Related Websites for Teachers and Librarians*
- *Children's Book-Related Blogs*
- *Author and Illustrator Websites*
- *Glossary of Book Terms*

"The art of teaching is the art of assisting discovery."—Mark Van Doren

SUGGESTED READ-ALOUD PLAN FORMAT

Include the following information in read-aloud plans you develop for the books you choose to share with your students:

- Publication Information
- Estimate of Read-Aloud Time
- Pre-Reading Focus
- While Reading Questions
- Follow-Up
- Extension Activities
- Additional Information (related titles, related poetry, information on the author or illustrator, related newspaper or magazine articles)
- Notes for Using the Book in Future Read-Aloud Sessions

Maintain a file of read-aloud plans organized according to themes, units of study, or months of study or, arrange plans in alphabetical order according to title, author, or subject.

In developing read-aloud plans, strive to involve the four strands of English Language Arts:

- Reading
- Writing
- Listening
- Speaking

SELECT PROFESSIONAL REFERENCES

Websites

- ✔ http://www.ala.org—American Library Association; check for a complete listing of the myriad prestigious awards given by ALA to children's books annually.

- ✔ http://www.cbcbooks.org—Children's Book Council.

- ✔ http://www.reading.org—International Reading Association.

- ✔ http://www.readwritethink.org—partnership of the International Reading Association, the National Council of Teachers of English, with support from the Verizon Foundation, and in association with the Thinkfinity consortium; peer-reviewed lessons; professional development; home-school connections.

- ✔ http://www.carolhurst.com—Carol Hurst's Children's Literature Site; book reviews; lessons; archives; free email subscription.

- ✔ http://www.MinnesotaStorytime.org—Minnesota Humanities Center; reading guides; resources; reading lists; great site to recommend to parents.

- ✔ http://www.ucalgary.ca/~dkbrown—The Children's Literature Web Guide is an amazing website devoted to children's and young adult books.

- ✔ http://www.indiebound.org/kids-indie-next-list—"best" books chosen by independent booksellers.

- ✔ http://www.bookhive.org—Charlotte Mecklenburg Library site; reviews of books; book-related activities for children.

- ✔ http://www.thinkfinity.org—supported by the Verizon Foundation; high-quality, standards-based Internet content for K–12 teachers and students: lessons, links, and professional development.

- ✔ http://www.cynthialeitichsmith.com—author's website offers ideas, inspirations, and information; an ALSC/ALA "Great Web Site for Kids."

- ✔ http://www.trelease-on-reading.com—website of Jim Trelease, author of **THE READ-ALOUD HANDBOOK** (Penguin Books).

- ✔ http://teach.simonandschuster.net—resources for "educators and librarians," powered by Simon& Schuster Children's Books,

- ✔ http://www.randomhouse.com/teachers/authors/results.pperl?authorid=10018—Teachers @ Random website offers resources for teachers.

✔ http://www.randomhouse.com/teachers/librarians—Librarians @ Random website offers news on latest award announcements, suggestions for book talks, and suggestions for activities on timely topics.

✔ http://www.candlewick.com/authill.asp?b=Author&pg=1&m=actlist&a=&id=0&pix=n—Candlewick's extensive list of excellent resources for teachers and librarians can be found here.

✔ http://us.macmillan.com/Content.aspx?publisher=holtbyr&id=373–Henry Holt Books for Young Readers teachers' guides, awards information, and free newsletter sign-up information.

✔ http://us.penguingroup.com/static/pages/youngreaders/teachers-librarians/index.html—Penguin Books for Young Readers page for teachers and librarians offers extensive material for use in schools: teachers' guides, activity kits, contests, and more.

✔ http://www.charlesbridge.com/client/client_pages/downloadables.cfm—Charlesbridge publishers' site offers curriculum connections; state standards compliance, downloadable guides, and more.

✔ http://www.holidayhouse.com/free_materials.php—Holiday House Books for Young People: educators' guides, readers' guides, and activities page.

✔ http://www.houghtonmifflinbooks.com/teachers/teachers.shtml—Houghton Mifflin Harcourt's teachers' resources page.

✔ http://www.guysread.com—Jon Scieszka's brainchild highlights books especially of interest to boys.

✔ http://www.ala.org/gwstemplate.cfm?section=greatwebsites&template=/cfapps/gws/default.cfm—American Library Association's "Great Web Sites for Kids."

✔ http://www.readkiddoread.com—James Patterson's site dedicated to engaging children with books; grade-level suggestions, reviews, reading guides, and more.

✔ http://www.nea.org/readacross—National Education Association's Read Across America site with a plethora of activities and suggestions, including details on the national Read Across America Day held on or near March 2, the birthday of Dr. Seuss.

✔ http://www.readingrockets.org—"Teaching kids to read and helping those who struggle" this site offers reading strategies, resources, lessons, reading lists, and activities designed to help young children learn to read and improved their reading skills; tips for parents, too.

Children's Book-Related Blogs

- http://readingyear.blogspot.com—"A Year of Reading" was created by teachers Franki and Mary Lee with one goal: to have read the Newbery winner before the award was announced. The blog offers an alternative to traditional review sources and is a great resource for teachers, librarians, and readers looking for good books.

- http://cynthialeitichsmith.blogspot.com—Cynthia Leitich Smith's highly regarded and widely read blog includes book reviews, resources, discussions and debates, interviews, and listings of other useful blogs. Smith is the author of fiction for young readers and is a faculty member at the Vermont College of Fine Arts MFA program in Writing for Children and Young Adults.

- http://www.hbook.com/blog—Read Roger: "The Horn Book Editor's Rants and Raves."

- http://blaine.org/sevenimpossiblethings—Seven Impossible Things Before Breakfast: Why Stop at Six? amazing children's book blog in which extensive interviews with illustrators and author/illustrators are offered.

Professional Reference Books

- **THE ALLURE OF AUTHORS: AUTHOR STUDIES IN THE ELEMENTARY CLASSROOM** by Carol Brennan Jenkins; Heinemann.

- **CHARLOTTE HUCK'S CHILDREN'S LITERATURE, TENTH EDITION** by Barbara Z. Kiefer; McGraw-Hill.

- **CHILDREN'S BOOK CORNER: A READ-ALOUD RESOURCE WITH TIPS, TECHNIQUES, AND PLANS FOR TEACHERS, LIBRARIANS, AND PARENTS**; Grades Pre-K–K, 1–2, 3–4, and 5–6; by Judy Bradbury; Libraries Unlimited.

- **CHILDREN'S WRITERS AND THEIR WEB SITES** by Jen Stevens; Libraries Unlimited.

- **EMERGING LITERACY: YOUNG CHILDREN LEARN TO READ AND WRITE** edited by Dorothy S. Strickland and Lesley Mandel Morrow; International Reading Association.

- **FAMILIES WRITING** by Peter Stillman; Heinemann.

- **HOME: WHERE READING AND WRITING BEGIN** by Mary W. Hill; Heinemann.

- **HOW TO GET YOUR CHILD TO LOVE READING** by Esmé Raji Codell; Algonquin.

- **INVITATIONS: CHANGING AS TEACHERS AND LEARNERS K–12** by Regie Routman; Heinemann.

- **RAISING LIFELONG LEARNERS: A PARENT'S GUIDE** by Lucy Calkins with Lydia Bellino; Heinemann.

- **READ TO WRITE: USING CHILDREN'S LITERATURE AS A SPRINGBOARD TO WRITING** by John Warren Stewig; Hawthorn.

- **READING MAGIC: WHY READING ALOUD TO OUR CHILDREN WILL CHANGE THEIR LIVES FOREVER** by Mem Fox; Harcourt.

- **RECONSIDERING READ-ALOUD** by Mary Lee Hahn; Stenhouse.

- **THE NEW READ-ALOUD HANDBOOK** by Jim Trelease; Penguin.

- **USING LITERATURE TO ENHANCE CONTENT AREA INSTRUCTION** by Rebecca Olness; International Reading Association.

- **USING LITERATURE TO ENHANCE WRITING INSTRUCTION: A GUIDE FOR K–5 TEACHERS** by Rebecca Olness; International Reading Association.

Professional Magazines

Periodicals to keep you abreast of new releases in children's materials:

- **Book Links** published quarterly by the American Library Association, this resource connects children's books, K–8, to curricula in science, social studies, and language arts. Included in each issue are suggestions for novels to teach, advice, author interviews, reviews, and thematic bibliographies. https://secure2.palmcoastd.com/pub/blst/newsubs.asp. Address: PO Box 615, Mount Morris, IL 61054-7566; Telephone: 888-350-0950; FAX: 815-734-1252.

- **Booklist** published 22 times per year, September through June and monthly in July and August by the American Library Association, this is a highly regarded source of reviews on all literature pertaining to children. http://www.ala.org/ala/aboutala/offices/publishing/booklist_publications/booklist/subscribe.cfm. Address: Booklist, PO Box 421027, Palm Coast, FL 32142; Telephone: 800-545-2433; email: mailto:booklist@emailcustomerservice.com.

- **Horn Book** published every other month, this magazine, founded in 1924, is chock full of reviews, publisher ads, editorials, and features reflecting a deep passion for and commitment to enduring quality in books for children and young adults. https://www.hbook.com/subscribe/Default.asp? Address: 56 Roland St., Suite 200, Boston, MA 02129; Telephone: 800-325-1170; email: info@hbook.com. Introductory rates; online newsletter.

- **LibrarySparks** nine issues per year; Targets librarians; ready-to-use lessons and activities. "Engaging Activities to Reach Every Reader." http://magazine-subscription.com/library-sparks.html Address: W5527 State Rd. 106, PO Box 800, Fort Atkinson, WI 53538-0800; Telephone: 800-933-2089; website: http://www.highsmith.com/librarysparks.

- **The Reading Teacher** published eight times a year for members of the International Reading Association, this magazine targets elementary school teachers. http://www.reading.org; Address: 800 Barksdale Road, PO Box 8139, Newark, DE 19714-8139; Telephone: 800-336-7323; email: mailto:customerservice@reading.org.

- **School Library Monthly** eight issues per year; for librarians K–12 who work collaboratively with teachers to provide instruction; http://www.schoollibrarymonthly.com/index.html.

"The important thing in science is not so much to obtain new facts as to discover new ways of thinking about them."—Sir William Bragg

Children's Book Publishers

Visit publishers' websites for ordering information and/or teaching suggestions. At larger publisher houses, such as Simon & Schuster, imprints are sometimes accessed from the main Web address. Within some of the larger publishing companies, imprints act independently of one another; in other publishing houses, they share departments. Often, ordering, and/or shipping departments are housed separately (sometimes in a different state!) from the publisher's business offices.

- **Harry N. Abrams Books for Young Readers**: http://www.abramsbooks.com/childrens.html

- **Bloomsbury Press**: http://www.bloomsburykids.com

- **Boyds Mills Press**: http://www.boydsmillspress.com

  - *Imprints*: **Calkins Creek, Wordsong**

- **Candlewick Press**: http://www.candlewick.com

- **Child's Play International**: http://www.childs-play.com

- **Clarion Books**: http://www.houghtonmifflinbooks.com

- **Disney Children's Book Group**: http://www.disneybooks.com

  - *Imprints*: **Disney Press, Disney-Hyperion**

- **Farrar, Straus & Giroux**: http://www.fsgbooks.com

- **Free Spirit Publishing**: http://www.freespirit.com

- **HarperCollins Children's Books**: http://www.harperchildrens.com

  - *Imprint*: **Greenwillow Books**

- **Henry Holt and Company**: http://www.henryholt.com

- **Holiday House**: http://www.holidayhouse.com

- **Houghton Mifflin Harcourt**: http://www.houghtonmifflinbooks.com

- **Kids Can Press**: http://www.kidscanpress.com/US

- **Kidwick Books**: http://www.kidwick.com

- **Lee & Low**: http://www.leeandlow.com

- **Little, Brown & Company**: http://www.hachettebookgroup.com/kids-teens.aspx

- **Meadowbrook Press:** http://www.meadowbrookpress.com

- **Penguin/Putnam** http://us.penguingroup.com/static/pages/youngreaders/children/index.html

- ○ *Imprints*: **Dial Books for Young Readers, Dutton Children's Books, G. P. Putnam's Sons, Philomel, Putnam, Puffin, Penguin, Viking, Grosset & Dunlap**

- **Random House** http://www.randomhouse.com/kids

  - ○ *Imprints*: **Knopf Delacorte Dell Young Readers Group, Random House Children's Books, Golden Books for Young Readers, Crown, Schwartz & Wade Books, David Fickling Books**

- **Scholastic** http://www.scholastic.com

  - ○ *Imprints*: **Scholastic Press, Cartwheel Books, Blue Sky Press, Arthur A. Levine Books, Orchard Books**

- **Simon & Schuster** http://kids.simonandschuster.com

  - ○ *Imprints*: **Atheneum, Margaret K. McElderry Books, Simon & Schuster Books for Young Readers, Aladdin, Little Simon, Simon Spotlight**

- **Albert Whitman & Co**.: http://www.albertwhitman.com

AUTHOR and ILLUSTRATOR WEBSITES

Jim Arnosky	http://www.jimarnosky.com
Esmé Raji Codell	http://www.PlanetEsme.com
Tomie dePaola	http://www.tomie.com
Kate DiCamillo	http://www.katedicamillo.com
Denise Fleming	http://www.denisefleming.com
Keiko Kasza	http://www.keikokasza.com
Laurie Keller	http://www.lauriekeller.com
Kathleen Krull	http://www.kathleenkrull.com
Loreen Leedy	http://www.loreenleedy.com
Yuyi Morales	http://www.yuyimorales.com
Linda Sue Park	http://www.lindasuepark.com
Patricia Polacco	http://www.patriciapolacco.com
Jack Prelutsky	http://www.jackprelutsky.com
Robin Pulver	http://www.robinpulver.com
Doreen Rappaport	http://www.doreenrappaport.com
Jon Scieszka	http://www.jsworldwide.com
Cynthia Leitich Smith	http://www.cynthialeitichsmith.com
Chris Soentpiet	http://www.soentpiet.com
Barbara Seuling	http://www.barbaraseuling.com
Carole Boston Weatherford	http://www.caroleweatherford.com
Mo Willems	http://www.mowillems.com
Karma Wilson	http://www.karmawilson.com

Visit also the websites of the authors and illustrators of the books featured in **Section II: In the Spotlight**. Websites for these authors and illustrators are listed below their comments on the making of the book.

For a list of "Great Web Sites for Kids: Author and Illustrators" generated by the American Library Association and the American Library Services for Children, go to: http://www.ala.org/gwstemplate.cfm?section=greatwebsites&template=/cfapps/gws/default.cfm.

Note: Although websites can be valuable resources that provide a wealth of information, the accuracy of their information or their safety for children cannot be guaranteed. Use the Internet wisely.

GLOSSARY OF BOOK TERMS

As in any field, there are specific terms used in the publishing industry to refer to various parts of a book or aspects of the publishing and marketing process. Some of the more common lingo is listed here as a handy reference.

book jacket	heavy paper cover surrounding a hardcover book.
bound galleys	uncorrected proofs; photocopy of a book used as "advance reading copy" for review purposes.
color separation	breaking down four-color artwork into four negatives—one for each of three colors (red, yellow, blue), plus black—for printing.
copyright	legal means of protecting one's work. Unless sold, this is automatic to anything written, published or unpublished, for the author's lifetime plus 50 years; found on the back of the title page of the book. Illustrations are also copyrighted and may not be reproduced without permission.
dedication	to whom the author and/or illustrator dedicate the book. Usually found after the title page before the body or text of the book.
endpaper	also **flyleaf**; the first sheet in hardbound books, attached to inside covers.
f&gs	folded and gathered sheets; prepublication copy of a picture book; for review purposes.
flap copy	information on the inside flap of the book jacket, usually about the story and an author profile.
spread	two facing pages that share one illustration; also referred to as **double-page spread**.
title page	lists the title, author, and illustrator of the work as well as the publisher. On the back of the title page you will find the copyright information.
trade books	books for the general public; sold in bookstores and book outlets and found in libraries.
trim size	the size of a book after it is bound.

". . . a book should serve as the ax for the frozen sea within us."—Franz Kafka

Author Index

Adler, David A., 37, 51
Agra Deedy, Carmen, 24
Ahlberg, Allan, 24, 28, 29, 52
Ahlberg, Janet, 24, 28
Alborough, Jez, 13, 48, 85
Alexander, Claire, 14
Aliki, 12
Allard, Harry, 29
Alsenas, Linas, 13
Anderson, Derek, 17
Anderson, Laurie Halse, 3, 10, 31, 124
Andreae, Giles, 13
Andrews-Goebel, Nancy, 6
Anno, Mitsumasa, 48, 129
Applegate, Katherine, 2
Armstrong, Jennifer, 25
Arnold, Tedd, 51
Arnosky, Jim, 40, 42, 134, 154
Askani, Tanja, 12
Auch, Herm, 25
Auch, Mary Jane, 25
Aylesworth, Jim, 3, 9, 122

Baker, Jeannie, 7, 20, 126
Bang, Molly, 10, 22, 37, 89
Banks, Kate, 24
Bar-el, Dan, 29
Barnett, Mac, 47
Barretta, Gene, 3, 23
Barry, Frances, 40, 134
Bauer, Marion Dane, 45
Beard, John, 14
Becker, Bonnie, 18
Bellino, Lydia, 150
Bennett, Kelly, 20, 21
Berger, Melvin, 43
Blabey, Aaron, 16, 17
Blackaby, Susan, 137, 142
Bloom, Suzanne, 17, 26, 85

Bluemle, Elizabeth, 5, 13, 15, 20, 56, 58–60
Bluthenthal, Diana Cain, 13
Boelts, Maribeth, 18, 94, 97, 98,
Boisrobert, Anouck, 21, 130
Bolden, Tonya, 8
Bond, Felicia, 12, 30, 85, 89
Bond, Rebecca, 46
Bottner, Barbara, 24
Bowen, Anne, 13, 35
Boyce, Natalie Pope, 137
Boynton, Sandra, 117
Bradbury, Judy, 150
Brenner, Martha, 124
Brett, Jan, 30
Brewer, Dan, 137, 143
Brewer, Paul, 125
Briant, Ed, 40, 48, 134
Brown, Don, 8, 10
Brown, Peter, 28, 38, 134
Brown, Ruth, 41, 134
Brown, Tameka Fryer, 19, 57
Browne, Anthony, 15, 25
Bruchac, Joseph, 20, 69
Buehner, Caralyn, 14
Bunting, Eve, 128
Burleigh, Robert, 9
Buzzeo, Toni, 32

Calkins, Lucy, 150
Cameron, Ann, 52
Campbell, Sarah C., 34, 118
Carle, Eric, 85, 137, 140
Carlson, Nancy, 13, 24, 37
Carr, Jan, 23, 45, 143
Carson, Mary Kay, 39, 134
Catrow, David, 51
Cazet, Denys, 27
Chaconas, Dori, 52
Cheney, Lynne, 133

Child, Lauren, 44, 135
Choi, Yangsook, 128
Choldenko, Gennifer, 14
Christelow, Eileen, 6, 27
Ciardi, John, 143, 144
Clark, Emma Chichester, 28
Clements, Andrew, 12, 23, 53, 85, 141
Cline-Ransome, Lesa, 10
Cocca-Leffler, Maryann, 14, 46, 126, 128
Codell, Esmé Raji, 150, 154
Cohn, Amy, 2, 8, 122
Cole, Joanna, 41, 134
Compestine, Ying Chang, 29
Conway, David, 12
Cooper, Elisha, 20, 130
Cooper, Melrose, 31
Corey, Shana, 3
Cowcher, Helen, 37
Cox, Judy, 7, 30, 46, 53, 89
Crawley, Dave, 85, 141
Crews, Donald, 49
Crum, Shutta, 26, 46
Cullinan, Bernice E., 140
Cummings, e.e., 101, 137, 141, 142
Cutler, Jane, 13

D'Agnese, Joseph, 34, 118
Dakos, Kalli, 141
Davies, Nicola, 43, 134
Davis, Jacky, 14
Day, Alexandra, 48
De Groat, Diane, 143
De Regniers, Beatrice Schenk, 143
DePaola, Tomie, 48, 154
DiCamillo, Kate, 52, 154
Dillon, Diane, 29, 32, 36
Dillon, Leo, 29, 32, 36
DiPucchio, Kelly, 31
Docherty, Thomas, 46
Donnelly, Liza, 48
Doodler, Todd H., 27, 32
Dorion, Christiane, 40, 134
Dotlich, Rebecca Kai, 11, 22
Dowson, Nick, 43
Durant, Alan, 30

Eaton III, Maxwell, 47
Edwards, Michelle, 30
Egan, Tim, 52
Ehlert, Lois, 41, 42, 135
Ehrhardt, Karen, 6
Elya, Susan Middleton, 7, 8, 30, 34, 47
Emmett, Jonathan, 46, 104

Falken, Linda, 2, 5
Falwell, Cathryn, 4, 11
Fearnley, Jan, 15, 85
Feldman, Eve B., 22
Fine, Anne, 47, 53
Flaherty, A. W., 28
Fleischman, Paul, 140, 141
Fleming, Denise, 11, 38, 141, 154
Fletcher, Ralph, 144
Florian, Douglas, 79, 101, 106, 140, 142, 143
Foreman, Jack, 17
Foreman, Michael, 17
Foster, Mark, 3
Fox, Mem, 150
Franco, Betsy, 142
Frasier, Debra, 32
Freedman, Deborah, 6, 17
French, Jackie, 14
French, Vivian, 38, 44
Furrow, Robert, 53

Garland, Michael, 24, 29
George, Jean Craighead, 38, 134
George, Kristine O'Connell, 85, 137, 142–44
Gerber, Carole, 40, 46
Gibbons, Gail, 38, 134
Gibson, Amy, 32, 37, 129
Giff, Patricia Reilly, 52
Giganti Jr., Paul, 34, 35
Golson, Terry, 47
Gonyea, Mark, 4
Goodman, David, 6, 36
Gorbachev, Valeri, 7, 15, 19, 27, 44, 85
Gore, Leonid, 19, 45
Graham, Bob, 13, 40
Grandits, John, 33, 129
Gravett, Emily, 14, 24, 25
Greenberg, Jan, 4, 8
Greenfield, Eloise, 141
Guiberson, Brenda Z., 41, 134
Gunning, Monica, 142

Hague, Michael, 137
Hahn, Mary Lee, 150
Harley, Avis, 141, 144
Harper, Charise Mericle, 19
Harper, Jamie, 20, 129
Harper, Lee, 45
Harrison, David L., 141
Hartland, Jessie, 21, 130
Heard, Georgia, 85, 137, 140, 144
Heide, Florence Parry, 18, 85
Heller, Ruth, 37, 42

Henkes, Kevin, 44
Hest, Amy, 5
Hill, Mary W., 150
Hines, Anna Grossnickle, 79, 143
Hoban, Tana, 48
Hoberman, Mary Ann, 141
Hogrogian, Nonny, 5, 12, 48
Holm, Sharon Lane, 32, 37, 116, 119, 120
Holub, Joan, 33, 40, 105, 107, 108, 109, 133
Hopkins, Lee Bennett, 11, 33, 85, 126, 128–29, 137,
    140–42, 144
Hopkinson, Deborah, 8, 27, 122
Hoppe, Paul, 13, 117
Horowitz, Dave, 33, 34, 46, 117, 129
Howe, James, 52
Hudes, Quiara Alegría, 8
Hughes, Langston, 20, 126–28, 141, 142
Hughes, Shirley, 36
Huneck, Stephen, 17, 21
Hurwitz, Johanna, 51, 52
Hutchins, Hazel, 36
Hutchins, Pat, 34

Isadora, Rachel, 8, 21, 29
Ives, Penny, 5, 11

Jackson, Elaine, 133
Jackson, Ellen, 124
Jacobs, Paul DuBois, 39
Janeczko, Paul B., 140–44
Jay, Alison, 6, 37
Jeffers, Oliver, 24
Jenkins, Carol Brennan, 150
Jenkins, Martin, 39
Jenkins, Steve, 41
Jocelyn, Marthe, 35, 118
Johnston, Tony, 144
Jonas, Ann, 49
Joosse, Barbara, 16
Jordan, Sandra, 4, 8
Joyce, Irma, 15
Judge, Lita, 38

Karas, G. Brian, 21, 44, 130
Kasza, Keiko, 16, 27, 154
Katz, Alan, 143
Katz, Bobbi, 143
Katz, Karen, 30
Kay, Verla, 3, 27
Keenan, Sheila, 133
Keller, Laurie, 12, 129, 132, 154
Kelly, Sheila M., 17, 126
Kerley, Barbara, 5, 8, 38

Ketterman, Helen, 29
Kiefer, Barbara Z., 150
Kinerk, Robert, 30
King-Smith, Dick, 37, 53
Klein, Abby, 53
Knudsen, Michelle, 14
Kontis, Alethea, 30
Krensky, Stephen, 45
Krull, Kathleen, 125, 154
Kruusval, Catarina, 44
Kuklin, Susan, 20, 126
Kumin, Maxine, 18, 126
Kvasnosky, Laura McGee, 52

Laínez, René Colato, 7, 20, 96
Lalli, Judy, 126, 141
Laminack, Lester L., 45
Lansky, Bruce, 142
Larson, Kirby, 18, 85
Lawlor, Laurie, 22, 25
Lear, Edward, 142
Lee, Dennis, 141
Leedy, Loreen, 22, 25, 33, 35, 42, 129, 134,
    136, 154
Lehman, Barbara, 49
Levenson, George, 138
Levine, Ellen, 128
Lewis, J. Patrick, 101, 140, 141, 144
Lichtenheld, Tom, 4, 117
Lies, Brian, 22
Lionni, Leo, 16, 35
Lipson, Eden Ross, 46
Livingston, Myra Cohn, 22, 44, 79, 140, 141, 144
Ljungkvist, Laura, 21, 25, 130
Lloyd-Jones, Sally, 11
Long, Loren, 16, 30
Longfellow, Henry Wadsworth, 143
Lowe, Ayana, 19, 57, 126, 140
Lowry, Lois, 12, 23
Lucas, David, 16
Lundell, Margo, 142
Lyon, George Ella, 32

Macken, JoAnn Early, 39
Madison, Alan, 18, 43
Manning, Maurie J., 14, 89
Marlow, Layn, 13
Martin Jr., Bill, 43, 44, 140
Marzollo, Jean, 24, 47
Matthews, Elizabeth, 5, 12
Mayer, Mercer, 48
McBrier, Page, 137
McCarthy, Meghan, 37, 42

McClintock, Barbara, 2, 32, 129
McCord, David, 143
McCourt, Lisa, 51
McDaniels, Preston, 16, 45
McDonald, Megan, 47, 51, 53
McElligott, Matthew, 34
McGhee, Alison, 52
McGinty, Alice B., 18, 21, 26, 33, 43, 61, 66, 67, 68, 73, 89, 129
McKelvey, Douglas Kaine, 142
McKenna, Colleen O'Shaughnessy, 53
McKissack, Patricia C., 2
McNamara, Margaret, 35, 46
McPhail, David, 11
Merriam, Eve, 140
Michelson, Richard, 2
Miller, Edward, 39
Miller, Heather Lynn, 21
Miller, William, 3, 6, 16
Miller, Zoe, 6
Mills, Claudia, 52
Milway, Katie Smith, 137, 138
Minor, Wendell, 4
Mitton, Tony, 5, 5, 23, 39
Modarressi, Mitra, 17, 21, 85
Moore, Eva, 143
Mora, Pat, 7, 13, 31, 88, 90, 91, 92
Morales, Yuyi, 7, 28, 35, 154
Mordhorst, Heidi, 143
Morgan, Mary, 28
Morgan, Michaela, 22, 30, 45, 99, 102, 103
Morrow, Mandel, 150
Moser, Lisa, 14
Muth, Jon J., 19, 22

Napoli, Donna Jo, 9, 10, 15, 18, 41, 43, 53, 134
Naylor, Phyllis Reynolds, 53
Nethery, Mary, 18, 85
Neuschwander, Cindy, 36, 118
Noda, Takayo, 141

O'Connor, Jane, 16
O'Malley, Kevin, 23
O'Neill, Alexis, 19
O'Neill, Mary, 79, 141
Olness, Rebecca, 150
Opie, Iona, 24, 28, 142
Ormerod, Jan, 49
Orr, Wendy, 53
Osborne, Mary Pope, 137

Page, Gail, 11
Paolilli, Paul, 137, 143

Parenteau, Shirley, 36
Park, Linda Sue, 20, 144, 154
Partridge, Elizabeth, 51
Patterson, James, 148
Paul, Ann Whitford, 27
Pelley, Kathleen T., 35
Pennypacker, Sara, 52, 76
Perkins, Lynne Rae, 11
Perry, Andrea, 40, 141, 143
Peters, Andrew Fusek, 141
Peters, Lisa Westberg, 43, 144
Petty, Kate, 39, 133
Pfeffer, Wendy, 39
Phelan, Matt, 49
Piernas-Davenport, Gail, 31
Pinkney, Jerry, 14, 28, 48
Pinkney, Sandra L., 17, 126
Pinkwater, Daniel, 4
Piven, Hanoch, 22, 25
Plourde, Lynn, 34, 42
Polacco, Patricia, 57, 154
Polhemus, Coleman, 48
Portis, Antoinette, 47
Potts, Professor, 40, 42, 134
Prelutsky, Jack, 85, 137, 141–43, 154
Priceman, Marjorie, 33, 129
Prosek, James, 38
Pulver, Robin, 25, 154

Rabin, Staton, 9, 122
Raczka, Bob, 45
Rampersad, Arnold, 128, 143
Rappaport, Doreen, 3, 9, 154
Raschka, Chris, 12, 23, 39
Reasoner, Charles, 36
Recorvits, Helen, 15, 126
Reid, Margarette S., 34, 118
Reinhart, Matthew, 39
Rennert, Laura Joy, 38
Rex, Adam, 47
Rex, Michael, 26
Reynolds, Aaron, 2
Ries, Lori, 51
Rigaud, Louis, 21, 130
Robbins, Jacqui, 21
Robbins, Ken, 34
Robinson, Sharon, 17
Rockwell, Anne, 19, 130
Roessel, David, 128, 143
Rogasky, Barbara, 79, 101, 106, 144
Rohmann, Eric, 49
Roop, Connie, 125
Roop, Peter, 125

Root, Phyllis, 23–25, 36
Rose, Deborah Lee, 37
Rosen, Michael, 14, 27
Rosenthal, Betsy R., 47, 96
Rotner, Shelley, 17, 126
Routman, Regie, 150
Rowden, Justine, 143
Rubin, Susan Goldman, 2, 5, 8, 9
Ruddell, Deborah, 137, 144
Rumford, James, 18
Russo, Marisabina, 18, 126
Ryan, Pam Munoz, 7, 10
Ryder, Joanne, 43
Rylant, Cynthia, 10, 46, 52, 57

Sabuda, Robert, 39, 129
Sachar, Louis, 53
Sakai, Komako, 31
Saltzberg, Barney, 44
Sattler, Jennifer, 17, 126
Sayre, April Pulley, 41, 43, 135
Scanlon, Liz Garton, 10, 64, 70, 74, 75
Schmidt, Amy, 85, 142
Schmidt, Suzy, 2, 8, 122
Schories, Pat, 48
Schubert, Leda, 39
Schwartz, David M., 35
Scieszka, Jon, 51, 144, 148, 154
Seeger, Laura Vaccaro, 36, 44
Serfozo, Mary, 49, 79
Seuling, Barbara, 154
Seuss, Dr., 41, 117, 134, 148
Shannon, George, 16, 29, 45, 85
Shapiro, Karen Jo, 140
Shapiro, Zachary, 27, 32
Sharratt, Nick, 5, 28, 111, 114, 115
Shaskan, Kathy, 40, 47
Shields, Carol Diggory, 37, 142
Shulevitz, Uri, 33, 48, 129
Shulman, Lisa, 24
Siddals, Mary McKenna, 138
Sidman, Joyce, 6, 26, 44, 77, 80–82, 143
Sierra, Judy, 4, 11, 15, 19, 22, 26, 28, 32, 38, 134
Silverman, Erica, 52
Singer, Marilyn, 23, 28, 39, 45, 113, 141, 142
Siy, Alexandra, 36
Small, David, 48
Smith, Cynthia Leitich, 149, 154
Smith, Lane, 2
Somar, David, 14
Spier, Peter, 48, 49, 79
Spinelli, Eileen, 4, 11, 16, 22, 73
Stead, Philip C., 17, 83, 86, 87

Steele, Mary Q., 79, 137, 140
Stein, David Ezra, 46
Stemple, Heidi Y., 140
Stevens, Jen, 150
Stewart, Sarah, 2, 23
Stewig, John Warren, 150
St. George, Judith, 3, 9, 42, 122, 124
Stiegemeyer, Julie, 34
Stillman, Peter, 150
Stohner, Anu, 11
Stone, Tanya Lee, 6, 42
Strauss, Linda Leopold, 32
Strickland, Dorothy S., 150
Suen, Anastasia, 44, 143
Sullivan, Sarah, 29
Sweeney, Joan, 33, 129
Swender, Jennifer, 39
Swinburne, Stephen R., 47, 96, 137, 142
Symes, Ruth, 5, 13, 104

Tafuri, Nancy, 48
Talbott, Hudson, 129
Tan, Shaun, 48
Tang, Greg, 36, 41, 44, 142
Tavares, Matt, 9
Teague, Mark, 23, 33, 129
Thomas, Patricia, 45
Thompson, Lauren, 13, 23, 35, 72, 73
Thong, Roseanne, 12
Tierney, Fiona, 14
Tobin, Jim, 26
Tokunbo, Dimitrea, 31
Trapani, Iza, 96, 143
Trelease, Jim, 147, 150
Truss, Lynne, 26

Updike, John, 79, 140
Urban, Linda, 15
U'Ren, A., 9

Van Allsburg, Chris, 48
Van Clief, Sylvia, 18, 85
Van Lieshout, Elle, 31
Van Os, Erik, 31
Vincent, Gabrielle, 12, 48
Viorst, Judith, 141
Voake, Steve, 40

Wadsworth, Ginger, 43
Walker, Rob D., 142
Walsh, Melanie, 43, 135
Warhola, James, 6, 10
Waters, Kate, 3

Wayland, April Halprin, 16, 30
Weatherford, Carole Boston, 3, 4, 154
Weisbud, Stefi, 96, 140
Westerlund, Kate, 31
White, Mary Michaels, 143
Whitehead, Jenny, 79, 141, 142
Wiesner, David, 48, 49
Willems, Mo, 12, 51, 85, 154
Wilson, Karma, 11, 33, 85, 129, 144, 154
Wing, Natasha, 4
Winnick, Karen B., 125
Winter, Jeanette, 9, 10, 15, 18, 19, 20, 41, 43, 135
Winter, Jonah, 40, 134

Winters, Kay, 47, 124
Wolf, Sallie, 26, 42, 143
Wong, Janet S., 141
Woodson, Jacqueline, 57, 128
Wooten, Deborah, 140

Yaccarino, Dan, 8, 23, 133, 138
Yang, James, 16
Yolen, Jane, 17, 31, 39, 140, 141, 143

Zalben, Jane Breskin, 142
Zemach, Kaethe, 6, 15
Zimelman, Nathan, 35
Zimmer, Tracie Vaughn, 143

Illustrator Index

Abolafia, Yossi, 141
Addy, Sean, 143
Adler, David A., 51
Ahlberg, Allan, 24, 28
Ahlberg, Janet, 24, 28
Ahlberg, Jessica, 44
Alborough, Jez, 13, 48, 85
Alcorn, Stephen, 33, 85, 129, 137, 141, 142
Alexander, Claire, 14
Aliki, 12
Alko, Selina, 133
Alley, R.W., 33, 52, 129
Alsenas, Linas, 13
Anderson, Derek, 4, 11, 17, 19, 28, 35, 38, 134
Anderson, Lena, 79, 137, 140
Anderson, Wendy, 18
Andrews, Benny, 128, 143
Andriani, Renée, 47
Angaramo, Roberta, 12
Anno, Mitsumasa, 48, 129
Arihara, Shino, 8
Armstrong-Ellis, Carey, 37
Arnold, Tedd, 51
Arnosky, Jim, 40, 42, 134, 154
Ashby, Gil, 140
Askani, Tanja, 12
Auch, Herm, 25
Auch, Mary Jane, 25
Avril, Lynne, 32

Baker, Jeannie, 7, 20, 126
Bang, Molly, 10, 22, 37, 89
Banyai, Istvan, 144
Barbour, Karen, 142, 144
Barretta, Gene, 3, 23
Barry, Frances, 40, 134
Bean, Jonathan, 53
Beard, John, 14

Beddows, Eric, 141
Björkman, Steve, 53, 128
Blabey, Aaron, 16, 17
Blackall, Sophie, 37
Blitt, Barry, 144
Bloch, Serge, 144
Bloom, Suzanne, 17, 26, 85
Bluthenthal, Diana Cain, 13, 30
Boiger, Alexandra, 53
Boisrobert, Anouck, 21, 130
Bolden, Tonya, 8
Bond, Felicia, 12, 30, 85, 89
Bond, Rebecca, 46
Booth, George, 29
Bowers, Tim, 12, 16, 23, 85, 141
Boynton, Sandra, 117
Bracken, Carolyn, 52
Breckenreid, Julia, 4
Brett, Jan, 30
Briant, Ed, 40, 48, 134
Briggs, Harry, 44, 142
Bright, Alasdair, 52
Broeck, Fabricio Vanden, 7, 20, 96
Brown, Alan, 133
Brown, Don, 8, 10
Brown, Kathryn, 14
Brown, Marc, 22, 38
Brown, Peter, 28, 38, 134
Brown, Ruth, 41, 134
Browne, Anthony, 15, 25
Brunkus, Denise, 141
Buckett, George, 15
Buehner, Mark, 14

Cabban, Vanessa, 30
Cable, Annette, 33, 129
Campbell, Richard P., 34, 118
Campbell, Sarah C., 34, 118

Carle, Eric, 29, 85, 137, 140
Carlson, Nancy, 13, 24, 37
Carpenter, Nancy, 124
Carpenter, Stephen, 142
Carrick, Paul, 44
Cassels, Jean, 18, 85
Catalano, Dominic, 143
Catrow, David, 51
Cazet, Denys, 27
Cecil, Randy, 5, 13, 15, 20, 24, 56, 59, 60
Chamberlain, Margaret, 14
Chamberlain, Sarah, 34, 118
Chapman, Jane, 11, 25, 36, 39, 43, 85
Chapman, Lee, 7, 34
Cherry, Lynne, 141
Child, Lauren, 44, 135
Choi, Yangsook, 128
Christelow, Eileen, 6, 27
Church, Caroline Jayne, 5, 13, 22, 30, 45, 46, 99,
     102, 104
Clark, Emma Chichester, 28
Clements, Andrew, 53
Cocca-Leffler, Maryann, 14, 46, 126, 128
Cohen, Lisa, 31
Cole, Henry, 15, 45
Collier, Bryan, 3, 9
Collins, Julie, 19, 57, 140
Colón, Raúl, 2, 33, 129
Cook, Donald, 124
Cooke, Jim, 141
Cooper, Elisha, 20, 130
Cooper, Floyd, 2
Cote, Nancy, 47, 96
Coverly, Dave, 26
Cowcher, Helen, 37
Cox, Steve, 47, 53
Crews, Donald, 34, 35, 49
Croft, James, 43, 134
Cyrus, Kurt, 27

Daigneault, Sylvie, 138
Davie, Helen K., 39
Davis, Jack E., 27, 32
Davis, Jacky, 14
Day, Alexandra, 48
Degen, Bruce, 41, 134
de Groat, Diane, 143
Demarest, Chris L., 45
Denton, Kady MacDonald, 18, 36
dePaola, Tomie, 48, 140, 154
Dewey, Jennifer Owings, 85, 137
Diaz, David, 6
Dillon, Diane, 29, 32, 142

Dillon, Leo, 29, 32, 36, 142
Docherty, Thomas, 46
Dominguez, Angela, 7, 89
Donnelly, Liza, 48
Donohue, Dorothy, 45
Doodler, Todd H., 27, 32
Dormer, Frank W., 51
Downing, Julie, 20
Dronzek, Laura, 16, 29, 45, 85
Dunbar, Polly, 141
Dunnick, Regan, 40, 47, 108, 133

Eaton III, Maxwell, 47
Ebbeler, Jeffrey, 30, 46, 89
Egan, Tim, 52
Egielski, Richard, 142
Ehlert, Lois, 41, 42, 135
Eldridge, Marion, 31
Emberley, Michael, 24
Ettlinger, Doris, 124
Evans, Leslie, 40, 46
Evans, Nate, 142
Everett, Leonard, 140

Falwell, Cathryn, 4, 11
Faulkner, Matt, 3, 10, 31, 122, 124, 140
Fearnley, Jan, 15, 85
Fernandes, Eugene, 137
Fink, Ben, 47
Fisher, Cynthia, 53
Fisher, Leonard Everett, 79, 141
Fisher, Valorie, 142
Fleming, Denise, 11, 38, 141, 154
Florian, Douglas, 79, 101, 106, 140,
     142, 143
Foreman, Jack, 17
Foster, Gerald, 3
Francher, Lou, 137, 143
Frasier, Debra, 32
Frazee, Marla, 10, 52, 64, 70, 74–76
Freedman, Deborah, 6, 17
Friend, Alison, 18, 126
Fucile, Tony, 52

Gammell, Stephen, 57
Garland, Michael, 24, 29
Gay, Marie-Louise, 52
Gerritsen, Paula, 31
Gerstein, Mordicai, 46
Giacobbe, Beppe, 140
Gibbon, Rebecca, 3
Gibbons, Gail, 38, 134
Gilchrist, Jan Spivey, 141

Glasser, Robin Preiss, 133
Gonyea, Mark, 4
Goode, Diane, 10
Goodman, David, 6, 36
Gorbachev, Valeri, 7, 15, 19, 27, 34, 44, 85
Gordon, David, 144
Gore, Leonid, 19, 45
Gorey, Edward, 144
Graham, Bob, 13, 14, 40
Gravett, Emily, 14, 24, 25
Greenseid, Diane, 29, 57
Grimly, Gris, 31
Guevara, Susan, 144
Gustavson, Adam, 45

Hafner, Marylin, 141, 143
Hague, Michael, 85, 137, 140
Halperin, Wendy Anderson, 20, 21, 26, 33, 43,
    61, 66, 68, 69, 73, 89, 129
Halsey, Megan, 143
Harley, Avis, 141
Harper, Charise Mericle, 19
Harper, Jamie, 20, 129
Harper, Lee, 45, 21, 130, 142,
Hartland, Jessie, 21, 130, 142
Hawkes, Kevin, 14, 18, 43
Heller, Ruth, 37, 42
Hendrix, John, 8, 27, 122
Henkes, Kevin, 44
Hillenbrand, Will, 22, 24, 44, 79, 140
Hines, Anna Grossnickle, 79, 143
Hoban, Tana, 48
Hogan, Jamie, 137, 142
Hogrogian, Nonny, 5, 12, 48
Holm, Sharon Lane, 32, 37, 116, 119, 120
Holub, Joan, 133
Hoppe, Paul, 13, 117
Horowitz, Dave, 33, 34, 46, 117, 129
Hughes, Shirley, 36
Huliska-Beith, Laura, 19
Huneck, Stephen, 17, 21
Hutchins, Pat, 34
Hyman, Trina Schart, 79, 101, 106, 140, 144

Ibatoulline, Bagram, 9, 12, 17, 31, 122
Ingman, Bruce, 29
Innerst, Stacy, 125
Isadora, Rachel, 8, 21, 29
Ives, Penny, 5, 11

Jabar, Cynthia, 36
James, Ann, 16
Jay, Alison, 6, 37

Jeffers, Oliver, 24
Jenkins, Steve, 41, 43, 144
Jeram, Anita, 37
Jin, Susie Lee, 143
Jocelyn, Marthe, 35, 118
Johnson, David A., 2, 8, 122
Johnson, D. B., 4
Johnson, Steve, 137, 143
Johnson-Petrov, Arden, 141
Jonas, Ann, 49
Jones, Noah Z., 18, 94, 98
Jorisch, Stephane, 16, 29, 30
Judge, Lita, 38

Kane, Henry B., 143
Karas, G. Brian, 21, 35, 44, 46, 51, 130
Kastner, Jill, 46
Kasza, Keiko, 16, 27, 154
Katz, Karen, 30
Keller, Laurie, 12, 129, 132, 154
Kellogg, Steven, 35
Kendall, Russ, 3
Kennedy, Anne, 4, 11, 16, 73
Kiesler, Kate, 137, 143, 144
Kneen, Maggie, 43
Kolar, Bob, 30
Koren, Edward, 143
Krall, Dan, 11
Kruusval, Catarina, 44
Kuklin, Susan, 20, 126
Kulikov, Boris, 6, 24, 42
Kvasnosky, Laura McGee, 52

LaMarche, Jim, 30
Langdo, Bryan, 36, 118
Lee, Huy Voun, 39
Leedy, Loreen, 22, 25, 33, 35, 42, 129,
    134, 136, 154
Lehman, Barbara, 49
Leijten, Aileen, 11, 22
Lessac, Frané, 142
Lewin, Betsy, 52
Lewin, Ted, 45, 128
Lewis, E. B., 127, 142
Lichtenheld, Tom, 4, 117
Lies, Brian, 22
Lionni, Leo, 16, 35
Lippincott, Gary, 140
Ljungkvist, Laura, 21, 25, 130
Lohstoeter, Lori, 137
Long, Ethan, 22, 23, 25
Long, Loren, 16, 30, 144
Lucas, David, 16

Magoon, Scott, 28
Maione, Heather, 53
Maizels, Jennie, 39, 133
Manders, John, 29
Manning, Maurie J., 14, 89
Mansfield, Andy, 134
Marlow, Layn, 13
Mason-Fry, Douglas L., 126, 141
Masse, Josée, 28, 113, 142
Matje, Martin, 52
Mattheson, Jenny, 8, 47
Matthews, Elizabeth, 5, 12
Mayer, Mercer, 48
McCarthy, Meghan, 37, 42
McClintock, Barbara, 2, 3, 9, 32,
    122, 129
McCue, Lisa, 52
McCully, Emily Arnold, 13
McDaniels, Preston, 16, 45
McElligott, Matthew, 34
McElrath-Eslick, Lori, 96, 140
McEwen, Katharine, 52
McGrory, Anik, 51
McKinley, John, 53
McPhail, David, 11, 141
McQueen, Stacey Dressen, 140
Meade, Holly, 18, 85
Meisel, Paul, 20, 142
Miller, Edward, 37, 39
Miller, Woody, 41
Minor, Wendell, 4, 38, 134
Modarressi, Mitra, 17, 21, 85
Moore, Cyd, 51
Morales, Magaly, 7, 31
Morales, Yuyi, 7, 28, 35, 154
Morgan, Mary, 28
Morley, Taia, 36, 41
Mourning, Tuesday, 22
Murdocca, Sal, 137
Muth, Jon J., 5, 12, 19, 22, 85

Nadel, Marc, 140
Nakata, Hiroe, 32
Narahashi, Keiko, 49, 79
Neilan, Eujin Kim, 12
Nelson, Kadir, 3, 9, 10, 15, 17, 18,
    41, 43, 134
Nelson, Michiyo, 21
Noda, Takayo, 141

O'Brien, John, 34, 118
O'Malley, Kevin, 23
Ormerod, Jan, 2, 49

Otani, June, 85, 142
Owings, Jennifer, 140
Oxenbury, Helen, 27

Page, Gail, 11
Paparone, Pam, 39
Paprocki, Greg, 36
Parker, Robert Andrew, 4, 8
Parker-Rees, Guy, 5, 13, 23, 39
Parra, John, 7, 13, 88, 90–93
Patterson, Annie, 43, 135
Perkins, Lynne Rae, 11
Peterson, Mary, 137, 142
Petrosino, Tamara, 85, 141
Phelan, Matt, 21, 49
Pinkney, Brian, 127, 128, 141
Pinkney, Jerry, 2, 14, 28, 48
Pinkney, Myles C., 17, 126
Piven, Hanoch, 22, 25
Plecas, Jennifer, 16
Polacco, Patricia, 57, 154
Polhemus, Coleman, 48
Portis, Antoinette, 47
Potts, Professor, 42, 134
Priceman, Marjorie, 33, 129
Prosek, James, 38

Qualls, Sean, 4

Rama, Sue, 21
Rand, Ted, 85, 141, 143
Rankin, Joan, 137, 144
Ransome, James E., 10
Raschka, Chris, 6, 12, 23, 39, 142,
    143
Ray, Deborah Kogan, 101, 137,
    141, 142
Reasoner, Charles, 36
Red Nose Studio, 40, 134
Reed, Lynn Rowe, 25
Reinhart, Matthew, 39
Rex, Adam, 47
Rex, Michael, 26
Reynolds, Peter H., 53
Riely-Webb, Charlotte, 16
Rigaud, Louis, 21, 130
Riley-Webb, Charlotte, 3, 6, 19, 57
Robbins, Ken, 23, 34, 39, 45, 141
Rockwell, Anne, 19, 130
Rogers, Jacqueline, 36
Rohmann, Eric, 49
Root, Barry, 3, 27
Root, Kimberly Bulcken, 3, 27

Roth, R. G., 6
Roth, Stephanie, 53
Rotner, Shelley, 17, 126
Russo, Marisabina, 18, 126

Sabuda, Robert, 32, 39, 129
Sakai, Komako, 31
Salerno, Steven, 142
Salmieri, Daniel, 32, 37, 129
Saltzberg, Barney, 44
Sampson, Michael, 140
Sattler, Jennifer, 17, 126
Schindler, S. D., 14, 35, 43
Schmidt, Ron, 85, 142
Schories, Pat, 48
Schuett, Stacey, 30, 125
Seeger, Laura Vaccaro, 36, 44
Seibold, J. Otto, 15, 28
Selznick, Brian, 5, 7, 8, 10, 38
Seuss, Dr., 41, 117, 134, 148
Shannon, David, 51, 144
Sharratt, Nick, 5, 28, 111, 114, 115
Shed, Greg, 43, 44
Shepperson, Rob, 101, 144
Shulevitz, Uri, 33, 48, 129
Sis, Peter, 85, 137, 143
Slavin, Bill, 35
Slonim, David, 2, 9
Small, David, 2, 9, 23, 25, 42, 48, 124
Smith, Charles R., Jr., 20, 126, 142
Smith, Jan, 33
Smith, Lane, 2
Snow, Alan, 40, 141, 143
So, Meilo, 143
Soentpiet, Chris, 11, 126, 128,
    140, 154
Somar, David, 14
Sorra, Kristin, 40, 105, 107, 109, 110
Spier, Peter, 48, 49, 79
Stead, Erin E., 17, 83, 86, 87
Stead, Judy, 45
Stein, David Ezra, 46
Stemple, Jason, 39, 143
Stevenson, Harvey, 141
Stevenson, James, 142, 143
Strugnell, Ann, 52
Sullivan, Barbara, 53
Sweet, Melissa, 26, 32, 52, 140, 141
Swiatkowska, Gabi, 15, 126
Swinburne, Stephen R., 47, 96

Tafuri, Nancy, 48
Talbott, Hudson, 129

Tan, Shaun, 48
Tavares, Matt, 9
Teague, Mark, 23, 33, 52, 129
Tharlet, Eve, 31
Thayer, Shmuel, 138
Thomas, Middy, 23
Thompson, Carol, 26, 46
Tilley, Debbie, 52
Tillotson, Katherine, 47
Timmons, Bonnie, 26
Torrey, Jesse, 143
Trapani, Iza, 96, 143
Tugeau, Jeremy, 31
Tusa, Tricia, 29

Uhlman, Tom, 39, 134
U'Ren, Andrea, 9, 39

Van Allsburg, Chris, 48
Vincent, Gabrielle, 12, 48
Voake, Charlotte, 38, 40

Walker, David, 7, 21, 23
Wallner, John, 79, 141
Walsh, Melanie, 43, 135
Ward, April, 144
Warhola, James, 6, 10
Wells, Rosemary, 24, 28, 142
Weston, Martha, 51
Whatley, Bruce, 14
White, E. B., 128
White, Michael P., 24
Whitehead, Jenny, 79, 141, 142
Wick, Walter, 24, 47
Wickstrom, Thor, 34, 42
Wiesner, David, 48, 49
Wilhelm, Hans, 140
Willems, Mo, 51, 154
Wilsdorf, Anne, 22
Wilson, Henrike, 11
Wilson, Karma, 154
Wimmer, Mike, 9
Winnick, Karen B., 125
Winter, Jeanette, 9, 10, 15, 18, 19,
    20, 41, 43, 135
Wolff, Ashley, 138
Wong, Janet S., 141
Wummer, Amy, 32
Wynne, Patricia J., 43

Yaccarino, Dan, 8, 23, 133,
    138
Yang, James, 16

Young, Beverley, 40, 134
Young, Ed, 41, 134

Zagarenski, Pamela, 6, 26, 44, 77,
    81, 82, 143

Zalben, Jane Breskin, 142
Zemach, Kaethe, 15
Zollars, Jaime, 13, 35

Subject Index

Abraham Lincoln, 2, 3, 9, 122–25
Addition, 33, 34, 35
Aesop fables, 14
Alarm clocks, 9
Alexander Calder, 6
Alphabet, 6, 8, 26, 27, 32
American history, 2–4
American Revolution, 2, 4
Andy Warhol, 6, 10
Anger, expressing, 15
Animal care, 13
Animals, 37–41
Antarctica, 37
Apostrophes, 23, 26
Appalachia, 10
Apples, 44
Art, 4–7
Art masterpieces, 5, 6, 36
Assimilation, 15, 19
Astronauts, 37
Attitude, 16
Author (career), 6
Author websites, 154

Barrio, 8
Beach, 46
Beetles, 38
Ben Franklin, 2, 3
Bilingual books, 7–8
Biography, 8–10
Birds, 26
Birthday, 31
Blogs, 149
Books, 5, 22, 24, 27
Book terms, 155
Bravery, 11
Bubble gum, 42

Bullying, 14, 19
Butterflies, 18, 43

Calendar, 22, 26, 30
Camp, 11
Careers, 19, 21, 47
Cats, 47
Chanukah, 30
Chapter books, 51–53
Character education, 10–18
Children's book publishers, 152–53
Christmas, 7, 30, 31
Climate, 41
Coco Chanel, 5
Collage, 4
Colonists, 3
Colors, 4, 5, 6, 26, 77–82, 116–20
Commas, 26
Commonality, 10
Communication, 12
Community, 19–22, 70–76
Community workers, 21
Conservation, 4, 28, 38, 41, 43, 134–38
Coral reefs, 38
Counting, 6, 7, 10, 12, 25, 28, 34, 35, 36, 37
Courage, 14
Cultures, 7, 8, 10, 11, 17, 18, 19, 20, 56–60, 61–69, 88–93

Dads, 15, 20, 21, 23
Dance, 5, 13, 14, 56–60
Degas, 5
Depression Era, 2
Dinosaurs, 5, 38, 39
Discrimination, 2
Division, 34

Dogs, 12, 48
Dolphins, 39
Drama, 11

Easter, 30
Egrets, 39
Electricity, 44
Emigration, 7, 15, 19
Endangered animals, 41
Energy, 42
English Language Arts, 22–27
Environment, 4, 28, 38, 41, 43, 134–38
ESL, 7–8

Fables, 14, 28–29
Fairytale characters, 5
Fairy tales, 27–29, 111–15
Fall, 40, 42
Family, 12, 14, 19, 22, 27, 70–76, 126–28
Farms, 20
Fashion, 5
Fear, 14
Fibonacci, 34,
Finicky eaters, 7
Fire safety, 39
Folktales, 16, 27–29
Friendship, 5, 7, 11, 12, 13, 14, 15,
    16, 17, 18, 19, 22, 26, 56–60, 83–87,
    99–104

Garbage, 40
Garden, 28
Geography, 2, 32–33, 61–69, 129–33
George Washington, 2
Getting along, 16
Gossip, 14
Grandparents, 14
Groundhog Day, 40, 105–10

Haiku, 12, 23
Halloween, 30–31
Hank Aaron, 9
Harriet Tubman, 3
Hats, 13, 32
Haym Salomon, 2, 9
Holidays, 30–31
Homophones, 23
Hope, 13
Hugs, 13
Hurricane Katrina, 18

Illustrator (career), 6
Illustrator websites, 154

Insects, 40
Intergenerational relationships, 19
Inventions, 9, 42
Inventors, 9
Invitations, 13
Iraq, 9

Jackie Robinson, 9
Jackson Pollock, 4
Jazz, 3, 4, 6
Jealousy, 19
John Coltrane, 4
John Hancock, 2
Josef Albers, 4
Juan Quezada, 6

Kindergarten, 32
Kindness, 12
Kwanzaa, 30

Leaves, 40, 42
Legends, 28–29
Letter writing, 23, 24
Library, 14, 22, 24
Loose tooth, 8

Manatees, 42
Manners, 11, 12, 14, 15, 16
Map skills, 32–33, 129–33
Marian Anderson, 7, 10
Martin Luther King Jr., 3, 9
Mary Smith, 9
Math, 13, 33–37
Measuring, 34, 35
Memoir, 8–10
Metaphor, 24
Migration, 38
Minerals, 39
Mobile art, 6
Moms, 15, 17, 21, 25
Monarch butterfly, 18
Money, 34, 35, 37
Monkeys, 41
Mother Goose, 24
Multiculturalism, 7, 8, 10, 11, 17–20, 56–60,
    61–69, 88–93, 126–28
Multiplication, 34
Music, 5, 6
Mystery, 47, 48
Myths, 28–29

New school, 17
New Year, 30

Noah's Ark, 27
November, 46
Numbers, 6, 7, 10, 12, 25, 28, 33–37
Nursery rhymes, 24, 28–29

Origami, 4

Parody, 26
Parts of speech, 26
Patterns, 34, 35, 36, 37, 116–20
Paul Revere, 2
Pelé, 10
Penguins, 39
Performance art, 5
Pet abuse, 12
Pet care, 12
Pilgrims, 3
Piñata, 7
Pizza, 28
Plants, 42
Playground, 14
Poetry, 23, 28, 33, 37, 139–44
Pond life, 38
Pony Express, 3
Pottery, 6
Preschool readiness, 32
Presidents, 9
Probability, 34
Professional references, 147–51
Pumpkins, 46
Punctuation, 23, 25, 26
Puns, 23

Quantity, 35

Rain, 49
Ramadan, 30
Read-aloud plan, 146
Reading, 5, 22, 24, 26, 27
Recess, 16, 19
Recycling, 40, 44
Resourcefulness, 13
Rhinoceros, 39
Riddles, 24
Rosh Hashanah, 16

Safety, 39
Sarah Hale, 3, 10
School picture day, 47
Science, 37–44
Science Fair, 42
Seasons, 26, 36, 43, 44–46, 77–82

Self-acceptance, 13
Self-esteem, 12, 14
Senses, 12
Shapes, 6, 36
Sharing, 34
Sharks, 42
Sheep, 39
Shoes, 47
Sibling rivalry, 6
Sign language, 21
Silent letters, 26
Similes, 22, 25
Skating, 4
Skipping, 16
Snow, 16, 31, 45
Snowman, 16, 45
Soccer, 10
Spiders, 42
Spring, 45
Storytelling, 22
Strangers, 15
Street signs, 25
Subways, 21
Summer, 26, 46–46
Summer vacation, 23
Supermarket, 19

Tad Lincoln, 9
Tattle-tale, 13
Thankfulness, 7, 10, 88–93
Thanksgiving, 3, 10, 30
Theodore Roosevelt, 10
Thunderstorm, 26
Tigers, 43
Time, 9, 36
Toads, 43
Tornadoes, 38
Travel, 32–33, 129–33
Turtles, 43

Underground Railroad, 3
Underwear, 40
Urban sprawl, 40

Valentines, 12
Veterinary care, 17
Visual art, 4, 6
Vocal art, 7
Volcanoes, 43

Wangari Maathai, 9, 10, 15
Wants and needs, 18
Waterhouse Hawkins, 5

Weather, 40, 105–10
Westward Movement, 2, 14
Willie Lincoln, 9
Winter, 22, 45, 99–104
Wordless books, 48–49
Word play, 23, 24
Word problems, 37

World War II, 3
Worms, 44
Worry, 16
Writing, 26
Writing process, 25

Zoo, 27, 32

Title Index

A B C: A Child's First Alphabet Book, 6
Abe Lincoln: The Boy Who Loved Books, 124
Abe Lincoln Crosses a Creek: A Tall, Thin Tale, 8,
    27, 122
Abe Lincoln Loved Animals, 124
Abe Lincoln's Hat, 124
Abraham Lincoln, 2, 8, 122
Action Jackson, 4, 8
Adéle & Simon in America, 2, 32, 129, 132
Adventure Annie Goes to Kindergarten, 32
Afternoon on the Amazon, 137
Aggie and Ben: Three Stories, 51
All around the Seasons, 44
All of Me: A Book of Thanks, 10, 22, 37, 89
All Pigs Are Beautiful, 37
All the World, 10, 64, 70, 73–75
Allure of Authors: Author Studies in the Elementary
    Classroom, The, 150
Alpha Oops! H Is for Halloween, 30
Amazing Faces, 11, 126, 140
Amazing Monty, 51
Amazing Pop-Up Geography Book, The, 133
America the Beautiful, 32, 129
An Egret's Day, 39
An Eye for Color: The Story of Josef Albers, 4
Angelina's Island, 19
Animal Friends: A Collection of Poems for Children, 85,
    137, 140
Animals Animals, 85, 137, 140
Animals Born Alive and Well, 37, 42
Anna's Garden Songs, 79, 137, 140
Anna's Summer Songs, 79, 140
Annie and Bo and the Big Surprise, 51
Anno's Journey, 48, 129
Anno's USA, 48, 129
Another Jar of Tiny Stars: Poems by More NCTE
    Award-Winning Poets, 140
Ant and Honey Bee: A Pair of Friends at Halloween, 51

Antarctica, 37
Apple Countdown, 33
Applesauce Season, 46
Around Our Way on Neighbors' Day, 19, 57
Around the World on Eighty Legs, 32, 129
Arrival, The, 48
Art & Max, 48
As Good as Anybody, 2
Astronaut Handbook, 37
Atlas of the World: The Ultimate Interactive, 130,
    131, 133
At the Supermarket, 19, 130
Autumnblings, 79, 140

Baby Beluga, 138
Back of the Bus, 2
Backseat Books: Kids' U.S. Road Atlas, 133
Badger's Fancy Meal, 16, 27
Ballyhoo Bay, 4, 11, 19, 28, 38, 134, 135
Barefoot: Poems for Naked Feet, 96, 140
Bats at the Library, 22
Bean Thirteen, 34
Bear Feels Sick, 11, 85
Bear's First Christmas, 30
Bear's Picture, 4
Beatrice's Goat, 137
Beat the Drum Independence Day Has Come:
    Poems for the Fourth of July, 140
Because I Could Not Stop My Bike and Other Poems,
    140
Beetle Bop, 38
Before John Was a Jazz Giant: A Song of John
    Coltrane, 4
Behind the Museum Door: Poems to Celebrate the
    Wonders of Museums, 140
Being a Pig Is Nice: A Child's Eye View of
    Manners, 11
Being Teddy Roosevelt, 52

Bella & Bean, 11, 22
Best Story, The, 22
Big Talk: Poems for Four Voices, 140
Big Whopper, 52
Bill Martin Jr. Big Book of Poetry, The, 140
Billy & Milly Short & Silly, 22
Bink & Gollie, 52
Bird, Butterfly, Eel, 38
Birds on a Wire, 140
Blackberry Ink, 140
Blast Off! Poems about Space, 140
Blockhead: The Life of Fibonacci, 34, 118
Blue Hat, Green Hat, 117
Bobo and the New Neighbor, 11
Book about Color: A Clear and Simple Guide for
    Young Artists, A, 4
Born to Be Giants: How Baby Dinosaurs Grew to
    Rule the World, 38
Born to Read, 22
Boy, a Dog, and a Frog, A, 48
Brave Charlotte, 11
Brave Charlotte and the Wolves, 11
Bread Comes to Life, 138
Breakfast for Jack, 48
Bridget's Beret, 4, 117
Budgie & Boo, 11
Buffalo Are Back, The, 38, 134, 135
Buffalo Storm, The, 2
Bunny Wishes: A Winter's Tale, 22, 30, 45, 99,
    102, 104
Buster Goes to Cowboy Camp, 11
Butterflies for Kiri, 4, 11
Button Box, The, 34, 118
Buying, Training & Caring for Your Dinosaur, 38
Buy My Hats!, 34, 117

Calendar, 22, 44, 79, 140
Callie Cat, Ice Skater, 4, 11
Cam Jansen, 51
Can You Find It? America, 2, 5
Cardboard Piano, 11
Carmen Learns English, 7, 89
Caterpillar Caterpillar, 38
Cat in the Hat, The, 117
Celestine Drama Queen, 5, 11
Charlotte Huck's Children's Literature, Tenth Edition,
    150
Chaucer's First Winter, 45
Children's Book Corner: A Read-Aloud Resource
    With Tips, Techniques, and Plans for Teachers,
    Librarians, and Parents, 150
Children's Writers and Their Web Sites, 150
Children Who Smelled a Rat, The, 52

Child's Calendar, A, 79, 140
Circle of Seasons, A, 79, 140
City Dog, Country Frog, 12, 85
Clementine, 52, 76
Come and Play: Children of Our World Having Fun,
    19, 57, 126, 127, 128, 140
Communication, 12
Compost Stew, 138
Cool Cat, 5, 12, 48
Coral Reefs, 38, 134
Cork & Fuzz: Good Sports, 52
Cowgirl Kate and Cocoa, 52
Crazy Like a Fox: A Simile Story, 22, 25
Creatures of Earth, Sea, and Sky, 85, 137, 140
Crocodile Blues, The, 48
Crow Call, 12
Curious Garden, The, 28, 38, 134

Dad and Pop: An Ode to Fathers & Stepfathers, 20
Danny's First Snow, 45
Dawn, 48
Day, a Dog, A, 12, 48
Day It Rained Hearts, The, 12, 30, 85, 89
Dear Bunny, 102, 103
Dear Deer: A Book of Homophones, 23
Dear Mother, Dear Daughter: Poems for Young
    People, 140
Dear Mrs. Larue: Letters from Obedience School, 23
Dear Santa Claus, 30
Dear World, 141
Degas and the Dance, 5, 8
Different Like Coco, 5, 12
Dinosaur Day, 48
Dinosaur Hunt, 51
Dinosaurs of Waterhouse Hawkins, The, 5, 8, 38
Dinosaurumpus!, 5, 23, 39
Dirty Laundry Pile: Poems in Different Voices, 141
Dodsworth in New York, 52
Doggone . . . Third Grade!, 53
Dogku, 12, 23, 85, 141
Dog Poems, 85, 141
Dog Who Cried Wolf, The, 16, 27
Dolley Madison Saves George Washington, 8
Dolphins and Sharks, 137
Dolphin Talk, 39
Doorbell Rang, The, 34
Do Unto Otters: A Book About Manners, 12
Down By the Cool of the Pool, 5, 23
Dragon Pizzeria, 28
Dream Keeper and Other Poems, The, 127,
    128, 141
Drummer Boy, 30
Duck Duck Moose, 33, 46, 129, 131, 132

Each Orange Had 8 Slices: A Counting Book, 34, 35
Each Peach Pear Plum, 28
Earthly Treasure, 39
Earth Songs, 140
Easter Egg, The, 30
*Eats, Shoots & Leaves: Why, Commas Really Do Make a
    Difference!*, 26
Eight Animals on the Town, 7, 34
Ellen's Apple Tree, 44
*Emerging Literacy: Young Children Learn to Read and
    Write*, 150
Emi and the Rhino Scientist, 39, 134, 135
Emperor's Egg, The, 39
Encyclopedia Prehistorica: Dinosaurs, 39
Errol and His Extraordinary Nose, 12
Every Friday, 8, 23
Everything Book, The, 141

Fabulous Fair Alphabet, A, 32
Families, 20, 126, 127
Families Writing, 150
Fantastic Undersea Life of Jacques Cousteau, The, 138
Farm, 20, 130
Farmer Joe and the Music Show, 5
*Farmer's Dog Goes to the Forest: Rhymes for
    Two Voices*, 141
*Fathers, Mothers, Sisters, Brothers: A Collection of
    Family Poems*, 141
Feeding the Sheep, 39
Festivals, 79, 141
Field Trip Day, 34
Fire Drill, 39
Fireboy to the Rescue!, 39
Fireflies At Midnight, 23, 39, 45, 141
Firekeeper's Son, 20
Five for a Little One, 12, 23, 39
Flip, Flap, Fly!, 23
Flip, Float, Fly: Seeds on the Move, 39
Flotsam, 48
Fly Free!, 12
Fly with Poetry: An ABC of Poetry, 141, 144
Foggy, Foggy Forest, 5, 28, 111, 114
*For Good Measure: The Ways We Say How Much, How
    Far, How Heavy, How Big, How Old*, 34
Four Valentines in a Rainstorm, 12, 30, 85, 89
Free Fall, 48
Friend Like You, A, 12
Frog Goes to Dinner, 48
Frog on His Own, 48
Funny Lunch, 51

Gardener, The, 2, 23
Geogra-Fleas!: Riddles All Over the Map, 108, 133

George Washington Carver, 8
*Gift of the Poinsettia: El Regalo De La Flor
    De Nochebuena, The*, 90
Gimme Cracked Corn & I Will Share, 23
Giraffes Can't Dance, 5, 13, 23
*Girl's Like Spaghetti: Why You Can't Manage without
    Apostrophes, The*, 26
Go, Go America, 131, 132, 133
Gobble Gobble Crash! A Barnyard Counting Bash, 34
Goin' Someplace Special, 2
Goldilocks and the Three Bears, 28
Good Books, Good Times!, 141
Good Dog, Carl, 48
*Good Garden: How One Family Went from Hunger to
    Having Enough, The*, 138
Good Luck Gold and Other Poems, 141
Goodnight Goon, 26
*Goof Who Invented Homework and Other School
    Poems, The*, 141
Gooney Bird Is So Absurd, 23
Grace's Letter to Lincoln, 125
Gracias Thanks, 7, 13, 88, 90, 91, 92, 93
Great Doughnut Parade, The, 46
Great Math Tattle Battle, The, 13, 35
Greedy Apostrophe: A Cautionary Tale, 23
*Greetings from the 50 States: How They Got Their
    Names*, 131, 132, 133
Groundhog Weather School, 40, 105, 107, 109, 110
Growing Patterns: Fibonacci Numbers in Nature, 34,
    118
Guess Again!, 47
Guttersnipe, 13

Hailstones and Halibut Bones, 79, 141
Hannah's Collections, 35, 118
Hansel and Gretel, 29
Harriet Dancing, 5, 13, 104
Hat, 13, 117
*Haunted States of America: Haunted Houses and
    Spooky Places in All 50 States and Canada, Too!*,
    108, 133
Have You Seen My Duckling?, 48
Haym Salomon: American Patriot, 2, 9
Hello My Name Is Bob, 13
Henry Aaron's Dream, 9
Henry and Mudge and the Tall Tree House, 52
Here Comes the Garbage Barge!, 40, 42, 134
Here's a Little Poem: A Very First Book of Poetry, 141
Here's What You Do When You Can't Find Your Shoe,
    40, 141
*Heroes and She-Roes: Poems of Amazing and Everyday
    Heroes*, 141
Hi! Fly Guy, 51

Hist Whist, 141
Holiday Stew: A Kid's Portion of Holiday and Seasonal Poems, 79, 141
Home: Where Reading and Writing Begin, 150
Hoofbeats, Claws & Rippled Fins: Creature Poems, 85, 137, 141
Hope Is An Open Heart, 13, 23, 72, 73
Houndsley and Catina, 52
How Do You Wokka-Wokka?, 5, 13, 20, 56, 58, 60
How I Learned Geography, 33, 129, 130, 131
How I Spent My Summer Vacation, 23
How Many Seeds in a Pumpkin?, 35, 46
How Many Snails? A Counting Book, 34, 35
How Much Is a Million?, 35
How the Second Grade Got $8,205.50 to Visit the Statue of Liberty, 35
How the World Works, 40, 134
How to Bake An American Pie, 33, 129
How to Get Your Child to Love Reading, 150
How to Heal a Broken Wing, 13, 40
How to Lose All Your Friends, 13
How to Make a Cherry Pie and See the USA, 33, 129, 131, 132
How Underwear Got Under There: A Brief History, 40, 47
Hug, 13, 48, 85
Hurry Up and Slow Down, 13

I Am Going!, 51
Ice Cream Store, The, 141
I Did It, I'm Sorry, 14
I Don't Like to Read!, 24
If I Were in Charge of the World and Other Worries, 141
If Not for the Cat, 85, 141
If You Lived Here You'd Be Home By Now, 40, 48, 134
If You Made a Million, 35
I Hate English!, 128
I Like Being Me: Poems for Children About Feeling Special, Appreciating Others, and Getting Along, 126, 127, 141
I'm a Turkey!, 40
I'm Not Invited?, 13
I'm Number One, 14
In November, 46
In the Land of Words: New and Selected Poems, 141
In the Small, Small Pond, 38
In the Tall, Tall Grass, 38
Inch By Inch, 35
Incredible Book Eating Boy, The, 24
Insect Detective, 40
Invitations: Changing as Teachers and Learners K–12, 150
I Spy A to Z: A Book of Picture Riddles, 24

It's a Spoon, Not a Shovel, 14
It's Picture Day Today!, 47
It's Probably Penny, 35
It's the 100th Day, Stinky Face!, 51
It's Valentine's Day, 141

Jack and the Missing Piece, 48
Jack and the Night Visitors, 48
Jack's Talent, 14, 126, 128
Jack Wants a Snack, 48
Jake Drake: Bully Buster, 53
John, Paul, George & Ben, 2
Jolly Christmas Postman, The, 24
Jolly Pocket Postman, The, 24
Jolly Postman or Other People's Letters, The, 24
Josephine Wants to Dance, 14
Joyful Noise: Poems for Two Voices, 141
Judy Moody Was in a Mood, 53
Jungle Grapevine, The, 14
Just a Minute: A Trickster Tale and Counting Book, 7, 28, 35

Kat's Mystery Gift, 51
Kick in the Head: An Everyday Guide to Poetic Forms, A, 142
Kids Pick the Funniest Poems: Poems That Make Kids Laugh, 142
Kisses on the Wind, 14
Kitchen Dance, 14, 89

Ladybug Girl and Bumblebee Boy, 14
Larue Across America: Postcards from the Vacation, 33, 129, 131, 132
Laugh-Eteria, 142
Leaf Jumpers, 40, 46
Leaf Trouble, 46, 104
Leaves, 46
Let It Fall, 46
Let's Save the Animals, 40, 134, 135
Let There Be Light: Poems and Prayers for Repairing the World, 142
Librarian of Basra: A True Story from Iraq, The, 9, 20
Library Dragon, 24
Library Lion, 14
Lincoln Tells a Joke: How Laughter Saved the President (and the Country), 125
Lion & the Mouse, The, 14, 28, 48
Lion's Lunch?, 14
Little Dog Poems, 85, 142
Little Mouse's Big Book of Fears, 14
Little Quack, 35
Little Tree, 101, 137, 142
Locust Pocus! A Book to Bug You, 142

Longest Night, The, 45
Look! Look! Look!, 48
Looking for Moose, 24
Loose Leashes, 85, 142
Lorax, The, 41, 134, 136
Lots of Spots, 41
Louder, Lili, 14
Luck of the Loch Ness Monster: A Tale of Picky Eating, The, 28
Lucy and the Bully, 14
Lunch Box Mail and Other Poems, 142
Lunch Money and Other Poems About School, 142

Magic School Bus and the Climate Challenge, The, 41, 134, 136
Magic Tree House Series, 137
Magnus Maximus, a Marvelous Measurer, 35
Mama Miti, 9, 10, 15, 18, 41, 43, 134, 135
Mama Says: A Book of Love for Mothers and Sons, 142
Manners, 12
Mapping Penny's World, 33, 129, 130, 132
Martin's Big Words, 3, 9
Marvelous Math: A Book of Poems, 142
Marvin Redport: Why Pick on Me?, 53
Mary Smith, 9
Mathematickles!, 142
Math Fables, 36, 41
Math Fables Too, 36, 41
Math for All Seasons, 36, 44, 142
Math-Terpieces, 36
Max's Words, 24
Meerkat Mail, 24
Meet the Howlers!, 41
Me on the Map, 33, 129, 130
Messing Around on the Monkey Bars and Other School Poems for Two Voices, 142
Miles to Go, 20, 129, 130
Millions to Measure, 35
Milo Armadillo, 15, 85
Mind Your Manners, B. B. Wolf, 15, 28
Mirror, 7, 20, 126, 127
Mirror Mirror: A Book of Reversible Verse, 28, 113, 142
Miss Brooks Loves Books! (and I Don't), 24
Miss Smith's Incredible Storybook, 24, 29
Mokie & Bik, 53
Molly Who Flew Away, 15, 85
Moon Bear, 41, 134
Moon Might Be Milk, The, 24
More Pocket Poems, 143
Moses: How Harriet Tubman Led Her People to Freedom, 3
Mother Goose Numbers on the Loose, 29, 32, 36
Mother Goose's Little Treasures, 24, 28, 142

Mouse Was Mad, 15
Mr. George Baker, 5
Mr. Lincoln's Boys, 9, 122, 123
Mr. Lincoln's Whiskers, 125
Ms. McCaw Learns to Draw, 6, 15
Muddy as a Duck Puddle and Other American Similes, 22, 25
My America: A Poetry Atlas of the United States, 33, 129, 131, 142
My Best Friend Is as Sharp as a Pencil and Other Funny Classroom Portraits, 22, 25
My Dog Is as Smelly as Dirty Socks and Other Funny Family Portraits, 22, 25
My Father, the Dog, 15, 59, 60
My Father Is Taller Than a Tree, 20, 69
My First Ramadan, 30
My Funny Book of Valentines, 142
My Lucky Day, 16, 27
My Mom, 15, 25
My Name Is Yoon, 15, 126, 127, 128
My People, 20, 126, 127, 142
My Shoes and I, 7, 20, 96
Mysteries of Harris Burdick, The, 48
Mystery, The, 47

Name Jar, The, 128
Negro Speaks of Rivers, The, 127, 142
Nest, Nook & Cranny, 137, 142
Never Smile At a Monkey, 41
Never Talk to Strangers, 15
New Kid on the Block, The, 142
New Read-Aloud Handbook, The, 150
New Year At the Pier: A Rosh Hashanah Story, 16, 30
Nicolas, Where Have You Been?, 16
Night Shift, 21, 130
No More, Por Favor, 7
No More Homework! No More Tests! Kids Favorite Funny School Poems, 142
Nonsense, 142
Not a Box, 47
Not a Copper Penny in Me House: Poems from the Caribbean, 142
Nouns and Verbs Have a Field Day, 26
Now & Ben: The Modern Inventions of Benjamin Franklin, 3

Ocean Soup: Tide-Pool Poems, 137, 142
Old Bear, 44
Old Elms Speaks: Tree Poems, 137, 143
Old Tree, The, 41, 134, 135
Olly and Me 1 2 3, 36
Once Upon a Baby Brother, 29
Once Upon a Banana, 25, 48

One Blue Fish: A Colorful Counting Book, 36
One Boy, 36
One Duck Stuck, 25, 36
One Frog Sang, 36
One Green Apple, 128
One Hen: How One Small Loan Made a Big
    Difference, 137
One Is a Feast for Mouse: A Thanksgiving Tale, 30,
    46, 89
One Tractor: A Counting Book, 36
1 2 3: A Child's First Counting Book, 6, 37
On the Mayflower: Voyage of the Ship's Apprentice &
    a Passenger Girl, 3
Oops!, 143
Orange Pear Apple Bear, 25
Other Side, The, 128
Otis, 16
Our Abe Lincoln, 3, 9, 122, 123
Our Fifty States: A Family Adventure Across America,
    131, 132, 133

Pablo's Tree, 90
Paint Me a Poem: Poems Inspired By Masterpieces of
    Art, 143
Pancakes for Breakfast, 48
Papa's Latkes, 30
Pass the Poetry, Please!, 144
Patterns in Peru: An Adventure in Patterning, 36, 118
Paul Revere's Ride, 143
Peace Week in Miss Fox's Class, 16, 73
Peanut, 16
Pearl Barley and Charlie Parsley, 16
Pencil Talk and Other School Poems, 143
People, 48
Pepi Sings a New Song, 21, 25, 130
Perfect Snowman, A, 16, 45
Peter and the Wolf, 6
Pieces: A Year in Poems & Quilts, 79, 143
Piñata in a Pine Tree: A Latino Twelve Days of
    Christmas, A, 7, 31
Pinky and Rex, 52
Pirate of Kindergarten, The, 32
Plants That Never Bloom, 37, 42
Players in Pigtails, 3
Please Is a Good Word to Say, 16
Plot Chickens, The, 25
Pocket Poems, 143
Poem-Making: Ways to Begin Writing Poetry, 144
Poetry for Young People: Langston Hughes, 128, 143
Poetry from A to Z: A Guide for Young Writers, 144
Poetry Matters: Writing a Poem from the Inside
    Out, 144
Poke in the I: A Collection of Concrete Poems, A, 143

Pop! The Invention of Bubble Gum, 42
Poppleton in Winter, 52
Popville, 21, 130
Pot That Juan Built, The, 6
Preschool Day Hooray!, 32
Pretty Salma: A Red Riding Hood Story from Africa, 29
Previously, 29
Princess and the Pea, The, 29
Princess Pig, 16
Probably Penny, 33
Pssst!, 47
Pumpkin Elf Mystery, The, 53
Punctuation Takes a Vacation, 25
Puppy Power, 53
Puzzlehead, 16

Rabbit and the Turtle, The, 29
Rabbit's Gift, 16, 29, 45, 85
Rain, 49, 79
Rain Talk, 49, 79
Raising Lifelong Learners: A Parent's Guide, 150
Rapunzel, 29
Read-Aloud Handbook, The, 147
Read a Rhyme Write a Rhyme, 143
Reading Magic: Why Reading Aloud to Our Children
    Will Change Their Lives Forever, 150
Read to Write: Using Children's Literature as a Spring-
    board to Writing, 150
Ready, Set, Skip!, 16
Ready for Anything!, 16, 27
Ready for Kindergarten, Stinky Face?, 51
Real Story of Stone Soup, The, 29
Reason for the Flower, The, 37, 42
Reason for the Pelican, The, 143
Recess Queen, The, 19
Reconsidering Read-Aloud, 150
Red Green Blue: A First Book of Colors, 6
Red Leaf, Yellow Leaf, 42, 135
Red Sings from Treetops: A Year in Colors, 6, 26, 44, 77,
    80, 81, 82, 143
Red Sled, 45
Relatives Came, The, 57
Rent Party Jazz, 3, 6, 16
Return of the Killer Cat, The, 47, 53
Rhyme Time, 143
Riddle-Iculous Math, 108
Rip-Roaring Russell, 52
Robin Makes a Laughing Sound: A Birder's Journal, The,
    26, 42, 143
Roman and Low Blast Off, 17
Roses Are Pink, Your Feet Really Stink, 143
Round the World on Eighty Legs, 37
Round Trip, 49

Roxie and the Hooligans, 53
Rufus and Friends: School Days, 96
Rufus and Friends Series, 96, 143
Runaway Bunny, The, 26
Runaway Mummy: A Petrifying Parody, The, 26

Sail Away, 49
Sally Gets a Job, 21
Sally Goes to the Vet, 17
Samuel Eaton's Day: A Day in the Life of a Pilgrim Boy, 3
Sandy's Circus: A Story About Alexander Calder, 6, 42
Sarah Morton's Day: A Day in the Life of a Pilgrim Girl, 3
Say Hello, 17
Say Hello!, 8, 21
Scarecrow's Dance, The, 17, 31
School Days, 143
School Mouse, The, 53
Science Fair Day, 42
Scrambled States of America, The, 129, 131, 132
Scrambled States of America Talent Show, The, 129, 131, 132
Scranimals, 85, 137, 143
Scribble, 6, 17
Sea Songs, 140
Second Is a Hiccup: A Child's Book of Time, A, 36
Seven Days of Kwanzaa, The, 31
Shades of Black: A Celebration of Our Children, 17, 126
Shades of People, 17, 126
Shanté Keys and the New Year's Peas, 31
Shape, 6, 36
Shape Me a Rhyme: Nature Forms in Poetry, 143
Sharing Christmas, 31
Shocking Truth About Energy, The, 42, 134, 135, 136
Sick Day for Amos McGee, A, 17, 83, 86, 87
Sign Language: My First 100 Words, 21
Silent Letters Loud and Clear, 26
Silver Seeds: A Book of Nature Poems, 137, 143
Sing a Song of Popcorn: Every Child's Book of Poems, 143
Sipping Spiders through a Straw: Campfire Songs for Monsters, 31
Sky Songs, 140
Sleepy Little Alphabet: A Bedtime Story from Alphabet Town, The, 26, 32
Slow Down for Manatees, 42, 134, 135
Sly the Sleuth and the Pet Mysteries, 53
Smash! Smash! Truck: Recycling as You've Never Heard It Before!, The, 40, 42, 134
Snack Smasher and Other Reasons Why It's Not My Fault, The, 143
Snow Day, The, 31
Snow Day!, 45
Snow! Snow! Snow!, 45

Snowy, Blowy Winter, 45
So You Want to Be An Inventor?, 42
So You Want to Be President?, 9, 124
Something Big Has Been Here, 143
Sound of Kwanzaa, The, 31
Space Songs, 140
Spinning Spiders, 43
Splendid Friend, Indeed, A, 17, 26, 85
Splish, Splash, Spring, 45
Spy A to Z: A Book of Picture Riddles, 47
Squeeze: Poems from a Juicy Universe, 143
Stand Tall, Abe Lincoln, 3, 122, 123, 124
Starlight Goes to Town, 29
Start Saving, Henry!, 37
Steady Hands: Poems About Work, 143
Stealing Home: Jackie Robinson Against the Odds, 9
Stories Julian Tells, The, 52
Storm in the Barn, The, 49
Stuart Goes to School, 52
Stuart's Cape, 52
Subway Ride, 21
Such a Prince, 29
Sue Macdonald Had a Book, 26
Summersaults, 79, 140, 143
Summer Wonders, 45
Sunday Chutney, 17
Sunshine, 49
Surprising Sharks, 43, 134, 135
Sylvie, 17, 126

Take Sky, 143
Taking Care of Mama, 17, 21, 85
Tap Dancing on the Roof: Sijo (Poems), 144
Teaching 10 Fabulous Forms of Poetry, 144
Teedie: The Story of Young Teddy Roosevelt, 10
Ten Things I Can Do to Help My World: Fun and Easy Eco-Tips, 43, 135, 136
Testing the Ice: A True Story About Jackie Robinson, 17
Thank You, Sarah! The Woman Who Saved Thanksgiving, 3, 10, 31, 124
Thank You, World, 18, 21, 26, 33, 43, 61, 62, 63, 64, 66, 67, 68, 69, 73, 89, 129, 130, 131
That's What Friends Are For, 18, 85
This Jazz Man, 6
This Place I Know: Poems of Comfort, 144
This School Year Will Be the Best!, 47
Those Shoes, 18, 94, 97, 98
Three Pigs, The, 49
Thunder-Boomer!, 26, 46
Tiger and Turtle, 18
Tigress, 43
Tillie Lays An Egg, 47
Time Flies, 49

Toad By the Road: A Year in the Life of These Amazing Amphibians, 43
Toasting Marshmallows: Camping Poems, 144
Today At the Bluebird Café: A Branchful of Birds, 144
Tomás and the Library Lady, 90
Tooth on the Loose, 8, 47
Tornadoes!, 38
To the Beach, 46
Trainstop, 49
Travel Game, The, 33, 129, 130, 131
Truckery Rhymes, 144
Tuesday, 49
Turkey Riddles, 109
Turning of the Year, The, 43, 44
Turtle, Turtle, Watch Out!, 43, 135
Twelve Dancing Princesses, The, 29
Twelve Days of Springtime: A School Counting Book, The, 37
Twenty-Odd Ducks: Why Every Punctuation Mark Counts!, 26
Two Bobbies: A True Story of Hurricane Katrina, Friendship, and Survival, 18, 85
Two of a Kind, 21

Ugly Duckling, The, 29
Uncle Andy's, 6, 10
Under the Kissletoe: Christmastime Poems, 101, 144
Underwear Salesman and Other Jobs for Better or Verse, The, 144
United Tweets of America: 50 State Birds Their Stories, Their Glories, 129, 131, 132
Up, Up, and Away, 43
Using Literature to Enhance Content Area Instruction, 150
Using Literature to Enhance Writing Instruction: A Guide for K–5 Teachers, 150

Velma Gratch & the Way Cool Butterfly, 18, 43
Very Big Bunny, A, 18, 126
Village Garage, The, 21, 44, 130
Visitor for Bear, A, 18
Voice from Afar: Poems of Peace, 144
Volcano Wakes Up!, 43, 144

Wangari's Trees of Peace, 9, 10, 15, 18, 41, 43, 135
We Are Extremely Very Good Recyclers, 44, 135
We Had a Picnic This Sunday Past, 57
Welcome to My Neighborhood! A Barrio ABC, 8
We're All in the Same Boat, 27, 32

We're Going on a Bear Hunt, 27
Whale Port, 3
What Color Is Caesar?, 18, 126
What Do Authors Do?, 6, 27
What Do Illustrators Do?, 6, 27
Whatever Happened to the Pony Express?, 3, 27
What If?, 44
What's the Big Idea, Molly?, 7, 19, 27, 44
What's the Weather Inside?, 144
When I Grow Up, 19
When I Was Young in the Mountains, 10
When Jack Goes Out, 48
When Lightning Comes in a Jar, 57
When Marian Sang, 7, 10
When Randolph Turned Rotten, 19
Which Shoes Would You Choose?, 47, 96
Whiff of Pine, a Hint of Skunk: A Forest of Poems, A, 137, 144
Whose Shoes? A Shoe for Every Job, 47, 96
Wild About Books, 22
Will You Read to Me?, 27
Winter Eyes, 79, 101, 106, 140
Winter Poems, 79, 101, 106, 144
Wired, 44
Wish, The, 31
Wombat Walkabout, 37
Wonderful Words: Poems About Reading, Writing, Speaking, and Listening, 144
Word Builder, 27
Worst Best Friend, The, 19
Writing Kind of Day: Poems for Young Poets, A, 144
Wynetta and the Cornstalk: A Texas Fairy Tale, 29

Yankee Doodle America, 4
Year Full of Holidays, A, 30
You Can, Toucan, Math, 37
You Know Who, 144
Young Cam Jansen, 51
Young Pelé: Soccer's First Star, 10
You Read To Me, I'll Read to You, 144
Your Daddy Was Just Like You, 21
Your Mommy Was Just Like You, 21
Yucky Worms, 44

Zelda and Ivy: The Big Picture, 52
Zen Ties, 19, 22
Zoe's Hats: A Book of Colors and Patterns, 32, 37, 116, 119, 120
Zoo I Drew, The, 27, 32

About the Author

JUDY BRADBURY (www.judybradbury.com) is a children's book author, reading specialist, and the author of the Children's Book Corner series. She teaches graduate-level children's literature courses and presents workshops nationally on the topic of connecting children's literature to the content areas. She resides in western New York.

Edwards Brothers Malloy
Thorofare, NJ USA
April 26, 2012